A PROJECT-BASED APPROACH TO TRANSLATION TECHNOLOGY

A Project-Based Approach to Translation Technology provides students of translation and trainee translators with a real-time translation experience, with its translation platforms, management systems, and teamwork.

This book is divided into seven chapters reflecting the building blocks of a project-based approach to translation technology. The first chapter identifies the core elements of translation environment tools and collaborative work methods, while Chapters 2 and 4 review the concept of translation memory and terminology databases and their purposes. Chapter 3 covers machine translation embedded in the technology, and the other chapters discuss human and technological quality assurance, digital ethics and risk management, and web-based translation management systems. Each chapter follows a common format and ends with project-based assignments. These assignments draw and build on real-time contexts, covering the consecutive steps in the workflow of large and multilingual translation projects.

Reviewing the many translation technology tools available to assist the translator and other language service providers, this is an indispensable book for advanced students and instructors of translation studies, professional translators, and technology tool providers.

Rosemary Mitchell-Schuitevoerder holds a PhD in Translation Studies from Durham University, UK, and has taught Translation Technology on the MA programmes at Durham University, UK, and Newcastle University, UK. She is a freelance translator of Dutch, Swedish, Norwegian, and Danish into English, and English into Dutch.

TRANSLATION PRACTICES EXPLAINED
Series Editor: Kelly Washbourne

Translation Practices Explained is a series of coursebooks designed to help self-learners and students on translation and interpreting courses. Each volume focuses on a specific aspect of professional translation and interpreting practice, usually corresponding to courses available in translator- and interpreter-training institutions. The authors are practising translators, interpreters, and/or translator or interpreter trainers. Although specialists, they explain their professional insights in a manner accessible to the wider learning public.

Each volume includes activities and exercises designed to help learners consolidate their knowledge, while updated reading lists and website addresses will also help individual learners gain further insight into the realities of professional practice.

Most recent titles in the series:

Note-taking for Consecutive Interpreting 2e
A Short Course
Andrew Gillies

Consecutive Interpreting
A Short Course
Andrew Gillies

Healthcare Interpreting Explained
Claudia V. Angelelli

Revising and Editing for Translators 4e
Brian Mossop

A Project-Based Approach to Translation Technology
Rosemary Mitchell-Schuitevoerder

For more information on any of these and other titles, or to order, please go to www.routledge.com/Translation-Practices-Explained/book-series/TPE

Additional resources for Translation and Interpreting Studies are available on the Routledge Translation Studies Portal: http://routledgetranslationstudiesportal.com/

A PROJECT-BASED APPROACH TO TRANSLATION TECHNOLOGY

Rosemary Mitchell-Schuitevoerder

LONDON AND NEW YORK

First published 2020
by Routledge
2 Park Square, Milton Park, Abingdon, Oxon OX14 4RN

and by Routledge
52 Vanderbilt Avenue, New York, NY 10017

Routledge is an imprint of the Taylor & Francis Group, an informa business

© 2020 Rosemary Mitchell-Schuitevoerder

The right of Rosemary Mitchell-Schuitevoerder to be identified as author of this work
has been asserted by her in accordance with sections 77 and 78 of the Copyright,
Designs and Patents Act 1988.

All rights reserved. No part of this book may be reprinted or reproduced or utilised
in any form or by any electronic, mechanical, or other means, now known or
hereafter invented, including photocopying and recording, or in any information
storage or retrieval system, without permission in writing from the publishers.

Trademark notice: Product or corporate names may be trademarks or registered trademarks,
and are used only for identification and explanation without intent to infringe.

British Library Cataloguing-in-Publication Data
A catalogue record for this book is available from the British Library

Library of Congress Cataloging-in-Publication Data
Names: Mitchell-Schuitevoerder, Rosemary, author.
Title: A project-based approach to translation technology /
Rosemary Mitchell-Schuitevoerder.
Description: London ; New York : Routledge, 2020. |
Series: Translation practices explained |
Includes bibliographical references and index.
Identifiers: LCCN 2020003466 | ISBN 9780367138820 (hardback) |
ISBN 9780367138844 (paperback) | ISBN 9780367138851 (ebook)
Subjects: LCSH: Translating and interpreting–Technological innovations. |
Translating and interpreting–Data processing.
Classification: LCC P306.97.T73 M58 2020 | DDC 418/.020285–dc23
LC record available at https://lccn.loc.gov/2020003466

ISBN: 978-0-367-13882-0 (hbk)
ISBN: 978-0-367-13884-4 (pbk)
ISBN: 978-0-367-13885-1 (ebk)

Typeset in Bembo
by Newgen Publishing UK

For John, Thomas, Benjamin, Simeon

CONTENTS

List of figures	*xii*
List of tables	*xiv*
Preface	*xv*
Acknowledgements	*xvi*
List of abbreviations	*xvii*
Glossary	*xix*
Introduction for instructors	*xxiv*
Introduction for students and translators	*xxxi*

1   Computer-aided translation tools and translation project
    management   1
    Key concepts 1
    Introduction 1
    1.1   Translation environment tools (TEnT) 2
    1.2   Compatibility 2
    1.3   Translation memory 4
    Food for thought... 6
    1.4   File management 6
        1.4.1   Filenames 7
    1.5   From Microsoft to CAT tools 10
        1.5.1   The ribbon 10
        1.5.2   Keyboard shortcuts 11
    1.6   The CAT tool 12
        1.6.1   CAT tool features 12
        1.6.2   Standalone and web-based CAT tools 13
        1.6.3   CAT tools and cognitive ergonomics 14

viii Contents

Food for thought... 15
1.7 Translation project management 15
    1.7.1 Volume and demands 15
    1.7.2 Translation workflow 16
    1.7.3 The translator in the workflow 17
    1.7.4 Project management by the language service provider 18
    1.7.5 Project-based assignments and project management 19
    1.7.6 Human resources database 20
1.8 Cognitive friction 21
Project-based assignment 22
Concluding remarks 23
Further reading 24

2 The translation memory database   25
   Key concepts 25
   Introduction 25
2.1 Creating a translation memory database 26
Food for thought... 28
    2.1.1 Segmentation 28
    2.1.2 The concordance and consistency 30
    2.1.3 The analysis feature and fees 33
Food for thought... 36
2.2 Metadata and subsegment matching 36
2.3 Boosting the translation memory 38
    2.3.1 Alignment 39
    2.3.2 Translation memory and reference files 39
    2.3.3 TMX files 40
2.4 Formats 41
2.5 Other functions and features on the ribbon 44
    2.5.1 Filters 45
    2.5.2 Regex 46
Project-based assignment 48
Concluding remarks 49
Further reading 50

3 Integration of machine translation in translation
   memory systems   51
   Key concepts 51
   Introduction 51
3.1 Artificial intelligence and machine translation 52
3.2 From statistical to neural machine translation in the CAT tool 53

3.3 Matches from the translation memory and machine translation compared 54

3.4 Machine translation – access and integration 56

Food for thought... 57

3.5 Translation memories train machine translation engines 57

3.6 Adaptive MT engines 58

Food for thought... 59

3.7 MT quality in the CAT tool 59

    3.7.1 Quality management 60

Food for thought... 62

    3.7.2 How to evaluate machine translation 62

    3.7.3 Evaluation models and metrics 63

Project-based assignment 66

Concluding remarks 67

Further reading 68

4 The terminology database   69

Key concepts 69

Introduction 69

4.1 Terms and terminology 71

    4.1.1 Glossary 71

Food for thought... 72

    4.1.2 Term extraction 72

    4.1.3 Metadata 74

Food for thought... 76

    4.1.4 Standardisation and quality assurance 77

4.2 Web searches 77

    4.2.1 Search techniques 78

4.3 Corpora 79

    4.3.1 Digital dictionaries 79

    4.3.2 Multilingual data corpora 80

    4.3.3 The creation of corpora 82

Food for thought... 83

4.4 CAT concordance 84

    4.4.1 External concordances 85

4.5 Morphology and the terminology database 86

4.6 Termbanks 86

Project-based assignment 88

Concluding remarks 90

Further reading 90

x Contents

5 Human and technological quality assurance 92
Key concepts 92
Introduction 92
5.1 Quality and standards 93
    5.1.1 Quality assurance and assessment 93
5.2 Quality in different TEnTs 95
    5.2.1 Quality assurance in CAT tools 95
    5.2.2 Quality assessment of MT technology 96
Food for thought... 97
    5.2.3 Web localisation and quality 97
5.3 Revision in CAT tools 99
    5.3.1 CAT revision of bilingual and monolingual files 100
5.4 ISO standards 101
Food for thought... 103
5.5 Revision and evaluation 104
    5.5.1 Human evaluation 105
5.6 The post-edit of wholly or partly machine translated texts 107
Food for thought... 108
    5.6.1 PEMT quality 108
Project-based assignment 109
Concluding remarks 111
Further reading 112

6 Digital ethics and risk management 113
Key concepts 113
Introduction 113
6.1 Intellectual property rights (IP) and ownership 114
6.2 Confidentiality and non-disclosure agreements 115
6.3 Business terms and conditions in relation to confidentiality and digital security 116
Food for thought... 119
6.4 Data sharing and data protection 119
    6.4.1 Google and GDPR 120
6.5 Digital ethics of shared TM and MT databases 121
6.6 Risk management 122
    6.6.1 Our security and intellectual property rights in translation projects 123
Food for thought... 124
    6.6.2 Risk factors 124
    6.6.3 Risk response 127
Project-based assignment 128
Concluding remarks 130
Further reading 130

7	Web-based translation environment tools	132

Key concepts 132

Introduction 132

7.1 Integrated translation environment 133

    7.1.1 Speech recognition 134

7.2 Servers and web-based CAT tools 136

7.3 Digital platforms 137

    7.3.1 Translator platform 138

    7.3.2 Marketplace platform 139

    7.3.3 Localisation platform 139

    7.3.4 Translation platform 140

    7.3.5 Knowledge platform 141

    7.3.6 Crowdsourcing platform 141

    7.3.7 The portal 142

Food for thought... 142

7.4 From content to translation management systems 143

7.5 Translation management systems 143

Food for thought... 145

7.6 Localisation of webpages and search engine optimisation 146

7.7 Translation technology and the users 147

Project-based assignment 149

Concluding remarks 151

Further reading 152

Bibliography	*153*
Index	*159*

FIGURES

1.1	Translator's parent folder	8
1.2	Subfolders generated by CAT tool	9
1.3	Ribbon in MS Word	10
1.4	A basic translation workflow chart	16
1.5	Translator's workflow	17
1.6	LSP's workflow in the cloud	18
2.1	File preparation dialog in SDL Trados Studio	29
2.2	Dialog box opened in concordance search in SDL Trados Studio 2019	31
2.3	Concordance target results for the term 'functional'	31
2.4	Search and find dialog in SDL Studio 2019	32
2.5	Search and Find function Ctrl+F	32
2.6	Concordance dialog in memoQ 9.1	33
2.7	Analysis report (statistics tab in memoQ 9.1)	35
2.8	Alignment with join-up lines between source and target segments	39
2.9	Pseudo translated PDF file	43
2.10	Ribbon in MS Word	45
2.11	Ribbon in CAT tool	45
3.1	CAT tool and adaptive MT	54
4.1	Translation Results window in memoQ 9.1	70
4.2	Term entry in memoQ 9.1	75
4.3	Bilingual data corpora in Linguee stating that 'external sources are not yet reviewed'	81
4.4	TAUS data cloud	82
4.5	The CAT concordance in operation	84
4.6	Termbank and lookup term in CAT tool (memoQ 9.1)	87
5.1	From i18n (internationalisation) to l10n (localisation)	98

6.1	Classification of technological and human risks in a translation project	125
6.2	PDF of three sides of a carton with text sideways and upside down	126
6.3	Risk response	127
7.1	Speech-to-text and text-to-speech software	136
7.2	File-based or cloud-based localisation	140

TABLES

2.1	MemoQ (M) and TRADOS 2007-like (T) counts compared in MemoQ 9.2 Statistics	36
3.1	Edit distance	55
3.2	LISA model for quality assurance	64
3.3	TAUS (2019) Dynamic Quality Framework (DQF) uses Multidimensional Quality Metrics	65
4.1	Example of term definition in SL	74
5.1	Positive and negative sides to revision in XLIFF or bilingual files	101
5.2	Random selection of criteria found in LSP evaluation statements (2019)	104
5.3	Error typology grid applied to a CAT tool with integrated MT	106
6.1	Selected terms and conditions for translation services	117

PREFACE

A Project-Based Approach to Translation Technology is about technological translation tools and how they learn through artificial intelligence. But the book is also about users and how they can learn to manage these tools. The pedagogy, the process of teaching and learning, is important in this book: it builds on the social constructivist theory in which knowledge is constructed collaboratively through social interaction in class (Kiraly 1995, 2000, 2005, 2012, 2014). Kiraly argues that collaborative learning teaches us more about our learning process as well as the translation process than, for example, a competence-based approach. This book moves on from this premise and includes the management of workflow through technological tools. Constructivist principles encourage interaction between professional activity and academic reflection, a thread that runs through all the chapters (Mitchell-Schuitevoerder 2013). Kiraly's constructivism requires learner-centred activities in which students are given a framework and then set their own objectives. Such activities constitute the project-based end-of-chapter assignments in this book.

'Learner empowerment' is a constructivist notion suggesting that if learner independence is initiated during the training, it will continue afterwards. This approach is essential: incessant developments in translation technology and the expanding range of tools requires the translator's continuous adaptation to new models and meanings. Therefore, it is important that ideas coming from the student are 'scaffolded', that they are given a real-time context, and are linked to supportive materials by the instructor (Kiraly 2000). If students set their own objectives, they must also know which tools and skills are required (Kiraly 1995).

A final comment about the importance of revision and evaluation in the book: because students actively construct their real-time technological translation skill in the assignments, they need to be involved in the evaluation of their own work to check whether they have met their objectives (Kiraly 2000). Suitable assessment methods are required to find out whether the translation project and process, including the use of technological tools, have been successful.

ACKNOWLEDGEMENTS

My gratitude goes first to hundreds of MA students at the universities of Durham and Newcastle who attended my translation and technology classes. I observed how they responded to the topic and my project-based style of teaching (at Durham University). I would like to thank Federico Federici and Ya Yun Yalta Chen for inviting me to teach. The project-based approach was Federico Federici's brain-child and my ensuing research path took me to conferences across the globe where I heard and exchanged ideas with many of the authors quoted in this book.

My thanks go to the Institute of Translation and Interpreting (UK) for the wide range of speakers they invited to their conferences and for their back-office support to me as a translator and author.

I thank my colleague translators in the ITI North East Regional Group in the UK for answering my questions about working practice.

A special word of thanks goes to Lucas Vieira Nunes who gave me the initial wink and useful answers to my questions about technological tools used in training institutions.

I would like to thank SDL Trados for giving me a personal licence to their CAT tool.

I am very grateful to the librarian of Bill Bryson Library University of Durham for giving me general access to their repository of (online) books.

I thank my friends: authors Jenny McKay and Simon Firth, editor Lynn Curtis, terminologist Sue Muhr-Walker, and URL adviser Xinyi WANG, for their advice and support.

And Lotte de Waal, thank you for your illustrations with a touch of humour.

Finally, my thanks go to the Routledge and series editors Kelly Washbourne, Louisa Semlyen, and Eleni Steck for making the preparation of this manuscript a smooth run. I received the support and answers I needed and I could work at my own pace without the translation deadlines I am used to.

ABBREVIATIONS

AEM	automatic evaluation metrics
AI	artificial intelligence
API	application programming interface
ASR	automatic speech recognition
BLEU	bilingual evaluation understudy
CAT	computer assisted/aided translation
CDA	confidential disclosure agreement
CMS	content management systems
CPD	continued professional development
DQF	data quality framework
DQF-MQM	data quality framework-multidimensional quality metrics
EAGLES	expert advisory group on language engineering standards
EEA	European economic area
EU/DGT	European Union directorate-general for translation
GALA	globalization and localization association
HR	human resources
HT	human translation
i18n	internationalisation
INDD	inDesign files
iOS	iPhone operating system (now including all devices)
IP	intellectual property
ISO	international organisation for standardisation
KWIC	key word in context
l10n	localisation
LISA	Localization Industry Standard Association
LQA	language quality assurance
LSP	language service provider

xviii Abbreviations

MS	Microsoft
MT	machine translation
NDA	non-disclosure agreement
NGO	non-government organisation
NLP	natural language processing
NMT	neural machine translation
PDF	portable document format
PE	post-edit
PEMT	post edit machine translation
PM	project manager
PO	purchase order
POS	parts of speech
Q&A	question and answer
QA	quality assurance
RBS	risk breakdown structure
RSI	repetitive strain injury
SaaS	software as a service
SEO	search engine optimisation
SL	source language
ST	source text
SR	speech recognition
STT	speech-to-text
T&C	terms and conditions
TAUS	translation automation user society
TBX	TermBase eXchange
TEnT	translation environment tool
TL	target language
TM	translation memory
Tmdb	terminology database
TMS	translation management system
TMX	translation memory eXchange
ToB	terms of business
TQA	translation quality insurance
TTS	text-to-speech
TT	target text
TU	translation unit
WCMS	web content management system
WWW	World Wide Web
XLIFF	xml localization interchange file format
XML	Extensible Markup Language

GLOSSARY

acceptability target text matches TL standards and end-user expectations

adequacy relates and qualifies the target text according to the source text

alphabetic language language based on roman letters

application programming interface a program that allows other programs to use its functions

authoring rights claim rights to the writing of an electronic document

auto-assembled string words in the target segment put together by the TM

automated speech recognition cloud-based AI technology for speech to text or text to speech

automatic evaluation metrics software programs that use a set of linguistic criteria for testing against a human reference translation

automatic speech recognition cloud-based AI speech technology

autosuggest prescriptive writing in the CAT tool

bilingual evaluation understudy an algorithm to evaluate the quality of an MT text

bootstrapped a glossary based on and derived from another glossary

code *see* language code/tag

cognitive ergonomics mental processes, such as motor response, which can affect interactions among humans and other elements of a system

cognitive friction resistance encountered by human intellect when engaging with a complex system of rules

collocates words that go together

Confidential Disclosure Agreement *see* non-disclosure agreement

content management system software application that allows users to collaborate in the creation of texts

context match a 100% TM match of a string of words

xx Glossary

Continued Professional Development   professional training in a variety of formats

copywriting   writing original texts

corpus-based MT   new data measured against data in the database

customisation   Tmdb phrases or terms in client glossaries

dialog   secondary window that allows users to perform a command

digital platform   facilitates exchanges between multiple parties in the cloud

domain knowledge   fields of specialism

domain-suffix   last part of a web address to define the type of website

drop-down menu   offers a list of options

Data Quality Framework   multidimensional metrics for quality assessment

Data Quality Framework-Multidimensional Quality Metrics   error typology

editor   *see* translation editor

encryption   converting data into a code for protection

error typology   measuring correct words against a benchmark translation

Extensible Markup Language   documents encoded in a format that is readable

false positives   potential but unsuitable matches

filter   searches for a specific item for a set purpose

fluency   target text matches TL standards and end-user expectations

fuzzy match   70%+ correct

fuzzy match threshold   proposal of matches only over 70%

gisting   a quality that gives a rough understanding

granular   tiny component

human resources   personnel

human translation   translated by a translator and not a machine

image-based   image files, not editable

indemnity insurance   an agreement to compensate for damage (through incorrect translation)

InDesign Files   image files, not processable in all CAT tools

intellectual property   ownership of ideas, intellectual creation and translation

intellectual property rights   legal right to claim ownership of ideas

interface   where two electronic components exchange data

International Organisation for Standardisation   group of experts to develop international standards

internationalisation   intermediary stage to remove culturally specific content

Key Word in Context   how the keyword is used with other words

language code   *see* language tag

language quality assurance *see* QA

language service provider   organisation offering language services

language tag/code   two letter endings to denote a language

leverage (of subsegment)   maximise the value

linear approach   read from beginning to end

Glossary **xxi**

local search   search in database
localisation   adapt terminology to culture and language of target country
Localization Industry Standard Association   produces a model for quality
  assurance
logographic languages   languages based on characters or symbols
lookup   quick term (phrase) search in databases
machine translation   text translated by machine translation engine
markup   tag with information
match   CAT tool term for TM proposal
natural language processing   a computer language to understand human
  language
neural machine translation   recent development of statistical machine
  translation
no match   no equivalence found in the TM
Non-Disclosure Agreement   signed document that promises not to divulge
  content
Non-Governmental Organisation   non-profit, voluntary group of people on
  international level
non-translatables   content that does not need to be translated
non-whitespace languages   character-based languages
offline editor   translation memory editor that works offline
on-demand software   companies pay a flat monthly fee for use of software
open-source   software that can be inspected, modified and enhanced by anyone
package   ZIP archive with XLIFF, TMX, TBX files for translation
paradigmatic approach   focus on the segment and its alternatives
parent folder   structured folder in Windows File Explorer
part of speech   category with similar grammatical properties
perfect match   equivalence keyword
plugin   small component in a larger piece of software and performs a
  specific task
Portable Document Format   uneditable image file
post-edit   MT edit
post-edited machine translation   machine translated text corrected
  by humans
post-editor   the linguist who post-edits MT
precision   the fraction of words in the MT output that is correct compared
  with the HT benchmark
pre-translate   CAT function to search TM/Tmdb for suitable matches
preview   separate window shows the target segments in context
project manager   member of project management team with specific role
propagate   CAT tool populates other occurrences in document
pseudo-translate   tests suitability of file for translation
purchase order   official document sent to translator with details about type,
  word count, deadline, and agreed price for the translation

xxii Glossary

push and pull approach proposals and requests

quality assessment quality measurement

quality assurance CAT tool function checks for errors

recall the total number of correct words (i.e. precision instances) produced by the MT

reference translation originally a human translation used to test the quality of speech recognition

regex mathematical theory to match recurrent patterns

repetitive strain injury pain felt in muscles due to overuse

ribbon taskbar in MS Word and CAT tools

Risk Breakdown Structure categories of risk

Search Engine Optimisation a technique used to move websites to the top of search engine rankings by means of search words or keywords

seed terms/list keywords on webpages

software as a service to access software in the cloud

speech recognition software to convert speech to text

speech-to-text speech converted to text on a digital device

standalone not web-based

standardisation technical specifications and criteria to ensure that materials and products are interconnected and interoperable

statistical MT MT based on data from bilingual text corpora

status bar horizontal bar at bottom of screen

string group of words that operate together

syllabic language *see* alphabetic language

tag symbol that contains formatting information

term extract extracts keywords and expressions in a new source text or a corpus of existing translations

terminology database database in CAT tool for manual entry of term pairs

terms and conditions general agreement between vendor and buyer of service

terms of business see terms and conditions

text-to-speech artificial voice reads text from PC

transcreation translation+creation: a marketing term that refers to the adaptation of ST to localised TT

Translation Automation User Society commercial organisation that develops MT testing metrics

translation editor/grid the interface with grids with ST and TT segments

translation environment tool translation technological tools

translation management system supports complex translation projects with integrated MT

translation memory key memory database in CAT tool

translation quality assurance *see* quality assurance

Translation Results window window that shows proposed matches

translation unit confirmed translation pair in the translation editor

Glossary **xxiii**

usability   MT quality criterion to determine level of usefulness

vendor   linguist who sells their services to the LSP

web content management system   web-based content management system (*see* CMS)

web localisation   making the text linguistically and culturally appropriate to the target locale (country/region and language)

whitespace languages   word-based languages

World Wide Web   internet

INTRODUCTION FOR INSTRUCTORS

This book is designed for instructors whose students are new to translation technology. It can also be used for students and professionals who want to learn more about translation technology and project management. This book is not a manual of technological translation tools, nor is it a guide to translation project management. If students have not yet been introduced to CAT tools, the suggestion is to throw them in at the deep end. The manufacturers of CAT tools and other translation software products provide detailed manuals, videos, Q&A pages, and knowledge base portals. It is important to point students to the Help sections in the CAT tool. Don Kiraly (APTIS Newcastle upon Tyne 2019) suggested that a 30-minute introduction to the CAT tool by the instructor should be enough to get students started, on condition that they use the CAT tool daily. The instructor's colleagues should allow and encourage students to deliver all their translation work in CAT tools. An introduction to CAT tools for teachers may be helpful. The key to CAT tool competence is regular use. A weekly instruction class is relatively unproductive, because it is not enough to consolidate a large amount of newly learnt skills, however small they may be.

The project-based approach aims to give the students an all-round perspective of translation projects, workflow, and of the teamwork required to complete large multilanguage translation projects using translation environment tools (TEnTs).

The book does not aim to be prescriptive: suggested TEnTs may not be accessible and they could become obsolete over time. One can only use what is available in the educational institution. There is the option to download demo versions on personal devices. The URL address www.routledgetranslationstudiesportal.com/ in the textbook points to the (editable) Routledge Translation Studies Portal. The double asterisks ★★ in the book are important markers that signify useful URL addresses in the Portal. The asterisks are followed by the title of the relevant section on the web page. If URLs are not accessible, you may be able to find alternative sites from your location.

The role of the instructor

The instructor is a guide and a supervisor. The project-based approach is student-centred. The instructor decides with the students on a framework that is suitable and feasible, makes suggestions and sets objectives, but does not determine the outcome. Meanwhile, the amount of new experiences for students may be such that clear guidance and a tight control of the steps in the process, especially in the assignments, is necessary. The instructor is free to decide on the running order in which chapters and assignments are presented to students. The instructor is the best person to gauge the students' competencies and skill levels. Equally important are the availability of hardware, software, and access to the web that will determine when or whether to discuss a chapter. A mix-and-match approach to the learning material in the chapter is possible.

The learning process

The project-based approach draws heavily on the ideas of Kiraly (2000, 2012) and Pym (1993). It is a constructivist way of learning in the classroom (Kiraly 2012) that requires long-term, interdisciplinary, and student-centred activities. It assumes that skills and competencies will be enhanced through social interaction in class. It encourages the analysis of problems and troublesome areas, which should ideally be managed collaboratively (Land and Meyer 2006). Pym (1993) underlines these notions: the starting process should not be the translation process, but an analysis of the problems ahead. If we start from a theory, we will be searching for matching examples – an approach that does not encourage the application of critical thinking. In this book the project-based assignments constitute the 'problem'. Students and instructors should start out by analysing them collaboratively. After the framework and clear objectives have been set, the instructor becomes the guide and supervisor, or an overall coordinator (Mitchell-Schuitevoerder 2014).

A project-based approach suits translation technology. Students need greater and more in-depth skills, knowledge and hands-on experience before they enter the profession. Humanities students are perceived to be more reluctant to engage with technology and if there is an element of fear this could limit the student's potential during and after studies (Doherty and Moorkens 2013). A translation project is complex with many stages from translation to revision and completion, and many more in between. Workflow [is important and] should ideally be discussed and designed first in each project-based assignment.

Student-centred project management

We know that the CAT learning curve is steep and that much effort goes into generating the first CAT target translation. Why then should we add the layer of project management? The answer is that the interplay between translation technology, situation, and context is best practised in project management. *Situatedness* brings the real world into the learning process (Rohlfing et al. 2003). A student who struggles with the CAT tool and does not experience the interplay, who cannot understand the context, and cannot visualise the situation, is likely to give up on translation technology. They must learn to see the whole picture: the situation is created by the source text with its characteristics and constraints (e.g. PDF formats), the context as a construct that depends on factors, such as language pair and direction (are there enough students in class with the same language pairs?), access to the internet, etc. The context controls and challenges the user. A CAT tool presents its own boundaries and limitations and they too are part of the context. The student is confronted with a situation and is challenged to act appropriately within it. They need to learn to shape translation technology instead of being shaped by it; in the book they learn about issues surrounding machine translation, translation quality in TEnTs, digital ethics, translating in the cloud and this knowledge should help them make choices and set parameters.

'Situated learning' gives the student a chance to reflect on the role and impact of translation technologies and to see the bigger picture (Bowker 2015). We need to create an authentic workplace in the classroom where students work and learn collaboratively in preparation for a career in the translation industry. The 'Food for thought' sections in this book invite discussion or reflection on the theory. The project-based assignments combine understanding, reflection, learning, and teamwork in practice.

Project-based assignments

The project-based assignments in the chapters offer frameworks which can and should be adapted by the instructor, in line with situation and context, and competencies. The assignments challenge the students to remember, understand, apply, analyse, evaluate, and create (Bloom's revised taxonomy 2001). The instructor leads discussions and offers support during planning and execution stages. After the team's self-analysis and evaluation, the instructor sits down with the students for a final assessment of their collaborative translation project.

Cross-curricular or modular approach

If the degree course includes a terminology module, a cross-curricular/modular execution of project assignments works well. Newly created glossaries – bilingual or monolingual – and corpora can be uploaded in a CAT terminology database. Cross-curricular/modular revision practices would support/could be supported by CAT tool quality assurance. If practice translations (homework) are completed in CAT tools and exchanged in bilingual doc. format, revised files with comments can be re-imported in the CAT tool and resubmitted as a clean target file. This working practice can be started early if the instructor's colleagues are willing to support a cross-modular/curricular approach to terminology and revision with translation technology tools. By the end of the book, students should have experienced most management and linguist roles pertaining to the creation and completion of a translation project. They will also have tried and managed a variety of technological features. They should have taken turns in managing multiple translation projects. Project management and other business-focussed or career-oriented skills must be consolidated in the final chapters. The instructor could arrange a presentation on project management by a colleague or student from the business school at any time.

Assessment

A project-based approach to translation technology is built on the premise that what happens in the industry should be trialled in class. Errors are made, outcomes may vary, and evaluation is essential to achieving improvement. Three types of assessment in collaboration between instructor and students can be used as a starting point (Robinson et al 2008):

- translation quality assessment

Students must not forget the ultimate objective of learning about translation technology, which is to improve translation quality. The submission of a final translation by a team can be graded by the instructor.

- peer/self-assessment of translation quality and efficiency through project management

The collaboratively agreed final team translation is the benchmark [translation] by which students assess and rate their individual translations. Although the focus in each project-based assignment is different, the students must recognise that the goal of a quality TM, good reference materials, and terminology databases or revision practice achieved with TEnTs, is *an error-free translation*. It is easy to lose sight of this goal and to concentrate on the success of the TEnT(s). Metrics and quality standards discussed in the book make it easy to switch to rating the TEnT rather than the translation!

- the individual student should assess their own translation quality and efficiency achieved through collaboration and project management

Individual assessment should be of the student's own translation against the benchmark translation.

- Project management assessment – both peer and individual – can be arranged in collaboration with the instructor and should include the assessment of work by the team and its individual members. It can be helpful to use a Likert scale for rating activities such as:

xxviii Introduction for instructors

- learning from each other
- dividing/sharing work
- clarity of task briefs
- time management
- collective decision-making
- communication
- motivation
- responsibility of self/peers
- tool management
- personal learning

A heuristic approach to learning or problem-solving allows the student to discover and learn from their own experiences through analysis and synthesis. Ultimately, students should be able to ask themselves: what should be my role / how can I solve the problem / should I act or refrain from comment / what can I do in this situation and what is the most practical solution? Regardless of the problem or the relevant technology, they should always adopt a can-do approach.

Team setup

Students who have not yet worked in the translation industry may not necessarily be familiar with concepts such as project management or project-based translation. Both concepts are explained in Chapter 1 but students will need guidance and support when setting up their teams to carry out a project-based assignment. The assignments vary between two kinds of team setup: the project team in which a team of students work together and a project management team that manages and contracts students to do the work. The boundary between the two types of team is not strict, and there may be situations where there are not enough students to form teams and assignments will have to be carried out collaboratively. Setting up a team is challenging and needs to be well organised:

- Project management teams need enough members to manage the different components of the translation project. If a project team is small, the members may have to take on multiple roles. Students who are members of a team may have double roles if they are contracted by other teams to translate. Students should have a chance to try different roles. There are arguments for and against continuing with the same teams. Variety is beneficial but continuity can give better results. The decision may depend on whether the translation project is short term or long term (see Shuttleworth 2017).
- Teamwork is vital. The establishment of teams may be dependent on the availability of students with similar language pairs. Diversity of target languages is

common in real-time project management teams. Linguists are asked to check for accuracy in languages they do not know.

Completion dates and source texts

There is a close link between completion dates and translation projects. The time between request and delivery is often a matter of days. Ideally, students should experience working under time pressure and it is wise to press for completion within a week. If the assignment drags on for much longer, students lose interest and become demotivated.

Trainee translator students do not generally have the knowledge and expertise to choose suitable source texts for TEnTs. They will need guidance from the instructor. There are several options:

1. the instructor prepares a range of URLs with suitable source texts containing short sentences and repetition. The digital format of the text matters, too. A text without layout requirements or HTML markup codes would be preferable in the initial assignment;
2. the instructor invites an external 'client' to supply their source material for translation. A good example is University College London (Shuttleworth 2017) where the translation trainee students collaborated with the Museum of Zoology with a repository of 68,000 specimens. The museum was delighted to have students translating for free and the students were highly motivated to produce translated material that would be published.

Finding organisations around the campus or your locality willing to supply e-materials in return for free translations by the students would undoubtedly be appreciated by all parties. They could be museums, transport companies, commercial companies, educational organisations, but also and particularly charities or not-for-profit organisations … the list is endless. If they have a website or materials that have been part translated, previously translated material would be ideal for text alignment and consistency.

Hardware and software

Suitable hardware and software are essential, such as enough desktop PCs with MS Windows, but when it comes to software, the instructor must decide what is feasible. It is not necessary to introduce students to multiple CAT tools. If they understand the basics of one, they may be able to adapt their skills to others. Software manufacturers are known to offer CAT tool licences with a server version to educational institutions. There is a huge range of freeware and shareware tools. Web-based TEnTs in Chapter 7 have the advantage of being comprehensive, including TM and MT features.

xxx Introduction for instructors

Technology is challenging, particularly when it comes to compatibility, the instructor needs ingenuity and lateral thinking.

Checklist for the instructor:

- source texts
- MS Word skills
- instruction to the instructor's colleagues
- instruction to students on self- and peer-assessment (it includes revision, but also personal and team skills)
- invitation to a business school teacher to give instruction on business and workflow models relating to project management

INTRODUCTION FOR STUDENTS AND TRANSLATORS

What the book plans to teach you

After thirty years as a freelance translator, I can honestly say it is a great profession. Technology has only made it better for me, because I can now work anywhere I choose. I open the computer-assisted translation (CAT) tool on my smartphone and speak the translation into the mic of my phone or else tap on a collapsible keyboard if I am in a public place. Amendments or additional paragraphs can be translated and added immediately. After six years as a teacher to post-graduate students of translation technology at two different universities in the UK, I have seen how former students have moved on and progressed in the translation industry. Recently, one student who is now a freelancer said that starting her career as a project manager of a language service provider (LSP) was the best thing she could have done. Another who worked with an LSP in the UK for 5 years, returned to Shanghai to be a project manager using a translation management system (TMS) either at home, at a hot-desk venue in the city, or at the LSP's headquarters in Dubai. Some have gone to work for LSPs abroad and returned as freelancers; others have used their acquired business-management skills and secured jobs with tech companies as software developers.

Fascinating as it has been to write a book on translation technology, it has also sometimes been a frustrating experience because of the ever-changing dynamics within the business. In the space of a year, long-established protocols and software can be completely overtaken by new developments. The most recent case in point was an observation I had made in one of the final chapters of this book that CAT tools do not have grammar checkers. This function has duly been introduced by one of the major tools, and undoubtedly other programs will follow suit. Translation technology is all about change and how to manage it. The Routledge Translation

Studies Portal is therefore *the* site to consult regularly for updates and additions and the names of products and tools. The URL address is www.routledgetranslationstud iesportal.com/. In the book URL links on the Portal are marked like this: **. The information in parentheses gives the title of the relevant section in the book on the Portal's web page.

Another concern has been deciding on the title of this book: outsiders interpret 'project-based approach' as meaning project management and 'translation technology' as machine translation. The project-based approach refers to the style of learning advocated and to the translation as a complex, frequently collaborative undertaking: volume and time constraints on source documents often mean that they must be split and shared among several translators. The translation technology component is best explained as the software that is used by translators and LSPs in large translation projects. The range of tools is infinite. The CAT (computer-aided translation) tool is the main player, because it is the tool into which so many other technological aids can be integrated. The machine translation engine is not the main player, even though it likes to compete with and within the CAT tool. It is, however, a very serious competitor both in terms of efficiency and improved translation quality. Watch this space!

The **project-based assignments** at the end of each chapter provide opportunities to practise translation technology skills, preferably within a framework of collaboration, through the use of appropriate tools. If circumstances do not permit organised collaboration, you will have to find other ways to collaborate: you can ask revisers anywhere in the world to revise target your files; you can ask teachers to comment on your work in bilingual CAT files; you can crowdsource; you can use digital platforms.

There may be several **setbacks** ahead of you while working through this book: the tool may not be available or work well, there may not be enough peers with the same language pair to facilitate collaboration or enough translators/revisers to tackle the job; or missed deadlines. These problems crop up in the working lives of professional translators too. This book aims to give you a better understanding, and **hands-on experience** within the assignments, of how translation technology is managed in the workplace. It also aims to help you use translation technology comfortably in your personal work environment. Translation technology is promoted as being a translator's best friend: manufacturers claim that it radically improves efficiency. Their often-used mantra is *less time, more profit, better quality*. We will put this to the test by using their translation technology tools and reviewing them through the eyes of the different parties involved.

This book is not only written for **trainee translators** and **aspiring translation project managers**, but also for **practising translators, project managers**, and **instructors.** Hopefully, practitioners within each category will appreciate being given an overview of translation technology tools and their impact on translation work. The project-based assignments at the end of the chapters are set up as frameworks and give users and readers of the book an opportunity to experience different roles, those of freelance or in-house translator, as well as reviser or project management team member ranging from project manager to human resources manager, client manager, terminologist, technology adviser. The translation project is viewed from the perspective of the software developers and the commissioning client who buys the translation service. Conflicts of interest are inevitable and it would be beneficial for all concerned if these could be aired and discussed during or after the assignment.

The **assignments** are an important component of the book. If they are read before an in-depth study of the chapter, they will give a preliminary indication of the skills and competences needed. They may also need modification in line with location, availability of tools, and language pairs. They should be planned together with the instructor, who can advise on suitable documents and files for translation and who will advise on time allowance for completion. Time for **reflection** must also be allowed: trainee and professional translators and managers should be encouraged to think about the tools they use and the quality of the product they hope to achieve. The 'Food for thought' sections are intended to promote discussion of potentially controversial issues. Time, for example, matters to all of us but in different ways. Clear deadlines must be set and met, and these should be tight in line with expectations and practice in the translation industry. A short deadline is important to the client who commissions a translation; having enough time to do the work properly matters to the translator who must deliver. The book highlights the paradox that although technology is supposed to help us reduce the time it takes to complete a job, sometimes it forces us to progress faster than we feel entirely comfortable with.

Other frustrations are that websites, webpages, and software programs are updated regularly, and web links are modified. Some cannot be accessed all over the world. For this reason, URL-links are not printed in the book but listed on the **Routledge Translation Studies Portal** where updates can be made as necessary. Technology companies and manufacturers come and go, the popularity of their products grows and wanes, and therefore the book makes limited reference to programs (see Portal).

Illustrations and data in the book are taken from the following CAT tool programs: DVX3, memoQ9, and SDL Trados Studio 2019. I started with Trados Workbench before the Millennium. I changed to DVX3, which was stable and straightforward but it did not keep up with SDL Trados Studio and memoQ. The competition between the latter two is fascinating to watch and experience. Other tools such as OmegaT, Lilt, and Wordfast decided not to compete but to move into the cloud where they are either open source or focus on machine translation.

This book is **not** a manual on how to use technological tools, nor is it a workbook. It is a practical textbook that aims to explain the ideas behind the technological tools available, their features and functions. The application in the project-based assignments depends on what is available where you study or work.

Although there is a gradual build-up from chapter to chapter in introducing new tools, it is possible to skip chapters or change their running order.

The book presumes a basic **knowledge of CAT tools**. Formal instruction may not be needed because the programs have made so much instructive material available, both within and outside the tool, that learning is best approached through doing. One of the foundations of CAT tool competence is a sound knowledge of MS Word and its functions.

The book touches on localisation, transcreation, and the technologies surrounding the translation of webpages. However, it does not cover these areas in detail. They are independent subjects, too extensive for a book that aspires to give an overview of generic technological tools. The book does not mention audiovisual tools for the same reason – they are specialist too. Nor does it explain machine translation (MT) as a product. MT is discussed purely as a supportive technological tool in relation to the CAT tool

Teamwork and code of conduct

The success of the project-based approach relies on good teamwork. The construct chosen is that of a language service provider. An LSP may consist of an in-house project management team with the following managers: (senior) project manager(s), relation managers, marketing and desktop publishing managers, recruitment managers, (human) resource managers, terminologists, technicians. The LSP will have an extensive database of linguists, including freelance translators and revisers. The project-based assignments require the formation of teams and the creation of a database of translators with different language pairs. Each team needs to set up a code of conduct to enable teamwork to progress smoothly. A code of conduct consists of a set of rules that will be respected by all team members: a commitment to meet agreed times, complete allotted tasks, maintain confidentiality, and show respect to others (this does not mean automatic agreement with other opinions, only that these must be respected). The rules should also include listening to each other, and a commitment to resolve conflict and tackle problems. There also need to be agreed measures to be taken should team members fail to meet set standards – intentionally or unintentionally – required to fulfil the project-based assignment.

There is no maximum or minimum number of team members. Under good management a larger team will achieve more than a small team. Good management means that senior managers will respect and listen to other team members and that decision-making is based on mutual consultation.

Pitfalls

Rather than my listing a whole string of recommendations here for avoiding potential problems with hardware and software, translation texts and resources, language pairs and direction, I suggest you discuss any specific concerns with your instructor in advance of beginning assignments, but here are a few general tips and warnings:

- internet

If there is no access to the internet, the project-based assignments cannot be carried out fully, nor can a translator or LSP do their work consistently. If the failure is temporary, it may be possible to use smartphones as hotspots for personal laptops. It is important that all files are kept backed up and available to meet this eventuality.

- texts for CAT tools

CAT tools work well with certain formats and love the repetition of terms and terminological phrases.

- hardware

If educational organisations cannot purchase software or licences, there are manufacturers that will offer licences for educational purposes. It is possible to download demos on personal laptops for limited periods of time.

- if there is a shortage of linguists in a specific language pair or direction, it is acceptable to source linguists outside your cohort. This is frequently a problem for LSPs and must be managed.

Remember, problem-solving is a prime requirement for users of translation technological tools!

1

COMPUTER-AIDED TRANSLATION TOOLS AND TRANSLATION PROJECT MANAGEMENT

Key concepts

- The translator, the language service provider (LSP), and computer-aided translation (CAT) tools have become partners in the translation process
- The computer-aided translation tool comes first among translation environment tools (TEnTs)
- The CAT tool is one of many TEnTs that can be linked or integrated
- The management of translation projects requires good teamwork, administrative and project-solving abilities

Introduction

CAT tools are invariably used in managed translation projects, but they can also be helpful in translation projects where the translator is working directly for the client. The CAT tool was built to assist the translator, it is shaped by the translator, it can efficiently process the work of collaborating translators and revisers, and it has become the tool used by project managers to help a team of linguists, in-house or freelance, to deliver a high volume of good quality translations, in multiple languages, shared among many contractees, and in the shortest period of time. Any difficulties associated with the tool must be solved by the users. Most likely, the problems were created by humans in the first place and not by the technology (Kenny 2016). This chapter builds on a basic level of CAT tool skills, good MS Word competence, the availability of Microsoft (MS) Windows operating systems and an appropriate CAT tool. In addition to MS Word and MS Windows expertise, your administrative skills will be challenged: effective personal file management is the precursor to successful CAT tool operations.

2 Computer-aided translation tools

1.1 Translation environment tools (TEnT)

The denotation 'translation environment tool' (TEnT) was coined in 2006 by Zetzsche, a translating professional, who realized that when translators refer to 'CAT tool', they are referring to the TM feature, which is only one component of a CAT tool. The acronym TEnT is meant to cover a broader spectrum. Currently, there does not seem to be much consistency in the usage of CAT or TEnT, so in this book CAT refers to the translation memory program, **TM** stands for the translation memory database, and TEnT covers a whole range of translation technology tools★★(go to www.routledgetr anslationstudiesportal.com/ – A Project-Based Approach to Translation Technology – links: The Tool Box; GALA's directory of language technologies). **GALA** (Globalization & Localization Association) lists language technologies ad infinitum. Some examples of lesser-known technologies are word-count software for all common file formats, terminology management software for multiple dictionaries or glossaries, and software that gives the user a clear picture of all their tasks and time expenses. The list continues to grow because the industry will provide new tools to help us manage our day-to-day operations and tools if they perceive a gap in the market. For example, **translation management systems** (7.5) allow us to manage not only CAT tools but administration, accounting, human resources, project management, etc.

Zetzsche's list (2003–17) of required technology tools for the translator heads off with Microsoft Windows (MS) and Office. MS software is the first essential. In a **standalone** and not web-based CAT tool, docx, Excel and PowerPoint files are uploaded and saved in MS Office, then imported in the CAT tool and exported to MS Office after translation. The translation, or target file, is then called a 'clean' file. Sometimes the client or LSP also need the bilingual CAT work file, the so-called 'dirty' file or XLIFF file (2.4).

Other examples of TEnTs are dictionaries, bookkeeping/financial tools, conversion tools (although CAT programs can convert Adobe PDF files (2.4), they do not always retain the original layout), web browsers (Firefox, Chrome, Opera, etc.) and programs for graphics and desktop publishing that enable the delivery of a ready-to-use product. Beyond the basics, such as indispensable security software, there are PDF fixing tools for recovery or repair, and screenshot readers which convert screen content to editable format. And then there are **APIs**, **plugin**s (7.1), speech recognition software (7.1.1) to name but a few, which can either be linked to the CAT tool or integrated. Different CAT programs have different strengths and weaknesses, which is why additional TEnTs can be helpful. Apparently, translators' most popular TEnTs lie in the field of terminology and will be discussed in detail in Chapter 4. And then there are the comprehensive translation management systems, which automate many parts of the translation process and include business management tools (Chapter 7), popular among LSPs. The trend to integrate many TEnTs is gathering momentum.

1.2 Compatibility

Most CAT tools operate on **MS** Windows systems. Users of non-MS Windows systems can either download virtual MS software or use CAT tools specifically designed for their systems. Currently the leading programs are only Windows-friendly. LSPs often prefer to contract translators who use MS operating systems for ease and compatibility. Many MS-based TEnTs are a challenge for non-Windows users.

OmegaT was launched in 2000 to work on multiple operating systems and others have followed. Whereas the big players in the MS Windows market are expensive to purchase and to maintain (annual service agreements, upgrades), OmegaT is an example of free **open-source software** for non-MS users. *Open* means that it can be inspected, modified, and enhanced by anyone, either producer or user. OmegaT's compatibility with other CAT programs is supported through filter plugins, which allow you to process XLIFF files, the standard workfiles in CAT (2.4). XLIFF is an **XML**-based format, created to facilitate the exchange of files between programs and users. Extensible Markup Language (XML) encodes documents in a format that is both human-readable and machine-readable. The demand to use iOS (Apple's operating system) software and not only Microsoft on desktops and laptops has increased so much that many suitable CAT programs have been designed since OmegaT entered the market★★(link: non-MS compatible CAT tools). Leading CAT tool competitors are Microsoft only programs.

Not only hardware-cum-software, but also the format of source files is an area where compatibility plays a role. CAT tools can handle major file types like Microsoft Office files and webpages, but more complicated file types such as image files are not always supported. For example, InDesign design files (INDD) are currently only supported by one CAT tool★★(link: INDD compatible), and even then, only after conversion in the cloud. XML files, in which text is created and stored in databases rather than in document files, can be converted in CAT tools, but not without limitations or applied filters. Once they are set up in the CAT tool the process is straightforward and they will be delivered as a perfect image product, ready for publication, if **tags** and **codes** have been applied correctly (2.4). PDF files can be problematic in relation to formatting. Hence, there are conversion TEnTs to make the import in a CAT tool straightforward (2.4).

A different kind of compatibility, or conflict, arises between web-based and standalone CAT tools (1.6.2). When the translator is required to work in a web or cloud-based CAT tool, such as a server managed by an LSP, the translator cannot take ownership of the data they have entered in the TM database. If the translator cannot download the XLIFF file or work in, for example, the program's **off-line editor**★★(link: offline mode), the translation units entered in the TM are no longer the translator's intellectual property. This loss of control often means that translators cannot build their own TMs. The technical and ethical aspects of TM sharing and online translation/collaboration will be discussed in more detail in Chapters 2 and 6.

Lack of compatibility between CAT tools has brought much frustration to working translators. The manufacturers are fully aware, and they improve compatibility to remain ahead of their competitors. Technology is often driven by manufacturers, who do listen if users make their voices heard. The user-friendliness of CAT tools today compared to the early programs in the 1990s has made the current tools intuitive and much more accessible.

4 Computer-aided translation tools

1.3 Translation memory

In this section we will scroll through reasons for using a CAT tool. The technology in the TM database will be studied in Chapter 2. But first, we should consider the learning curve that appears to deter some practitioners from using CAT tools. Over the years, the curve has become less steep for two reasons: the manufacturers compete to make their software user-friendly; they have included clearly written Help features and videos that can be accessed from within the CAT tool and the internet has opened many opportunities for users and learners to find instruction and answers to questions. If you consider yourself a newbie and feel unsure about how to use a CAT tool, demo versions can be downloaded for a month and the manufacturers' training videos will get you started. If you need more help, there are translator platforms which offer advice through Q&A; translator support is offered on mailing lists and in online support groups, and professional organisations**(link: professional organisations) offer **continued professional development (CPD)** webinars to members.

We owe the following definition for the TM to EAGLES (Expert Advisory Group on Language Engineering Standards). It describes a TM as a text archive of matching source and target units with appropriate metadata to support the ranking. The definition also points to variations between programs:

> A translation memory is a collection of multilingual correspondences with optional control information stored with each correspondence. [...] The control information can include information about the source text [...], its date, author, company, subject domain. This information may be used in ranking matches. [...] A given query with a current source segment may return a number of correspondences with matching stored source segments.
>
> CAT programs differ as to the information stored along with the raw texts and the retrieval methods. [...]
>
> *EAGLES 1996*

In 2010, two decades after the software had entered the market and competition had flourished, TAUS, the Translation Automation User Society, predicted a more advanced future for translation memory**(link: TAUS). The EAGLES definition of TM as a text archive from which translator select, has changed to programs which are highly compatible. They use a ranking system to suggest and propose and it is up to the user to reject or accept. TAUS wants to prove that algorithms, metrics, ranked matches in TM, and machine translation (MT) are on a par. They believe that TM will move into the cloud, like its MT sibling:

> The opportunities for advanced leveraging using sub-segment matches and a combination of **statistical** algorithms and linguistic intelligence have unfortunately been ignored for too long by the mainstream industry.

TM will now finally become a smart tool, bridging the gap with its more intelligent MT sister and significantly increasing the recycling of previous translations. At the same time, TM will move into the cloud. Leveraging of translations will be done in the cloud through web services links in desk-top and enterprise translation tools. The combination of advanced leveraging and the sharing of TMs in the cloud will boost translation productivity by 30% to 50%. And just as important, we will see greater consistency and accuracy in translations.

TAUS Predictions Webinar, 21 January 2010

Why should we use TM? According to the industry's mantra, we need TM to reduce our time investment, to improve efficiency/productivity and profit. They claim that the translator will spend less time recalling terminology they translated previously, because **matches** are proposed each time the TM identifies repetition. Not only does the program increase our efficiency, but it will also boost profit: less time means more money. *Repetition* has gradually become a keyword with the negative connotation that creativity is irrelevant because we need consistency. Indeed, the TM works extremely efficiently in texts with high repetition rates, but repetition should not be the only criterion for using TM. The CAT tool has many advantages over and above translations performed outside the tool:

- clear side-by-side presentation of ST and TT
- segmentation of text helps prevent omission
- the search function facilitates searches in large texts and multiple texts
- power loss does not affect the TM, hence no loss of translated text
- autocorrection and accuracy checks support 'tired eyes'
- well-structured revision features
- text sharing and third-party revision or collaboration across different computers
- the integration of many tools (dictionaries, glossaries, API machine translation) in one program
- the history of previous matches

The listed features show that the CAT tool can be supportive in different genres or styles of text and in a variety of formats. TM supports our personal working memory; it remembers what might have slipped our mind.

The formatting function, a helpful characteristic of the CAT tool (1.6.1) is a great time saver. It replicates the layout of the ST in the TT and it facilitates the translation of file formats which cannot be processed in MS Word. The CAT tool automatically converts the different formats to its standard bilingual interface (2.4). Web formats are one example of the many new technological features that have leveraged translation above the pure act of translating. They have placed more demands on the translator. CAT tools can help (Melby and Wright 2015: 665).

6 Computer-aided translation tools

Food for thought…

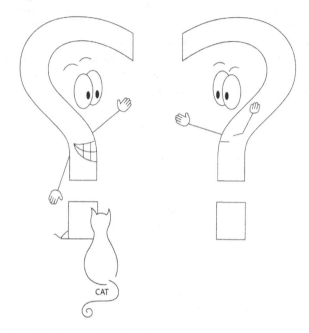

What value does the CAT tool add to the translation process?

1.4 File management

A file is a container in a computer system for storing information. Good management of electronic files as soon as we receive them is crucial to learning how to manage CAT tools. It prevents 'loss' of files in the many new folders set up by the CAT tool. CAT programs have different systems of storing files, but they share the creation of many new files and their way of naming them. For example, one source file will generate the following files:

- source file
- bilingual doc file (for review)
- XLIFF file (the work file that can be shared with others)
- TM database
- terminology database
- target file

The total files and folders vary between programs, as well as the storage system. The translator cannot control the generation of files but can control where they are stored. Before importing the source file in the CAT tool, it is important to

- name the source file clearly, and
- to store it in a clearly marked folder

1.4.1 Filenames

Do not change filenames

The naming of a computer file should be done with care, clarity, and precision. Once in the CAT tool the name cannot be changed. LSPs request a filename not to be changed because a different name would prevent it from being imported in their system.

Label files with short names or numbers and language tags

The filename should be clear and short and not exceed the width of the column in File Explorer, where it is stored. Do not add spaces but underscore: AB_2020_IT.

Numbers provide a better chronology than alphabetic ordering: 01_ASD precedes ASD_01

01_ASD
ASD_01
BSD_04
BSD_15
BSD_7

Non-alphabetic languages

If the language is non-alphabetic and contains characters the computer will have its own method to order filenames, by strokes or sounds, for example in pinyin. To achieve a degree of conformity and homogeneity between languages, filenames generally begin with numbers.

Language codes or tags

The ending of source and target files should always be with the relevant **language codes**, also called **language tags**. Some languages have different two-letter codes due to variations within a language. Language codes (ISO 639-1)★★(link: ISO standards) and country codes (ISO 3166)★★(link: ISO standards) are not the same. The filename 0123_en_GB indicates that the source text is in British English.

Target language tags/codes

The CAT tool adds TL tags to filenames, or it creates folders with the relevant language/country tags where it stores exported files. We can make the CAT tool send our files to the folders where we want them. We need to be systematic and create a good **parent folder** with subfolders (Figures 1.1 and 1.2) before we open the CAT tool.

8 Computer-aided translation tools

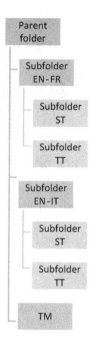

FIGURE 1.1 Translator's parent folder

Parent folder

A parent folder is the higher directory and can be filled with subdirectories or subfolders. Figure 1.1 is an example of a parent folder with subfolders set up by the translator who set up a parent folder with three subfolders:

TMs EN-FR and EN-IT

The translator's TM folder in Figure 1.1 may have two TM databases for EN<>FR and EN<>IT respectively. The language subfolders contain subfolders for ST and TT. If CAT tools generate their own directories, it is best to keep your directory simple and just create a folder as in Figure 1.2 where the translator has one folder for CAT projects and one client folder (Agency F).

CAT tool folder

In Figure 1.2 the CAT tool generated seven subfolders for source text, target text, review files, TM, reports, and retrofit (re-import of final target text). If we set up a 'project' in the CAT tool, rather than a 'single document', we can then add files to the project later.

Computer-aided translation tools 9

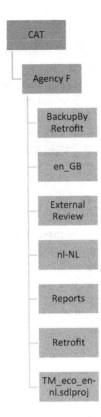

FIGURE 1.2 Subfolders generated by CAT tool

Tips

[...] symbol

If you are not familiar with operations, and you want to export or generate a target file, do so slowly and click on the [...] symbol next to the filename. It opens your browser and allows you to select a folder where you want to store the target files. By clicking on 'next' or 'finish' without opening your browser, the CAT tool takes control and place files in its program folders or generates new folders. The general rule of thumb is that if we click on Next, Next, Next, without much consideration as to what is happening, we allow the CAT tool to make choices that tend to ignore *our* directories.

Do not move files

Moved files can no longer be opened in the CAT tool because the CAT tool classifies them as '*lost*'. The error message 'file cannot be found' is final and future updates will not be possible.

1.5 From Microsoft to CAT tools

A more than basic familiarity with Microsoft Windows and Microsoft Word is extremely helpful. CAT tools replicate MS software with windows, **dialog** boxes, ribbons, menus, toolbars, and functions. Dialog boxes are the small windows that can be moved by clicking on the ribbon and dragging them to a position where you want them. A good level of MS Word skills and knowledge of keyboard shortcuts is useful too. There are many free MS Word skill tests on the internet to test or improve your skill levels**(link: MS Word test).

1.5.1 The ribbon

CAT software and MS Word**(link: Microsoft glossary) have similar **ribbon**s, **status bar**s at the bottom, windows, **interface**s and dialog boxes. We can access the ribbon by using the mouse (mousepad) or by typing shortcut codes. The mouse has two buttons, the left click and right click, which operate different functions. The left click is the main button by default (it can be reversed for left-handed users) and we use it to select objects and double click to open them. The right mouse button can open the contextual tabs on the ribbon and a drop-down menu in a CAT tool segment. Generally, a right click will open a menu**(link: mouse functions).

Right click

- opens **drop-down menu**s (also accessible through tabs on the ribbon)
- opens a function icon on the ribbon which gives access to a toolbar with new functions

Left click

- on an icon or the little triangle underneath opens a drop-down menu.** (link: MS Word).

FIGURE 1.3 Ribbon in MS Word

The ribbon, in MS Word and the CAT tool, is a powerful command bar that has organised the program's features into a series of tabs at the top of the window.

Several MS Word core functions are quite similar to CAT tool functions:

- The Application button, top left, which presents a menu of file-related commands, such as Save, Open, Close. It is advisable to make good use of this button, particularly when closing a file (avoid the temptation to click the cross in the right top corner – it is not a saving function).
- The quick Access Toolbar is the smallest toolbar (top left): it displays most frequently used commands, such as Save.
- Core tabs are the tabs that are always displayed, such as Home and Review.
- Contextual tabs are displayed within certain types of files and remain grey if not applicable.
- Galleries are lists of commands or options presented graphically as icons, for example, on the toolbar with descriptors and icons, such as Thesaurus and the icon of a dictionary.
- Dialog box launchers are buttons (or tiny arrows) at the bottom of some groups of tabs that open dialog boxes with features relating to the group. 'Font' opens a broad range of options, such as Strikethrough or Uppercase.

The functions on the ribbon operate the program. We tend to use the functions we think we need, and ignore others. The CAT tool ribbon contains functions that override the default status and make it more adaptable to our needs, for example, our language pairs. Our productivity, quality, and efficiency will benefit from taking time to become familiar with the ribbon.

1.5.2 Keyboard shortcuts

Many keyboard shortcuts**(link: keyboard shortcuts) are identical in MS and CAT tools. Keyboard shortcuts open functions just like the mouse. Shortcuts are accurate, immediate and appropriate, and they may even help us prevent repetitive strain injury (RSI), associated with the mouse. An example of a keyboard shortcut in Word and CAT:

Alt+A highlights the entire file or a smaller section
Ctrl+C copies the selection
Ctrl+X cuts, and
Ctrl+V pastes

Shortcuts help us work faster and are more precise than moving the mouse to commands on the ribbon. If there is shortcut, it can be found by hovering over an icon on the ribbon and the code will appear. Apparently, we save time by keeping our fingers on the keyboard and it prevents clicking on the wrong icon or command.

12 Computer-aided translation tools

1.6 The CAT tool

LSPs generally expect their contracted freelancers to own a CAT tool and to be competent users. In the following sections we will discuss what the CAT tool does, the different types and the relationship between the translator and the CAT tool.

1.6.1 CAT tool features

A CAT tool has four main features: firstly, it segments the text into units and presents the source and target segments next to or below each other (2.1.1) in a translation grid (also called **translation editor**); secondly, a source segment and target segment form a pair, called a **translation unit** (TU); thirdly, the translation memory stores TUs which are recalled as perfect or fuzzy matches when the TM recognises a source segment (2.1); finally it employs an automatic lookup in its TM and terminology databases to display search results for insertion (2.1).

The following list of additional features was partly compiled by GALA (Globalization and Localization Association), an international non-profit organisation whose members specialise in language services, translation, and technological applications in the translation industry. All the functions and features are incorporated in CAT tools to support the translation memory:

- Spellcheckers autocorrect the spelling of alphabetic languages, but most do not support logographic languages based on characters or symbols. The spellcheckers rely on delimiters such as spaces and punctuation to identify words. In **alphabetic** or **syllabic languages**, they automatically highlight errors and fix spelling and grammar mistakes. CAT programs rely on the MS Word spellchecker and Hunspell, an open-source program which is used in Google Chrome. The default spellchecker varies between CAT tools, but either program can be used.
- The in-context preview allows translators to preview their translation in real time in a separate window on their screen, which gives a better overview of ST and TT than the editor's segmentation window.
- Integrated machine translation is possible in CAT tools but must be enabled in the CAT program. An **API** key (7.1) is usually required, so that you can pay the provider of the MT engine for the data you send to the MT engine.
- Adaptive machine translation learns from user input in the CAT tool★★(link: examples of adaptive MT programs).
- A **concordance** is a text search tool that looks for examples of a word or an expression in a **string**, i.e. within context, in the translation memory database, when requested. It checks usage, not meaning. Results can be inserted in the editor.

Computer-aided translation tools **13**

- Electronic dictionaries can be linked for additional term searches inside the tool.
- The alignment function helps you build translation memories by aligning source and target texts that were translated previously outside the tool.
- Terminology databases and term extraction tools.
- Word counts and match statistics, the basis of quotes for translation services.
- File conversion processes many different formats.
- Predictive typing as in smartphones.
- Quality assurance, which is an error-spotting function during the entire translation process (Chapter 5).

Most CAT tools support MS Office formats, such as .docx, .odt, .csv, .xlsx, plus .html files and .xml. The translation industry has introduced the **XLIFF** file (interchangeable CAT tool format) and **TMX** file (interchangeable format for databases) which improve compatibility and homogeneity. Advanced CAT tools also support software formats, such as .json, which is a language independent format, Visual Studio and software for layout and building plans, such as InDesign, Corel Draw and sometimes AutoCAD. The usefulness of CAT tools cannot be denied when translating multimedia formats. They extract text for translation, rebuild and reformat the file in the target language after the translation is finished. The translator works in the standard bilingual CAT tool text display and is not distracted by metadata or, for example, the autocompletion function in Excel (2.4 Formats). The spellchecker is automatically operable in the CAT tool, contrary to Excel and other formats.

1.6.2 Standalone and web-based CAT tools

CAT tools are available for online or offline usage. Web-based (cloud-based) CAT tools are accessed online and require a licence, which is often supplied by the commissioning LSP for the duration of the project; standalone desktop CAT tools must be purchased and the programs can be downloaded. Compared with web-based CAT tools, they have the advantage that they do not depend on internet connection stability. Although CAT tools were originally designed to work in standalone mode, a server version has cloud-computing features. The server is used in environments where collaboration is required, for example in training centres or project management teams. LSPs may switch from servers to comprehensive translation management systems (TMS). They automate the translation process and give the project manager an overview of operations ranging from translation projects to accounting, marketing, buying and selling translation services (7.5)★★(link: web-based and TMS systems). The advantages and disadvantages of working with web-based tools are discussed in more detail in 7.2.

14 Computer-aided translation tools

A new type of web-based CAT tool entered was launched in 2019, the smartphone or tablet version★★(link: web-based and standalone parity). Obviously, the phone version cannot show all the functions, but it works well as a backup for the translator on the road who is asked to make quick changes or add a paragraph. The developers of CAT tools are constantly bringing changes with modified or new features. The similarity between the main tools has increased greatly, and so has their compatibility. Many LSPs prefer translators to work on their servers and if this trend continues it will be interesting to see if it will at all be necessary to invest in standalone tools.

1.6.3 CAT tools and cognitive ergonomics

Despite all the improvements in TM software programs, there appears to be little consideration for cognitive ergonomics, in other words, the well-being of the user of TEnTs. The International Ergonomics Association (IEA) defines **cognitive ergonomics** as 'mental processes, such as perception, memory, reasoning and motor response [i.e. physical movements], which can affect interactions among humans and other elements of a system' [i.e. human-computer interaction]. Surveys carried out by researchers show that translators are concerned about the constraints imposed on them by translation technologies (Ehrensberger-Dow and Massey 2014). These constraints have arisen due to technological developments and range from lower rates paid for fuzzy and exact matches, added time pressure because CAT tools surely support faster translations, and the translator's irritation with tag handling in highly formatted files.

In practice the tools we use should lighten our load, cognitively and physically. The benefits of computer-aided translation mean that we do not have to search files for terminology, that windows and dialog boxes can be opened simultaneously on our screen, that HTML files and Excel sheets are converted in the CAT tool and presented as an editable bilingual segmented page, and that files for editing, generated by other translators, have a standardised format in the CAT tool. However, the regular upgrades, new designs, features, and functions are often found to be counter-intuitive by the user who must process and remember them (Ehrensberger-Dow and Massey 2014).

There are reasons for some translators not to adopt CAT tools. They find that multiple screens and functions, the requirement to manage external terminology tools, dictionaries, and to integrate machine translation in the tool, make them feel overloaded. The industry's mantra, 'speed, quality, and efficiency', can be felt as a curse, because if the use of a CAT tool means tighter deadlines, the tools are seen to become counter-productive. It cannot be denied that the advancement of translation technology is a controversial topic if we consider how TEnTs affect the translator. Some tools may suit the LSP but will the ensuing work practice please the translator?

Food for thought...

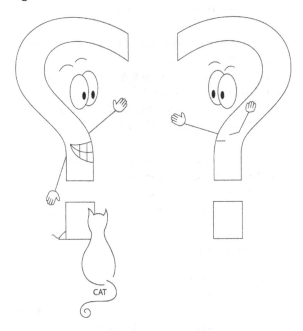

What advantages and disadvantages does the CAT tool bring to the translator?

1.7 Translation project management

LSPs used to be called 'translation agencies'. Today they go under different titles; we will use the LSP acronym. CAT tools play a central role in translation project management: they control the workflow, they help coping with volume, they support the mantra of quality, efficiency, and profit, be it sometimes at the expense of the translator's sense of well-being.

1.7.1 Volume and demands

Since the Millennium, the amount of required translation has increased enormously. Undoubtedly, the internet is the driver. Global communications generate masses of text for different purposes in an unprecedented range of formats. Translation practices have changed accordingly. By 2011, translation buyers already outsourced 90% of their translation work (Dunne 2011). Even organisations such as the European Union cannot manage the vast quantities in-house and will outsource to freelancers or LSPs. New formats have emerged, many new TEnTs have been developed, expectations (speed and pricing) have changed and the translator must manage the changes, or at least cope. Dunne (2011) makes the following observations about change:

- clients outsource because translation is not one of their competencies.
- large translation projects need more revision, terminology management, localisation.
- book translations and manuals with tens of thousands of words are often shared among several freelance translators.
- collaboration can be arranged through CAT tools which enables translator to share TMs and terminology databases.
- real-time collaboration in the cloud is possible on servers or in translation management systems, often managed by LSPs (7.2; 7.5).

Translations have become projects and translation is only one component in the workflow. The translation project requires management of communications and accounts in addition to the actual translation process. Sheer volume demands a different approach to how we translate and deal with demands.

1.7.2 Translation workflow

The translation project consists of many stages, ranging from job offer, translation to revision, and delivery. A simple workflow chart (Figure 1.4) shows the relationship between client, translator, and LSP. The chart can be extended: the translator may involve additional parties by sending queries to colleagues or posting questions on mailing lists or forums. Even if an LSP is involved, a translator may need to consult third parties if the dedicated project manager does not know the source or target language. The client can often only explain, which leaves the translator dependent on other sources to find equivalent terms in the target language.

An LSP may have a team of managers with different roles under a senior project manager. The number of stages and substages are infinite: the first stage will most likely require briefing, and negotiating about time and remuneration between

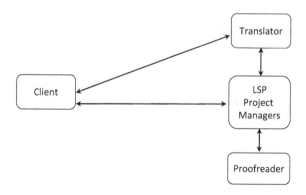

FIGURE 1.4 A basic translation workflow chart**(link: workflow diagrams)

Computer-aided translation tools 17

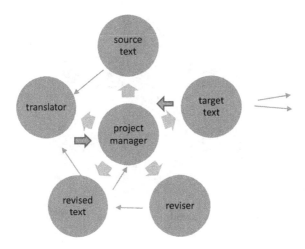

FIGURE 1.5 Translator's workflow

client and translator. The LSP must source translators (and other linguists, such as revisers). A **purchase order (PO)**, which is the first official document with details about type, word count, deadline, and agreed price for the translation service, needs to be sent to the translator to complete the first stage. Translation is the second stage followed by the third stage of revision; the final stage in the workflow includes delivery and invoices from translators to the LSP, and from the LSP to the client. If the contracted translator uses a CAT tool, stage 2 consists of:

receipt of file > preparation > ST import > translation > self-revision > return to LSP > third-party revision > return to LSP > return to translator > export of XLIFF file or generation of target text > return to LSP.

During the process additional nodes of interaction are generated through contact with the project manager at different points such as delivery, return of revised translation, review by the translator and return to the LSP project manager (Figure 1.5). If the translator translates in a web-based CAT tool, controlled by LSP, it will produce a smoother cycle because the entire workflow is in the cloud (Figure 1.6).

1.7.3 The translator in the workflow

Complex translation processes require good project management. Translation requests, additional paragraphs and modifications to documents need a prompt response. Freelancers are their own project managers. Their challenge is to prevent unreasonable time reduction: their productivity can be driven to unreasonable volumes due to inflated expectations linked to technological advancement. As a result of TEnTs, translators may be given 'less time' instead of the promised 'more time'.

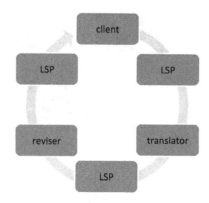

FIGURE 1.6 LSP's workflow in the cloud

The time allowance for the following translation request is three hours from receipt of email to delivery of the translation. The subject is technical (cosmetics) and requires research. Note that self-revision is more effective the following day than immediately after completion:

> Good morning,
>
> I hope you are well today. We are currently looking for a translator to help with a translation for our Cosmetics client.
> The text is about a new range of summer products for 2020; there are 414 words. Please take note of the source file in which you can also see the product names for reference.
> Would you have capacity to translate this by 2pm UK time today?
>
> *Email from LSP (2019)*

Translation work has generally become more complex with less remuneration (see 2.1.3) Good translation management is crucial for well-being and satisfaction. It needs to be more comprehensive than the delivery of quality translations.

1.7.4 *Project management by the language service provider*

Language service providers (LSPs) are well equipped to manage multilingual translation projects. LSP project managers do not generally translate, they manage projects and contract external translators, although they may also have in-house translators. They manage sales, human resources such as **vendors** (linguists who sell their services to the LSP), and marketing. They recruit vendors and will ask for evidence of language pair competence, domain knowledge (fields of specialism), tool use, and the types of service(s) they offer such as translation, proofreading, post-edit of machine translation, desktop publishing, transcription.

Project management can be mapped into five processes (Dunne and Dunne 2011):

- initiation
- planning
- execution
- monitoring
- signing-off

The processes contain nine knowledge areas:

- management of project integration
- scope
- time
- cost and pricing structure (2.1.3)★★(link: word rates)
- quality
- human resources
- communications
- risk (6.6)
- procurement

A shorter formulation of the project manager's responsibilities is as follows (Chan 2015:63):

- plan, execute, and close projects
- set achievable objectives
- build the project requirements
- manage cost, time, and scope of projects

Increasingly, LSPs automate the process and use either CAT tool servers or web-based translation management systems.

1.7.5 Project-based assignments and project management

Each chapter ends with a project-based assignment for which you will need to set up a project management team. We will now explain the construct. An LSP operates through a project management team. Its members manage others: it recruits, requests, monitors, and contracts linguists. In this book, you will be asked to build your own project management teams to fully appreciate the benefits of technology and experience the challenges of collaboration and teamwork. If in class your circumstance do not allow you to recruit, the 'project management team' can be modified (reduced) to a 'project team' in which the members perform tasks themselves. Very often project team members then become project managers because they need third parties to assist them in their roles and functions. Thus, the project team may evolve into a project management team. There may be circumstances when teamwork is not at all possible in class: the components in the translation project can then be performed from the perspective of a contracted freelance translator who collaborates with others.

In the real world, a project management team will ideally consist of linguists with different native languages and language pairs. Team members have different functions and can therefore be assigned different tasks. The teams usually have one senior project manager, responsible for leading the team, ensuring that the members have everything they need to complete their tasks to achieve goals and objectives. The project management team will have any number of project managers to manage the tasks through contracted external linguists (freelancers).

The project-based assignment will always have a set time frame in which members fulfil their roles. After completion the team is dissolved. Teams can reconvene, be modified, or reconfigure for new project-based assignments. If the team works well, it can stay together. For the duration of the project the team members work towards a set common goal of delivering the project within time and budget constraints and according to agreed standards. Third parties are the stakeholders, such as clients and service providers. If the service providers are translators, they are contractees. The project managers may well spend much time overseeing and managing their team of service providers. Completion and quality checks of the translation should be performed by team members, such as revisers, quality assurers. Project managers within a team are accountable to the senior project manager and need to communicate effectively with their colleague project managers and stakeholders to deliver a successful project.

Although there is a distinct difference in the distribution of tasks performed by project teams or project management teams, hybrid project (management) teams are quite acceptable.

1.7.6 Human resources database

A database is any collection of data, or information that is specially organised for searches and retrieval by a computer. Human resources (HR) is generally understood to be personnel. An LSP will undoubtedly have an invaluable HR database consisting of linguists, the contractees, who carry out or revise translations. There may even be a team member whose job it is to recruit linguists and manage the database. The process of recruitment and human quality control needs a set of criteria agreed by the team, based on qualifications and records of experience, language expertise, and specialist fields so that freelancers can be vetted before they are contracted.

1.8 Cognitive friction

Before we move to the project-based assignment where we will experience managing a translation project, we should return to the translator and their relationship with technological translation tools. We have seen how the well-being of the user can be affected by TEnTs. In addition to cognitive ergonomics (1.6.3), the user may also experience '**cognitive friction**'. This is the 'resistance encountered by a human intellect when it engages with a complex system of rules that change as the problem changes' (Cooper 2004). This kind of conflict occurs not only between the user and their tools, but also on another level, for example, when the freelancer becomes part of a translation project and collaborates with other linguists. Translators often disagree with, for example, the revision of their translations, translators often argue about appropriate target terms, translators protest against reduced rates of pay. The list can be continued. The translation is a multilevel system (Ehrenberger-Dow and Massey 2014) with rules that play at different levels:

- the rules that matter to the client are standard, style, price, and speed;
- the project management team is faced with hierarchical rules of seniority in the team, which also affect external translators and revisers;
- the translator requires fair pay, sufficient time, helpful resources, and support.

Speed and rates are common causes of friction because the different parties do not share the same objectives: the translator generally asks for more time than the client/LSP is willing to give, and the same applies to rates. The contracted translator may experience stress that they will lose their contracts with the LSP if they do not abide by the rules.

Cognitive friction also exists on a technological level. What is the impact of TEnTs on the translator?

- upgrades and new versions of their own CAT tools have a negative impact on time
- translating in the LSPs web-based tools challenges routine and habit
- financial depreciation in relation to the pricing of TM matches
- reduced word fees for **post-edited machine translation (PEMT)**
- prohibited use of integrated MT in a CAT tool in relation to potential breaches of confidentiality (6.2)

There has always been cognitive friction, but its nature has changed since the arrival of TEnTs. LSPs find themselves in a difficult position between the translation buyer and the translation vendor where the parties have a different understanding of time, efficiency and quality. Good LSPs will try to satisfy the needs and wishes of either party. Project managers must be skilled and diplomatic negotiators.

22 Computer-aided translation tools

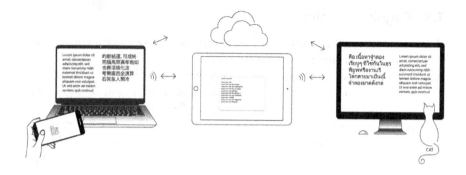

Project-based assignment

Objective:
A hands-on experience of managing translation technology and human resources in a translation project.

Assessment and outcome:
Peer/self-assessment of product (translation), process and performance. The outcome should be the ability to manage the workflow in further assignments with expertise and understanding, using different or additional tools.

Method:
The assignment is designed for teamwork, but collaboration between individuals is possible.

Tools:
CAT-tool (a server version is not necessary at this stage)

Suggested resources:
Digital source text (for example a brochure for museums, cars, domestic products, services, hotels and catering, promotional university websites, health and safety in organisations, **non-government organisations**). Consult your instructor to check if the text is suitable for a collaborative translation in a CAT tool.

Language pairs and direction:
Multiple language pairs; both directions, if TM is reversable

Assignment brief

In this project-based assignment we will try our hands at managing a translation project. The LSP team consists of different roles and the project offers different perspectives: the project requires project managers (PM) and translators. The LSP manages a translation project and contractees, but does not translate. The translator managed by the LSP will be asked to translate or to revise. TEnTs play an important part. The brief is as follows:

The client requests the translation of a brochure into multiple languages. The LSP is asked for a quote and best turnaround time. The brochure has an approximate word count of 3000+ words. Consider this request as an LSP and work through the following stages as a team:

- Set up a project management team (or a project team if human resources (contractees) are limited (see 1.7.4.1)), find a suitable source text and check the availability of your contractees. The timescale needs to be decided with the instructor.
- Draw up a quote for the client (samples of quotes, purchase orders, and invoices can be found on the internet).
- In the team, decide on the steps from quote to delivery and design a workflow.
- Compose an email with a job offer and send to freelance translators in your database (recruitment 1.7.4.2). Send the email stating the word count and the deadline, with a sample of the source text in an attachment.
- Draft a purchase order (PO) and email it to the translators that have accepted the offer. This email is a formal notification to the translator to proceed and start the translation.
- Request contractees to return self-revised translations in two formats: clean target file and an XLIFF work file (more details in 2.4).
- Self-assess your task as a project manager by scoring according to agreed criteria, or in line with component(s) in the workflow diagram, or in relation to the responsibilities suggested in 1.7.4. Discuss areas for improvement.

Possible pitfalls

- Unsuitable material for translation. The TM in CAT tools is effective when there is repetitive terminology. Consult your instructor.
- Shortage of translators
- Role overlap
- Formats: it is advisable to use uncomplicated formats in this assignment, such as docx. Other formats often require tags, which are discussed in the next chapter (2.1.1 and 2.4).

Concluding remarks

This chapter has introduced you to a range of translation environment tools with an overview of the the CAT tool, the TM, its features and functions. We have considered the benefits and challenges of the CAT tool from the translator's and the client's or LSP's perspectives. We have considered the similarities of ribbons and commands in CAT tools and MS Office, and their usefulness. We have seen the importance of good file management in respect to the CAT tool. We have learnt how to manage translation projects that involve multiple target languages, managed by LSPs who collaborate with the client, contracted freelance translators, take care of accounts and quality standards in translations. We have looked at the different roles in a translation project management team with project managers and in-house or contracted translators and other linguists. You have been given an opportunity to organise the setup of a project management team and to determine the roles of its team members, create workflow charts and operate features and functions in the CAT tool. All these activities help us reflect on not only our different roles and contribution to the outcome and quality of translations, but also on the use of CAT tools in the translation process.

Further reading

Dunne, Keiran J. and Elena S. Dunne (eds) (2011). *Translation and Localization Project Management*. Amsterdam and Philadelphia: John Benjamins.

Ehrensberger-Dow, Maureen and Sharon O'Brien (2014). 'Ergonomics of the translation workplace: Potential for cognitive friction'. In: Deborah A. Folaron, Gregory M. Shreve, and Ricardo Muñoz Martín (eds), *Translation Spaces,* 4(1): 98–118. Amsterdam and Philadelphia: John Benjamins.

Melby, Alan K. and Sue Ellen Wright (2015). 'Translation memory'. In: Chan Sin-Wai (ed.), *The Routledge Encyclopedia of Translation Technology,* pp. 662–77. London and New York: Routledge.

Walker, Andy (2014). *SDL Trados Studio – A Practical Guide*. PACKT Publishing.

Wright, Sue Ellen (2015). 'Language codes and language tags'. In: Chan Sin-Wai (ed.), *The Routledge Encyclopedia of Translation Technology,* pp. 536–49. London and New York: Routledge.

2

THE TRANSLATION MEMORY DATABASE

Key concepts

- The translation memory database can be filled to suit our individual needs
- The translation memory database accepts several methods to boost its content
- The translation memory database can be customised to suit our language pairs
- The translation memory database includes features to improve translation quality and productivity
- The translation memory database can affect profit margins

Introduction

'Translation memory' means TM database. In the translation industry the terms 'TM' and 'CAT tool' are often interchangeable: TM meaning CAT tool or vice versa. We will try to avoid this confusion. The TM is a database consisting of translation units (TUs), which we have entered over time. We can increase the size of our TM by importing **TMX** files (interchangeable TMs) from colleagues or LSPs for our use or reference purposes (2.3.3). A TM needs to be managed intelligently to be effective. The TM is more than a useful storage system. Regular edits and good maintenance make the TM a resource that is customised to our own needs and keep it up to date. The TM is the primary database in the CAT tool.

The TM's special feature is that it automatically stores TUs when we confirm a translated segment, whereas the terminology database (Tmdb) must be built manually: we must highlight and add the terminology pairs we want to store. The Tmdb is integrated in CAT tools. One CAT program prefers an external Tmdb, because it can then also be used outside the CAT tool. In the tool it can

26 The translation memory database

be linked to the translation project and integrated like any internal Tmdb★★(link: External Tmdb).

The TM in a new CAT program arrives empty and it can take quite a while to fill, depending on the amount of translation we do. If you are a student who uses a public PC, the TM will be cleared each time the PC is shut down. Therefore, we must be careful to export our TMs as interchangeable TMX files and save them in our personal accounts for importation when we open a public CAT tool (2.3.3). If we want to fill a TM before we start a new project, we can import resources (2.3.1) or TMX files (external TMs).

In this chapter we will explore how we can best use and boost the TM to suit our needs, even in the short term, and make it a superb tool to increase and enhance quality, efficiency, and potential profit. Although translators and LSPs share the objective of better quality and more productivity through the TM, translators often cross their swords with LSPs about word rates when costing a project (2.1.3). Manufacturers constantly update their programs, adding new features. The cloud plays a crucial part in CAT tool development; it gives access to infinite new opportunities. In the project management assignment, you can experience TM features and view them from different perspectives, through the eyes of the LSP and the translator.

2.1 Creating a translation memory database

When the TM recognises an identical or almost identical source segment, the target results or **matches,** appear in the **Translation Results** window. When the TM performs a **lookup**, it compares the content in the source segment you are about to translate against segments in the TM. It looks for source segments that have enough content in common. It then presents the **translation units (TU)** that it has found. The identical degree of the match between the source segment and a TM segment is expressed in percentages. For example, if the content of a translation memory segment matches the document segment exactly, it is a 100% or **perfect match**. If a new segment and a translation memory segment match precisely, including tags, numbers, punctuation, etc., it is a **context match**. Some CAT tools identify a context match as a 101% match. A less than 100% match is a **fuzzy match**. The default fuzzy match threshold generally is 70%. This cut-off point is known as the '**fuzzy match threshold**': there is insufficient usable content below this level.

You can accept or reject proposed matches in the Translation Results window, edit fuzzy matches in the target segment after you have accepted them, or translate from scratch in the target segment because **no match** was found. Your confirmed translated segments are sent to the TM, which is updated when you confirm revised TUs. Your entire TM can be edited at any time.

In the interchangeable TMX format, a TM can be shared with other translators. It is a useful procedure to maintain consistency if several translators are working on the same translation project. It flags up matches (in the Translation Results window)

The translation memory database **27**

each time it identifies a previously translated unit. A shared TM becomes more effective when all the project translators are linked to a central server, because the TUs of all translators are then confirmed in real time. A shared TMX offline can only serve as an up-to-date reference at the time it is received and imported. LSPs therefore use CAT systems with servers or translation management systems (TMS) to maintain real-time consistency in translation projects with multiple translators (7.2, 7.5).

We are not limited to the creation of only one TM in our CAT tool. In fact, it is advisable to create several TMs, customised according to domain, subject field, or client. A large TM may present too many matches, and it will need more maintenance and editing. It is therefore advisable to use several smaller and customised TMs. If we have one large comprehensive TM in addition to smaller TMs, it can be set to read-only mode in the Translation Results window. The TM is complemented by the terminology database (Tmdb). The TM stores whole segments and the longer the string, the less likely the TM will find a perfect match, whereas term pairs are concise and are more likely to generate matches.

The CAT tool has a **pre-translation** feature, which relies entirely on the TM. We can ask the CAT tool to pre-translate a document before we start translating. It looks up every segment in the TM and inserts the best match. If there is no match, the program can use a fragment-assembled match or machine translation (depending on our setting). It can also try to join or split segments automatically if it results in better matches. Pre-translate is a powerful feature, but it generally requires revision of the proposed TUs. Unless set otherwise, the TM will propose matches in the Translation Results window. If we enable **autosuggest**, the TM will guess while we are typing and we can accept its suggestions on the fly.

Regardless of the quantities we store in our TMs, it is quality that matters. Good work practice means regular maintenance. We can do so in the TM editor where we use filters to remove old entries, duplicates, 'blacklisted' terms. In the TM editor our eyes spot-check errors. **False positives,** for example, are TM matches that are not suitable in context. Other important features are the repair resource which re-indexes entries and the reverse lookup that reverses the language direction in the TM for use in both directions. Reversed matches should not be used indiscriminately: source segments in reverse generate a different set of synonyms in the target language. For example, 'express' has different meanings as a noun (fast train) and as a verb (to squeeze). If you translate the respective target terms back into English, depending on the context, they may not bring you back to 'express'.

The TM can be a time-saver and ensure consistency in large files. The conditions are that the source text is consistent and error-free, external TMs are maintained and supplied glossaries are reliable (4.1.1, 4.1.4). We must be prepared to spend time editing proposed matches to guarantee the quality of our own TMs. If an unsuitable match is accepted, it will be **propagated** until we reject it. The TM is as good as we make it, control it and maintain it.

Food for thought...

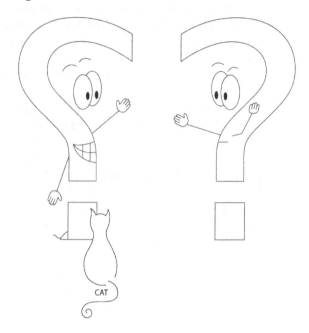

What might be the advantages and disadvantages of using the Pre-translate feature?

2.1.1 Segmentation

The CAT tool splits a source document into segments so that the TM can store the TUs systematically for recall. File preparation, after importing a document in the CAT tool, is an automated procedure that happens almost unnoticeably in the CAT tool. 'Project preparation' is the process that is clearly displayed in one of the CAT tools (Figure 2.1). The first task, '*Convert to Translatable Format*' (Figure 2.1), is the **segmentation** process and converts the source text to a segmented bilingual CAT tool format. By default, the segment boundaries are spaces or punctuation marks, which works well in word-based languages such as English where a full stop signifies the end of a sentence. The segmentation is defined by rules specific to each source language and may vary between different CAT tool programs. We can to some extent edit the rules to suit our needs, but they are designed to support match searches and our intervention could prevent recall. The inclusion or exclusion of one word in a new string will not generate a perfect match. In non-whitespace languages (character-based languages in East and South East Asia) segmentation has been traditionally defined by characters. CAT tools are now enabling a choice so that words instead of characters can be ticked as the basic unit for segmentation in Chinese and Japanese source languages.

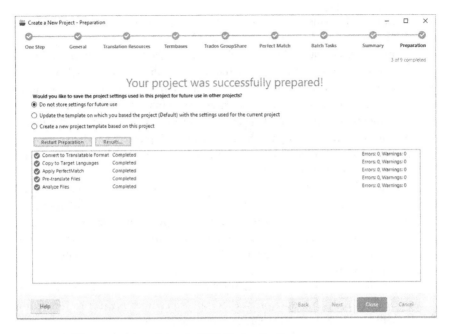

FIGURE 2.1 File preparation dialog in SDL Trados Studio

A smooth operation of the TM relies on segmentation. Researchers claim that our eye movements are affected and constrained by segmentation in the source language boxes. Pym (2008) and Dragsted (2005) argue that the translator only sees what is in the box without realising syntactic or semantic relationships with the preceding or following units or sentence(s) which leads to non-contextual translation.

Manufacturers have done their best to address the perceived limitations of segmentation. Firstly, the translator can join and split segments (depending on the file type and the segmentation rules in the CAT program). Joining segments can be helpful if cohesion is important within and between sentences, or if segmentation prevents the insertion of a suitable term in the target segment. However, when we join and thus extend SL segments, the TM may have more difficulty finding matches because of longer strings. Another drawback is that splits or joins insert (inconvenient) tags to maintain the ST layout (2.4). Secondly, the **preview** feature has been introduced in many CAT tools to compensate for segmentation and the suggested lack of context. The preview window allows the translator to see their translations on the fly in monolingual format instead of having to wait for the final export. Thirdly, it is possible for the translator to review and revise the exported target text outside the CAT tool and then re-import the revised monolingual target text to update the TM. Revision of a smooth unsegmented monolingual text, which is kinder to the eye and the brain, can give better revision results. Errors are sometimes picked up in the generated translation that have been missed during a bilingual review in the CAT tool editor, the interface with grids containing the segmented ST and TL units.

Despite improvements and new developments in the tools to help us deal with segmentation, opinions on the ultimate translation quality are divided. Pym (2008) claims that TM software may help maintain terminological consistency, but it requires too much management to bring about great productivity gains. Meanwhile, LSPs are great advocates of the TM. Their priority is to meet the client's requirements which is made possible through a shared TM in large projects. Furthermore, segmentation structures source texts, improves repetition rates, guarantees consistency, and leads to cost reduction (2.1.3).

Ultimately the translator is the decision-maker regarding acceptance or modification of segmentation rules. We need to be aware of syntactic differences in relation to our language pairs so that we can change segmentation rules to suit our needs (2.5.2). We can also control segmentation rules by being critical of the way in which source texts are formatted before we import them. Editable source texts can be formatted or reformatted by the translator in MS Word. For example, we can use the formatting features in MS Word, rather than spaces, tabs, and hard returns or line breaks. A reduction of these special characters prior to importing the file will greatly reduce segmentation and reduce the number of format tags (2.4). The translator should prioritise precision over recall, favour quality over productivity (Bowker 2005). Precision refers not only to content, but also to source formatting.

2.1.2 The concordance and consistency

The **concordance** feature makes it possible to look up specific words or word sequences in our TMs. The dialog box, or concordance search window, presents all the entries, including the surrounding words, in our TM(s). The purpose of a concordance is to show how a term or phrase is used in context (see 4.4). It also helps the translator retrieve a TU that is not shown in the Translation Results box, a 'no match'. This is helpful when the term or phrase was previously entered within a string that is not identical and therefore will not even present a fuzzy match. Other explanations for 'no matches' could be another layout and therefore a different set of tags, an extra space, missing punctuation or other numbers. Seemingly minor differences prevent matches.

In Figure 2.2 we see the concordance search feature on the CAT ribbon. One click opens the dialog box with a choice between source and target searches in the concordance. Note that there are also keyboard shortcut codes to the concordance. The CAT concordance is bilingual and shows source and target segments.

The highlighted results of a target concordance search of the term 'functional' are displayed in Figure 2.3. The translator can compare the five results and match them with the source segments to determine why the second entry is 'functional

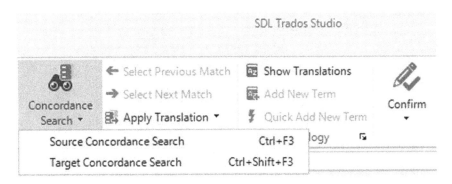

FIGURE 2.2 Dialog box opened in concordance search in SDL Trados Studio 2019

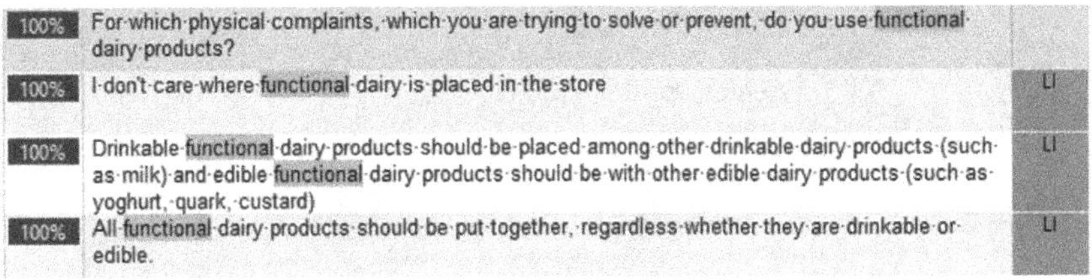

FIGURE 2.3 Concordance target results for the term 'functional'

dairy' without 'products'. The concordance contributes to consistency. As the SL segments are identical in all matches, consistency would require the translator to select 'functional dairy products' in the TL.

The CAT concordance is a popular feature. Translators are known to rely on the concordance to find term translations in the TM instead of building a Tmdb. The additional effort to add term pairs to the Tmdb, may be a deterrent, but the reward is that Tmdb matches are presented together with the TM matches in the Translation Results window.

A quick way to check for consistency is to highlight a term in either source or target segments and press Ctrl+F (Figure 2.4). The dialog box then pops up in View on the ribbon. Figure 2.5 shows that Search and Find is performed on the term 'limited'. By pressing the enter key or clicking 'Find Next' the translator can search for all the occurrences of, for example, the term 'limited' in the target segments of the active file or project files.

The search function and use of the concordance are popular shortcuts to check consistency. Good work practice requires consistency checks in the quality assurance (QA) feature in the Review tab on the CAT ribbon. The QA feature flags up inconsistencies and we will discuss this in more detail in 5.2.1. The bilingual concordance is not designed to achieve consistency. It presents matches in context to focus on terminology usage. It can however support consistency and

32 The translation memory database

FIGURE 2.4 Search and find dialog in SDL Studio 2019

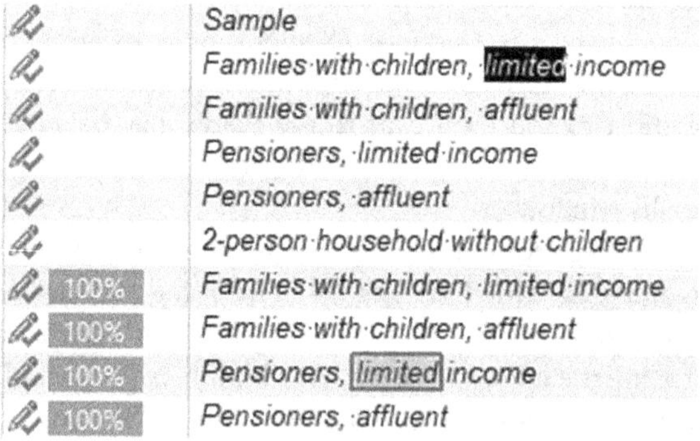

FIGURE 2.5 Search and Find function Ctrl+F

is often used for that purpose. In Figure 2.6, the concordance dialog highlights four search results for 'supplied' in the source language but there are only two identical matches in the target language. Adjectival endings in the target language prevent matches. However, if you highlight the stem of the word in the concordance search, it will show results with and without the adjectival ending. A more

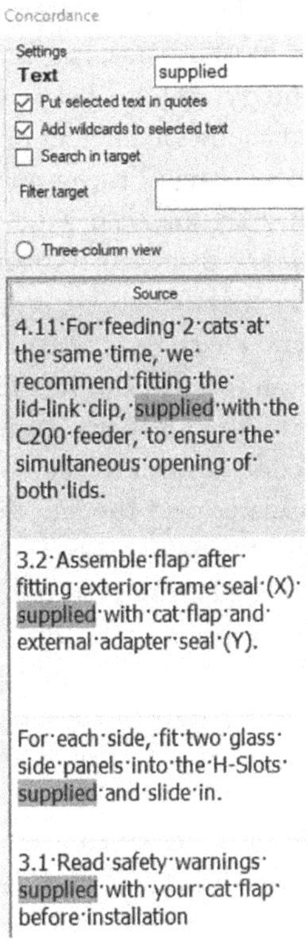

FIGURE 2.6 Concordance dialog in memoQ 9.1

professional search method is described in 4.5. Morphological changes are not understood by the TM. This problem can be addressed in the Tmdb by adding metadata (4.1.3).

The consistency of terms and phrases is important in technical documents. It is important when the source document is split and shared between several translators, each with their individual translation style. The TM can ensure that the client will receive a document with consistent terminology, and translators benefit greatly from consistency alerts or match proposals in large or updated documents. In a shared project alerts and consistent match proposals are only possible if all translators are working on the project in the cloud. Even then the project manager must do a final consistency check and smooth over potential disagreements between translators.

2.1.3 The analysis feature and fees

Translators run the analysis/statistics feature before they start to check the word count. They will see the amount of repetition which should speed up the job, because the TM will propagate perfect matches. LSPs use the feature to cost the translation project (Figure 2.7). They expect a translator to offer a discount for repetitions, 75% discount for 90–100% matches, 50% discount for 70–90% fuzzy matches and no discount for (fuzzy) matches below 70%. Alternatively, the LSP sets up a Purchase Order (PO) and chooses a different breakdown against their TM and it is up to the translator to accept or reject the translation job. Some translators will reject discounts altogether. Their arguments may be that they purchased an expensive CAT tool for their benefit and that even 100% matches need to be checked in context. They risk not being offered the job.

The analysis gives word and character counts and other statistical data, such as the number of new words and repetitions in a file, before or after translation. In Figure 2.7 the ribbon at the top gives the name of the project, file(s), active document, or part of the document from the cursor, and counts. It gives a status report of what has been translated and the amount of repetition in the ST. It also gives the option to calculate the word count in another program, as CAT tools vary. The variance is caused by the method chosen to identify and count numbers or tags, and different segmentation rules. The analysis in the lower half of Figure 2.7 shows that there is repetition in 15 segments and in 37 source words. A calculation in the other tool showed the same number of segments but less repetition, a lower source word count and fewer words with no match (Table 2.1).

There are also language-specific variances in pricing. For example, 1000 Chinese characters will usually be translated into about 600–700 English words; 1000 English words will be translated into about 1500–1700 Chinese characters (depending on the nature of the text). A Dutch target text generally scores a 15% higher word count than the English source text, and this variance within language pairs is not uncommon. It is due to a different syntax. In other languages a letter or character count per line may offer a more reliable fee basis. Fees are generally based on the source text because these counts are available at the initial negotiation stage. Ideally fees should be set per language direction.

In German, a language that joins many noun compounds into single long words, fees tend to be based on standard lines consisting of 55 characters including spaces between words. Fees can also be based on hourly rates, page rates, and flat fees (minimum fees).

The analysis feature in the CAT tool is convenient for costing, both for translators and LSPs. When CAT tools first entered the market and introduced match matrixes in the analysis feature, the agencies began to ask contracted translators for reduced rates for repetitions. Many translators felt let down because they saw their increased profit margins fall below the level prior to CAT tools. Translators argued that fuzzy matches needed editing and that revision included a critical review of context matches and therefore there should not be any discounts. One of the manufacturers' selling points was that CAT tools would increase productivity and increase profit. The question many translators ask is 'whose profit'.

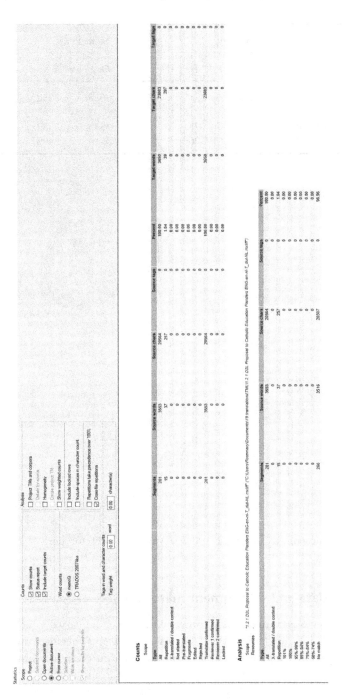

FIGURE 2.7 Analysis report (statistics tab in memoQ 9.1)

TABLE 2.1 MemoQ (M) and TRADOS 2007-like (T) counts compared in MemoQ 9.2 Statistics

	Segments		Source words	
	M	T	M	T
All	281	281	3553	3532
Repetition	15	15	37	35
Translator confirmed	281	281	3553	3532
No match	266	266	3516	3497

Food for thought...

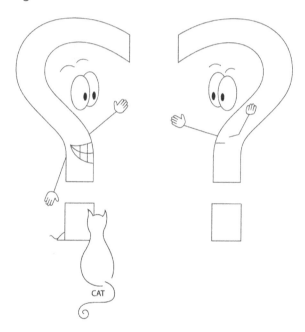

What are arguments to defend a 100% payment of fees for perfect and fuzzy matches?

2.2 Metadata and subsegment matching

It is important to add metadata, in other words data about data, which can be done in the Tmdb but not in the TM that only accepts metadata during the project setup. When we create a new project and add or create the TM, we can add information such as date and name, domain, client, and deadline. These data are visible in dialog boxes while we translate in the translation editor. They are important if several TMs are open. Several and different matches may appear in translation results. We can see in which TM, associated with which client or domain, they occur. Displayed dates are significant too and may remind us that it is time to clean a TM if obsolete terms present themselves. Although we cannot add metadata to the TM database on the fly, we can use the Tmdb for this purpose. It may be useful to know the part of speech (POS), gender or number, so that we can account for declensions and inflections. The TM searches in authentic strings, while the Tmdb searches term pairs or phrases, which we can modify, extend, make plural, etc. Fuzzy matches are only generated if there is a high level of similarity. Although it is possible to lower the fuzzy match percentage in the settings, it is not recommended. The TM will propose many unhelpful suggestions. If translators find the TM's recall disappointing, it is because matches are part of longer strings in segments. In this respect, the recall by Tmdb is superior (Flanagan 2014).

Software developers are working hard to develop subsegment matching in the TM to improve match results. TAUS, the Translation Automation User Society★★(go to www.routledgetranslationstudiesportal.com/ – A Project-Based Approach to Translation Technology – link: TAUS), was set up in the Netherlands in 2009. The association consists of major translation buyers and other organisations and companies interested in the advance of translation technology, especially machine translation. It offers webinars to educate its members and other stakeholders, and conferences to generate networking possibilities. TAUS has developed a frame-work to test (machine) translated data and to collect and disseminate data among members (Zetzsche 2019 (297th Journal)).

TAUS has launched a new product called Matching Data. Its developers recog-nise that adding metadata to the TM could in fact be counterproductive if metadata cause TUs to be locked into one domain. Their solution to inadequate matching lies in receiving huge quantities of parallel language data from different sources and owners, which are then transformed into unique corpora, i.e. bodies of text, such as glossaries. They are not only domain-specific (e.g. associated with a client's product, field or science) but are also customised to individual search requirements. In Matching Data, the matches are based on **granular** subsegments, which means they focus on much smaller units, with more lexical or morphemic detail and descrip-tion. TM manufacturers have adopted this approach. Many TMs can now search at subsegment level in the TU to give a partial perfect match, rather than a fuzzy match which needs post-editing. This kind of subsegment **leverage** (Flanagan 2014) has been given different names by different CAT tool manufacturers: 'Deepminer', 'Uplift', or 'Longest Substring Concordance'. The TM looks for a matching string of words within another TU and that substring is not affected by any surrounding words which would previously have prevented a match.

The identification process is straightforward, but CAT programs operate dif-ferently when their respective TMs reassemble or auto-assemble new and longer strings, and results vary. 'Uplift' which matches subsegments in the TM works better if the TM is smaller and more specific. The program claims that Uplift saves us using their external terminology database. This might be true if the searched terms are

38 The translation memory database

stored in the TM, but if they are new or stored in external resources the suggested match may be less perfect without access to terminology and reference features. CAT tool developers are trying to remedy this short coming, and some CAT tools give the translator more control over resources that can be used in addition to the TM. 'Deepminer' was the first form of subsegmentation. The TM 'mines' for subsegments and uses statistical data to analyse TM content (DTA=Dynamic TM Analysis). DTA was called 'Guess Translation' in another CAT tool. What all CAT tools do is perform a concordance search, i.e. find subsegment pairs in source and target strings and present the subsegments combined with the non-matching word strings in the Translation Results window. This procedure allows the translator to select the target subsegment, insert it, and translate the remainder of the string. The feature Auto-assemble was also a product of data analysis. It was a laudable attempt to create good matches, but the edit distance was high. Autosuggest is not unlike predictive writing in smartphones: it recalls potential matches in the TM, triggered by the translator's keystrokes. Subsegmentation in CAT tools is work in progress. CAT tool upgrades bring new features.

Obviously, the quality of subsegment matching will depend on the quality and specificity of the TM. A random TM will give random matches, whereas a customised, domain-focused, well-maintained TM will deliver higher quality matches and a lower edit distance. Again, it is the translator who holds the controls. Sophisticated features need data, and they are provided by the translator.

2.3 Boosting the translation memory

Any translator using a CAT tool and expecting that it will immediately speed up their translation, may be disappointed. A new CAT tool arrives with an empty TM. The building process can be slow if, for example, your translation work is non-specialist, you have many different clients in different domains, or if your texts have little in common. Students, who use their institution's CAT tools several hours a week and are given texts from different domains to provide translation challenges, may find themselves in a similar situation: the TM will not provide many matches.

A repeated warning for users of public PCs in training centres regarding TM creation: public PCs shut down without storing data. They do not allow you to build a TM. You must remember to export TMs in the transferable and exchangeable TMX format at the end of a session and store the files in personal folders.

Despite these precursors of data loss, CAT tools have good features to boost the TM. They enable us to import monolingual or bilingual reference files which will give us bilingual or monolingual ST/TT matches in the Translation Results window. We can import external interchangeable TMX files to boost our TM; **alignment** is the pairing of source and target texts that have not been translated in the CAT tool; and importing reference materials within the project is another helpful feature. TM edits and maintenance are important, but so is the preparation of translation projects, which includes the need to boost the TM prior to translating.

2.3.1 Alignment

The alignment feature in the CAT tool turns previously translated documents and their source texts into translation units (TUs) so that we can add them to a TM. Performing alignment to boost the TM can be useful but it is time-consuming. CAT tool developers have tried to facilitate and automate the alignment process. It has become more intuitive and one CAT tool claims it is now integrated and automated. Different programs have different names for the alignment feature. In one CAT program (memoQ 9.1), we add reference files to a LiveDocs corpus and the program will then align them automatically. It claims that the aligned results are correct in most cases, but that human revision is needed each time a match presents itself to ensure good results. It is advisable to make yourself familiar with the alignment feature before the need arises. Automated alignment is a great improvement compared to the manual adjustment of join-up lines between segments which used to be the standard method in CAT tools (Figure 2.8).

CAT tools offer five types of alignment: alignment with review, which means checking the join-up lines between segments or review in the translation editor on the fly, alignment of single files and multiple files. The fifth type is the monolingual review (5.3.1): the translator can revise an exported clean target file. When the reviewed target file is re-imported, the TM performs an automatic alignment and updates changes. The alignment of source and target texts, and external reference material is not the only way to boost a TM, we can create TM content with existing public translations or public, bilingual corpora (4.3).

2.3.2 Translation memory and reference files

The phrase 'reference material' is commonly used by LSPs. The translator will receive additional files with information or terminology. LSPs tend to send **packages**, a CAT tool term for ZIP archives that are created in the CAT tool containing: project files for translation, TM, Tmdb, analysis report, and reference files. The package is imported and opened in the translator's CAT tool and after completion it is emailed or uploaded as a return package. Competition and the need for compatibility has made packages interchangeable between programs.

FIGURE 2.8 Alignment with join-up lines between source and target segments

40 The translation memory database

Packages can also be prepared on a server. The translator is given a temporary licence for the relevant CAT tool. This is a trend which might outstrip the use of personal CAT tools (7.2).

Reference material can be contextual, containing extra-linguistic information to explain the topic, images of products, applications and packaging or illustrations to help the translator understand the subject of the source text. It can also be a linguistic resource with relevant terminology, glossaries (mono or bilingual), or previously translated TTs. CAT tools can now import and process reference material in suitable formats such as MS Word (PDF files are image files and would first require a conversion to editable text) without performing an alignment. Keywords in context are then presented as reference material in the Translation Results window. Colours and icons are used to differentiate between references and translation matches.

Reference files can be included in a package, or sent by email, or made available online. Programs deal with the import of reference material in different ways, either as a separate feature after or during import when you tick 'reference' in a drop-down box to identify them as non-translatable files. The benefit of importing reference files in your CAT tool is that the TM does the searching and presents relevant matches, explanations, and definitions on the fly, which saves the translator having to scan or highlight relevant phrases in reference files before or during translation. The benefit of reference material supplied to the translator by client or LSP depends on its relevance and quality.

2.3.3 TMX files

A TMX file is a TM that is exported in an interchangeable format which can then be imported in another CAT tool. TMX files can also be exchanged between colleagues or team members working on the same job if they are not sharing a TM on a server. It should be noted that shared TMX files are best used in Read Only format. If a proposed match is accepted by the user, it will then be entered in their own TM, contrary to importing an entire TMX without checking the content. Many open-source TMX files are available on the web (some can be downloaded, but with the same warning: to be used as Read Only files):

- MyMemory is a TMX file★★(link: external TMX) with a collection of translation memories from the European Union and United Nations, produced by a company called Translated.net. The TMs can be downloaded in TMX format, and they are also available as plugins in CAT tools. Translators have reported on websites that MyMemory TMX does not come without errors and could be compared with MT regarding quality. If it is used in the CAT tool as an online plugin, it is in effect an MT tool.
- The Directorate General for Translation has compiled TM databases in EU languages ★★(link: external TMX)
- For other multilingual **corpora** see Corpora (4.3)

Boosting a TM is tempting when your TM is empty. Alignment, importing reference files, external TMX files are methods worth exploring but expectations should not be high and time investment is best limited to prevent disappointment. Small, customised TMs work best, but we must create, edit, and manage these ourselves.

2.4 Formats

Source text files for translation come in many different formats (up to 50) and CAT tool manufacturers compete to keep up with changes and the interchangeability of new formats. CAT tools have made it possible to translate files that were previously inaccessible or not readable on translators' desktops. There are image files or files with such complex layouts that reformatting the TT would put the translation job beyond the scope of the translator and the budget of the client. Before accepting an unusual file format, it is advisable to check if your CAT tool can process it. You may receive files in formats with formatting instructions hidden in tags, which must be observed in the target segments. Tags are entered in the TM as part of the string. Tags affect not only the word count but also the identification of strings. The TM may not identify a string as a match due to an added or missing **tag**. Tags are considered inconvenient, their insertion takes extra time, but they are the best way to retain difficult formats. Some formats are easier to manage within the CAT tool because of its standardisation of all formats in the translation editor. Formats such as Excel spreadsheets, web-based HTML files, PDF files, and PowerPoint files all conform to the segmented grid in the editor. The only difference is that their formatting must be kept by means of tags. There are format tags in the SL segments and they must be inserted in the target segments by the translator.

MS Excel

The translation process of an MS Excel file format is more convenient in a CAT tool than in Excel: the text does not hide behind other cells, furthermore, it can be spellchecked, the word count feature operates and the predictive aspect is absent in the CAT tool. Although Excel spreadsheets were not designed for translations, they have become popular with LSPs to manage short or fragmented source texts such as instructions or specifications that need translating in multiple languages. All the target languages can be assembled in one spreadsheet. When working in Excel, the translators must insert translations in the respective language columns, and if their language is in the P column, it is difficult to see the source text in the A column without moving the scroll bar. The CAT tool imports and converts the Excel format to its clear bilingual editor interface and exports the translation in its original Excel format. One CAT tool (DVX3) has a function that excludes red text (fonts) in spreadsheets. If the translator copies the source text to their column and changes the font colour to red in the A column, the source text will remain in the

42 The translation memory database

A column and not be overwritten in the CAT tool and the target text is exported in the required column.

HTML

HTML (HyperText Markup Language) files have a computer '**markup**' language which although readable, has tags with all the information needed to define structure and layout for the text on the World Wide Web. The tags are placed within these symbols <>, which is what the eye can see. The CAT tool reads all (hidden) instructions and presents them with its own set of tags (also called codes) in the source segments. To replicate the original layout, the CAT tags must be included in the right places in the target texts. Translators complain about tags, because they require extreme accuracy and cost extra time. If the syntax of SL and TL is very different, the insertion of tags in the right place can be demanding. The CAT tool flags up error warnings if tags are forgotten or misplaced and the file cannot be exported until the omission is corrected. CAT tool manufacturers are working hard to simplify and automate the insertion of tags. It would be impossible to post HTML target files on the web without the markup and we must therefore respect the CAT tool tags.

XLIFF and TMX

XLIFF (text files) and TMX (TM databases) are **exchange formats**, which means they are interchangeable between desktops/laptops and compatible with a variety of CAT programs. The terminology database is interchangeable in TBX format. Interchangeable files are helpful when collaboration is required between translators who are not working on a server or in the cloud. Despite the interoperability of TMX, we need to be aware that CAT programs have different ways of doing things such as segmenting the ST and storing the information in tags. Consequently, what is considered a segment in one CAT tool might not be in another and the imported TMX file may not present anticipated matches due to a different segmentation process or tag coding systems, or simply because the translator joined or split sentences prior to conversion.

Target files are exchanged in XLIFF format and have a similar problem: there are so many different file formats and so many different programs that although most tools can process XLIFF files, some loss of data or features during the transfer process is possible. If we want to be sure that our CAT tool can handle the imported XLIFF file, we can apply the 'pseudo-translation' feature in the CAT tool. It translates a source text in a pseudo target language to test if the XLIFF file can be handled and processed (Zetzsche 2003–2017). The bilingual XLIFF in the CAT editor in Figure 2.9 shows a pseudo translated PDF file in dollar symbols. It looks fine and has imported well. However, the export gives the following message:

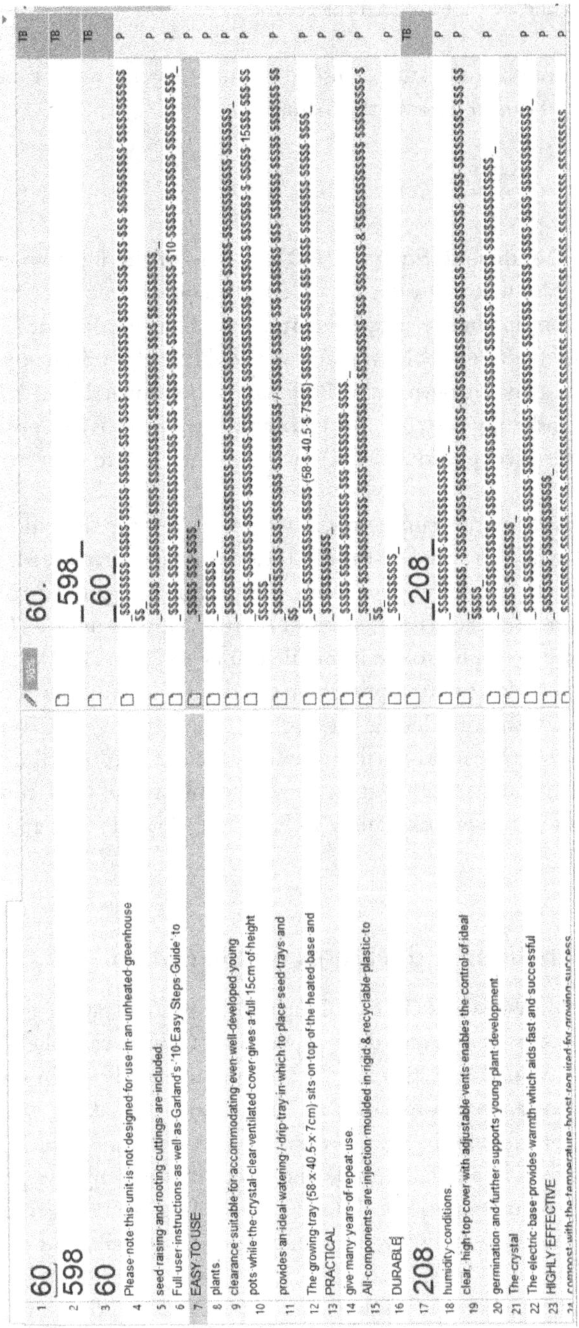

FIGURE 2.9 Pseudo translated PDF file

> Adobe Acrobat Reader could not open 'xxx.pdf' because it is either not a supported file type or because the file has been damaged. For example, it was sent as an email attachment and was not decoded correctly

The pseudo-translation feature is useful because it generates a timely warning that the CAT tool cannot process the format.

PDF

The **Portable Document Format (PDF)** is one of the most widely used file formats. It is an easy method to secure a file and change it from an editable format in MS Word to an uneditable image file. It is a problematic format for the translator. Translation in a CAT tool is not always possible and if it is, sentence sequencing and format may change. If the PDF file is **text-based** you will find that you can search and copy text, but if it is **image-based** this is not possible and an Optical Character Recognition (OCR) program is needed to convert the file and make it editable.

It is important to understand why CAT tools have more difficulty converting some files, and why the success of the TT layout is not guaranteed. The clearer the text, the better the conversion result, but a scanned text file saved in PDF format is enough to make a translator and their CAT tool despair. The pseudo-translation feature is helpful to see if the file can be exported and what the target file will look like prior to attempting a translation. If a translator receives many PDF files, it is worth considering the use of a high-quality OCR program to convert PDF files prior to importing them in the CAT tool. It guarantees the retention of format and sentence structures. In comparison, CAT tools can process other common formats extremely well, such as PowerPoints, and formatting results are good.

2.5 Other functions and features on the ribbon

The ribbons in MS Word and CAT tools operate in similar ways (Figures 2.10 and 2.11). They have tabs, icons, and drop-down boxes which vary slightly between CAT tools. A thorough investigation of the ribbon will bear fruit in the long term. A minimalist approach to using a TM, i.e. how to make it work with the least effort, may be efficient in the short term, but will not give much satisfaction. The program arrives in a default mode and needs customising and personalising. Each translator's requirements are different, depending on text genres, domains, and language pairs. We will discuss filters and regex, which allow us to personalise the TM. And if this is not possible because we are not the administrators but users of the CAT tool, it is good to study the menu, so that we know which features and functions are available. We could then ask the administrator to change a few settings to suit our needs.

The translation memory database 45

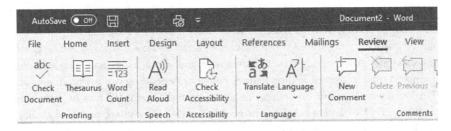

FIGURE 2.10 Ribbon in MS Word

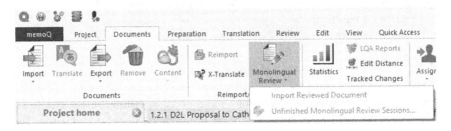

FIGURE 2.11 Ribbon in CAT tool

2.5.1 Filters

We have stressed the importance of maintaining and editing the TM. CAT programs have their own servicing mechanism and we should apply the TM repair tool regularly. It does most of the 'maintenance work' for us by re-indexing the database and we can set the edit tab in the TM to remove duplicates. This process is called setting up **filters**. The TM editor has many filters and deserves our attention:

- Edit filters can be used to search for a specific source/target term or phrase in the TM.
- We can check modification dates in 'history' to recall previous versions for comparison.
- We can set or add filters. For example, TM maintenance is made easier if we set the filter to show duplicates, because they can then be deleted on the fly each time they appear in the Translation Results window.
- We can set a filter to capitalise certain words in our languages or we can tell it *not* to capitalise.

All these functions and more are available in the TM editor. When a TM slows down because of its size, or if we use several TMs simultaneously in a project to recall as many matches as possible, filters help improve matches and prevent false positives.

46 The translation memory database

Some programs have a filter that sets **penalties**. They produce percentages in the margin and alert us to matches which may be 100% identical but include a tag or a space. If we ignore this penalty it will affect the format. A percentage of, for example, 90% will alert us to differences and allow us to accept or edit the proposed match. We can add or remove penalties depending on our requirements. Furthermore, if one of our clients requests the term 'item' (ST) to be translated as 'product' (TT) and another client prefers 'article', we can set penalties to alert us that our clients use different terms. Penalties are also useful when we import a TM from a colleague. A penalty set for the entire external TM will tell us that its search results are not our matches. Penalties are not 'punishments' but alerts that matches need closer scrutiny. Filters give us a means to control the TM regarding the matches it recalls.

2.5.2 Regex

Our texts are full of patterns, such as dates, which are ordered differently per country and language. Regex in the CAT tool is set up to apply transfer rules for different formats of date and time, currencies, metrics, numbers, and email addresses. The transfer rules will adapt dates from, for example, US 03.13.22 ST to UK 13.03.22 TT. Regex helps the TM recognise the string and it will match the digits in the source and target segments on the fly.

Regex, which stands for 'regular expressions', is a mathematical theory on which pattern matching is based. MT and CAT could not operate without regex. It is not about regular language expressions but about matching recurrent patterns. Why is regex important to us? If we recognise and understand pattern matching, we can change segmentation rules and improve our error checking in the CAT tool's QA (quality assurance) functions. Here follows an example where the TM will not recognise the sentences as identical because they lack automatic numbering:

> This is a new model.
> (a) This is a new model.
> 1) This is a new model.
> B) This is a new model.
> 1.1. This is a new model.

Matching is improved if we change the segmentation as follows:

> This is a new model.
> (a)
> This is a new model.
> 1)
> This is a new model.

B)
This is a new model.
1.1.
This is a new model.

If you go to segmentation rules in the CAT tool you can add the following regex:

^\(?[a-zA-Z0-9]+\)[\s\t]*

It means: look for all segments that start with any lowercase letter or uppercase letter or any number between 0 and 9, which repeats itself one or more times, is preceded or not by a left parenthesis, is followed by a right parenthesis, then by a space character or a tab character, which repeats zero or more times. To change this rule we then add #!#, which means apply a segment break here. Regex may not immediately appeal to linguists, but translators who have learnt a few codes find it extremely helpful and an excellent way to customise their TMs.

Regex codes consist of metacharacters, which are standard. Here are some examples:

?	makes the preceding character optional
\d	a number character (digit)
\w	a word character (letter)
\s	a space character
\b	a word boundary
[4,]	four or more of the preceding character
|	'or'
★	zero or more of the preceding characters
+	one or more of the preceding characters

If you want to check for inconsistencies, and you realize/realise that you may have confused GB and US spelling, you can click on Find and Search for one spelling and then again for the other spelling. The regex metacharacter | enables one search: realiz|se.

Many regexes are pre-set: if boxes in the CAT tool settings are ticked, currency in the English group should appear in the target format as 1,234.56 and in the German target format as 1.234,56. This feature is automatically enabled when we select source and target languages. However, we may have a client who requires a space instead of a dot as the decimal separator, in for example, 2 000, and it is helpful to set the regex accordingly in the custom list in auto-translation rules★★(link: regex).

CAT tools explain how to create a regex list in their Help sections and although it requires some code writing, it is a skill that can dispel irritation: it prevents the TM from producing repeated errors or fuzzy matches or what we call false positives, or unwanted matches in Search and Find. MT and TM systems both rely on regexes to match TUs; MT needs regexes as a fully automated system. CAT tools and MT systems are gradually merging, based on the same modus operandi. The next chapter discusses integrated and adaptive MT in CAT tools, which would not be possible without regexes.

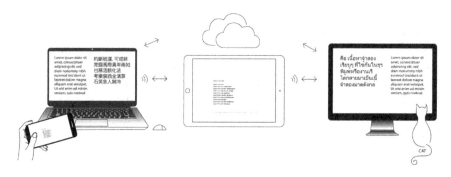

Project-based assignment

Objective:
Collaboration in a translation project and the management of one or more shared TMs either online or offline

Assessment and outcome:
Self/peer assessment of the collaboration with special focus on TM/TMX management, the exchange of XLIFF files and their impact on consistency in the translation

Method:
The assignment is designed for a project management team but collaboration between individuals is possible

Tools:
A desktop CAT-tool to test the exchange of TMX and XLIFF files. A server version is not necessary but would facilitate real-time collaboration between collaborating translators.

Suggested resources:
Digital source text and digital reference materials (monolingual for reference, bilingual for alignment)

Language pairs and direction:
Multiple language pairs; both directions if TM is reversable

Assignment brief

Set up a project management team (1.7.4.1) to include a senior project manager, a relations manager, who is responsible for negotiations with the client and translators, a resource/reference manager, and other managers as appropriate.

Your translation project involves a client, contracted translators, and one translation with a high word count plus adequate reference materials. The source text for translation into one or more languages is split and shared between two or more translators per language pair/direction. The main objective is to build a useful TM (to be shared as a TMX) and supply reference materials to maintain consistency in the translation. Consistency can be measured according to key terms in the TMX and reference materials.

In this assignment most time should be spent on project and TMX preparation within the team.

The following actions are suggested, the order is not set:

- distribution of team management roles
- recruitment of translators
- selecting the source text (PDF files are not suitable for this assignment) in consultation with your instructor
- performing initial alignment(s) within the team to build the TM/TMX before sharing
- sourcing suitable digital reference files
- if using a server, creating packages with source, reference files and TMX/ TBX files
- creating POs and briefs for translators, including the analysis/statistics report
- offering a price scale for repetition according to analysis/statistics report
- checking consistency in returned translation
- TMX files from translators should be imported in the master TM
- the master TM should be edited, including removal of duplicates.

Possible pitfalls

- duplicates in the TMX
- poor quality of the source text. Manipulate the ST if needed. Consistency in the ST can be helpful.
- import and export of TMX files impact (sub)segmentation
- loss of data in TMs and TMXes during migration – keep backups
- forgetting to attach a TM(X) to the project

Concluding remarks

This chapter has illustrated how the TM as the main component in the CAT tool can improve translation quality and increase your productivity. The industry's

50 The translation memory database

mantra has been reviewed in the light of quality and consistency, productivity and quantity, and the impact of the TM on the profit margins of manufacturer, LSP, and translator. The CAT tool is an extremely sophisticated and comprehensive program. The TM is however relatively inflexible. We cannot make alterations or additions in the TM on the fly, as it can only accept our TUs, store them and recall matches with high similarities. Improved translation quality depends on the user's maintenance of TM quality. The TM can only increase productivity if it is well filled and customised, possibly accompanied by a range of smaller customised TMs, rather than one big master TM. Furthermore, if we do not use filters and regex, and we must change smart apostrophes to curly apostrophes manually after completion, we are not using the tool efficiently. If we are asked by the client to use terminology consistently and there are multiple translators involved, we must check matches from an external TMX file before we insert them. We need to know their origin, date, and version history. If our TM is boosted with TMX data, it might be preferable to view it in Read Only mode. Alternatively, we can create a new TM for the client and import the TMX data into the customised TM. Productivity and quality are ultimately controlled by the translator and not by the CAT tool.

Further reading

Dragsted, Barbara (2005). 'Segmentation in translation. Differences across levels of expertise and difficulty.' In: *Target*, 17(1): 49–70. John Benjamins. https://doi.org/10.1075/target.17.1.04dra.

Flanagan, Kevin (2014). 'Subsegment recall in Translation Memory – perceptions, expectations and reality', *JoSTrans*, 23.

Garcia, Ignacio (2015). 'Computer-Aided Translation'. In: Chan, Sin-Wai, *The Routledge Encyclopedia of Translation Technology*, pp. 68–87. London, UK: Routledge.

Gintrowicz, Jacek and Jassem Krzysztof Jassem (2007). 'Using regular expressions in translation memories', *Proceedings of the International Multiconference on Computer Science and Information Technology*, pp. 87–92.

Zetzsche, Jost (2003–17). *A Translator's Tool Box for the 21st Century: A Computer Primer for Translators*. Winchester Bay: International Writers' Group.

Zetzsche, Jost (2019). 'The 297th Tool box Journal'. *The International Writers' Group*.

3

INTEGRATION OF MACHINE TRANSLATION IN TRANSLATION MEMORY SYSTEMS

Key concepts

- The translation industry has embraced technology in response to high volume translation requiring a fast turnaround
- Artificial intelligence (AI) and the further development of machine translation (MT) meet the high demands
- Translation technology developers have invested significantly in research to improve MT
- We can combine MT search engines with the TM in the CAT tool to improve and speed up our translation work

Introduction

Machine translation (MT) is an important TEnT. In this chapter we will evaluate MT's added value to translation when it is integrated in the CAT tool. The MT function requires little preparation or action. When it is enabled in the CAT tool, its proposals pop up in the Translation Results window for the translator to accept or reject. TM matches take priority and MT matches may appear at the bottom of the list, depending on the CAT tool.

The MT database cannot be edited: it is part of the external search engine. We can only accept, reject, or post-edit proposed matches. Our discussion of MT is specific: MT as a TEnT, integrated in the CAT tool and potentially adaptive. For example, if we accept and edit an MT match, the TU enters the TM when it is confirmed. Next time, the previously edited MT match will be proposed as a TM match. Developers have caught on to this and designed closed circuits in which the MT learns from the TM and becomes adaptive. This is not possible in an independent MT engine such as Google, which learns from huge corpora and not from the individual translator's CAT tool entries.

It is important to understand the operation of TM and MT in the CAT tool. We must also know how to estimate and evaluate MT quality in the CAT tool. If we have a better understanding of MT features as a TEnT and use the tool appropriately, we can reduce the need to post-edit (PE) after the translation is completed. We can do the editing on the fly. We will therefore discuss MT as a TEnT in a supportive capacity, its integration in CAT tools, the quality it delivers, and the evaluation of its quality through models and metrics. All this can be tried and tested in the project assignment.

3.1 Artificial intelligence and machine translation

Artificial intelligence (AI) is a machine's ability to perform the intelligent tasks we do without thinking. Machine translation (MT) is an AI system. Through AI, machines can solve problems, interact with our immediate surroundings and think creatively. The following four AI categories are relevant to MT: machine learning, deep learning, neural networks, and natural language processing. Machine learning is the science of programming computers to act in an automated way. It uses systems that can learn from data, identify patterns, and sets of rules, thus creating algorithms to make independent decisions with limited human invention. Deep learning is a subcategory of machine learning. It analyses huge amounts of data to complete tasks like speech recognition (7.1.1), translation, TM and terminology databases, and more. Neural networks drive the analysis and consist of a set of algorithms modelled after the human brain, designed to recognise patterns in data. Algorithms cluster and classify data. They can be trained. And finally, there is natural language processing (NLP) which enables computers to understand and process human languages. NLP teaches computers to use speech and understand language. Computers do not yet understand the nuances of language, such as body language, facial expressions, tone of voice, and intonation, but considering that humanoid robots can give witty, sarcastic replies and understand random, ambiguous human utterances, we anticipate improved performance in MT.

More and more CAT programs are paired with machine translation engines and offer adaptive MT based on algorithms within the tool. They learn from the data provided by the translator in the cloud, in standalone or web-based CAT tools. The learning process is called deep learning, which digs deeper into TU segments. It can offer improved suggestions for fuzzy matches by piecing together subsegments (2.2). Up to now, MT suggestions in CAT tools have often led to much time spent on error repair. The roll-out of neural machine translation (NMT) in CAT tools has lifted MT output to such a level that post-editors cannot always identify errors in a monolingual review because of smooth and fluent NMT output. The difference between NMT and statistical MT (SMT), its predecessor, is discussed in the next section.

3.2 From statistical to neural machine translation in the CAT tool

Corpus-based statistical machine translation uses a database with infinite pieces of text, monolingual, bilingual, and multilingual, and it applies statistics to present matches from its huge database at random. The SMT translation decoder is an algorithm that searches for the best equivalent in its database. Zetzsche (2019 (298th Journal)) compares the search technique to looking for suitable 'LEGO bricks': you know what you want to achieve and pick the pieces that might produce the best fit. You slot them into place in a top-down movement. SMT works like that: its chunks give us the correct meaning, but the sentences are awkward with incorrect word order or syntactic relationships. NMT works differently: it is a deep learner and uses neural networks to understand and identify the best sequences for the translation of full sentences instead of phrases. It has an attention-based encoder/decoder model in which the encoder takes the source sentence and all available knowledge (metadata) and generates/decodes a target sentence. The 'attention' mechanism looks for suitable alternatives. It is not always helpful because it can pay too much attention to a term or phrase. Furthermore, the system tends to struggle with proximity, the closeness of pairs. Nevertheless, it supersedes NMT when it comes to sequences, because the preceding and following words and phrases help determine the outcome. The sequential relationship is quite different to dropping and forcing individual LEGO bricks into place.

SMT generates a higher level of word accuracy but NMT scores higher in word order and **fluency** and **adequacy**, two MT descriptors. Toury (1995) used the term 'adequacy' and '**acceptability**' (called 'fluency' in MT) when the focus moved from text-based to context-based or functionalist approaches in the 1980s. 'Adequacy' relates and qualifies the target text according to the source text, and the 'acceptability' of a translation follows TL standards and end-user expectations. The descriptor for SMT matches is more likely to be 'adequacy', whereas NMT is best assessed in relation to 'acceptability' or 'fluency'.

Slight mistranslations in NMT are difficult to recognise and require more editing time. NMT is less efficient in specialised domains. It uses general data up to a certain level and then switches to domain-specific data. NMT has a fragmented view of a text, which explains inconsistencies in word matches. Its strings operate well at sentence level but do not respond well to the predictive features (2.2) in TMs or translation management systems. The NMT wants to predict, based on what is available in the database.

Although NMT gives superior results, its non-interactive nature does not facilitate integration in CAT. The translator must review all the ready-made MT matches and accept/reject or edit. In contrast, the TM offers matches which have been entered by the translator or are stored in an external or imported TM. TMs can be maintained, edited and improved at any time, whereas the database of the MT engine cannot be edited by the translator. In the CAT tool, TM matches supersede MT matches. The TM will indicate the quality of the match in

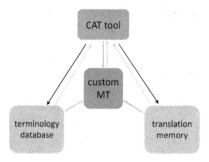

FIGURE 3.1 CAT tool and adaptive MT

percentages (2.1), whereas MT matches are not rated or scored. This is an imbalance that is detrimental to MT matches. If algorithms were given more dominance, the TM might be able to select from the MT database, but NMT requires such a large amount of training data that it would be too large for the TM to hold and process.

Most CAT tools enable the integration of NMT and various programs list the NMT engines that can be used. Although the integrated MT comes second in the CAT tool, TM matches and MT matches are recycled in each other's databases. If the TM does not leverage a match, the MT will generate one, which will then be entered in the TM after it has been edited or confirmed by the translator. It will populate the segment next time as a TM match. In an adaptive MT system (3.6), TM matches enter the MT through deep learning (Figure 3.1). The searches of TMs and MT engines in their respective databases follow a similar pattern, but the qualitative outcome is quite different.

3.3 Matches from the translation memory and machine translation compared

When we enable the MT engine in the CAT tool, the search function scans the TM and MT databases. If we have enabled matches to populate the target box, then by default, the TM is given priority over an MT match. If there is no context or perfect match, the TM may present a fuzzy match. We know that fixing fuzzy matches below a certain threshold of around 70% is not viable, and it is not recommended to lower the threshold level. MT matches do not have a scoring system: they may need serious post-editing. MT would benefit from a similar scoring system. For example, if MT matches were rated **gisting** quality, which gives us only a rough understanding of the meaning, we could decide to reject them like fuzzy matches. The TM does the rating by matching new TUs with previous TUs in the database. If MT could be scored, it would preclude much unnecessary post-editing (Garcia in Chan 2015: 81).

TABLE 3.1 Edit distance

The	president	confirmed	that		employees	should be	informed
The	CEO	said		the	employees	should be	told
	S	S	D	I			S

CAT systems have shown improvement in MT match accuracy. They can now apply another layer of metadata to segments to indicate whether an MT translation will reach an acceptable level of quality (TAUS). Web-based CAT tools can predict which MT engines are likely to give the best integration into CAT workflow. This development is called machine translation quality estimation and its development is still in its early stages.

TAUS (2019) compares the different levels of productivity between TM and MT. The study shows that segments translated with TM have a shorter edit distance on average and are translated faster. The minimum edit distance between two strings of words is the minimum number of editing operations that are needed to transform one to match the other. Editing operations are generally insertion (I), deletion (D), and substitution (S). The example shows how the MT translation (line 2 in Table 3.1) compares with the 'ideal' reference translation (line 1 in Table 3.1):

The edit distance is determined by the weighting given to each edit distance. If S (substitution) scores 1, D (deletion) scores 2, and I (insertion) scores 3, the edit distance in this sentence is 8.

DQF, the TAUS Data Quality Framework, looks at the distribution of **MT+PE+TM+HT** in hybrid TM/MT processes. Any process will require some post-editing (PE): MT matches, TM fuzzy matches, and human translation (HT) without matches. What TAUS discovered was that 100% matches in the TM were more reliable than any MT match, and that fuzzy matches which by default have a correctness threshold level of around 85% are less reliable than MT: the lower the fuzzy match percentage, the more reliable the MT match. Their study of efficiency in the different processes shows that a combination of all processes (MT+PE+TM+HT) is given an efficiency percentage over 45%, TM achieves a percentage of nearly 45% in suitable word matches and HT is given the highest percentage of time spent on each segment. TAUS' findings indicate that the edit distance in TM is longer than in MT and yet TM productivity is higher. A suggested explanation is the translator's familiarity with their TM and the awareness of the level of editing that is required in fuzzy matches according to their percentages. TM fuzzy matches are, however, a grey area because of the different match rates. TAUS concludes that there is no clear point where MT efficiency proves to be higher than TM efficiency. They also found that the target language plays a role in quality and output. If English is the source language, MT productivity in Western European languages can be up to three times higher than in Asian languages. In terms of productivity, MT comes close to the lower fuzzy matches.

56 Integration of machine translation

We can draw several conclusions: the TM match supersedes the MT match in time and quality, and while MT matches and TM fuzzy matches compare well, a combination of all processes in which HT has the final word gives the best results. Language pairs and text genre affect MT quality: TM efficiency and time may vary between different language pairs, depending on syntax or script. Current developments in TM data training and adaptive MT (3.6) aim to leverage the integration of MT in the CAT tool and may resolve the imbalance between TM and MT matches.

3.4 Machine translation – access and integration

MT is free/open-source software, which means that it may be used freely for any purpose (Forcada in Chan 2015: 152). MT needs to be free/open-source, because engines used in CAT tools are statistical corpus based and depend on the availability of data, ideally in sentence-aligned parallel texts (2.3.1). However, open source does not mean that anybody can interfere with the software, because it is legally copyright protected and relies on experts and skilled computer programmers to make changes. If software is free of charge, it is called freeware. CAT tools list appropriate MT engines for their programs and ask you to enter the API key code to link up with the cloud-based MT database of your choice. Some engines are free of charge, others charge per character and require API subscriptions.

The challenge for free/open source MT technology is its integration in CAT tools. As mentioned in the previous section 3.3, TAUS made two pertinent observations: TM matches override MT matches and MT suggestions are not rated. MT would also benefit from being more user-friendly and unified across the different search engines (Forcada in Chan 2015: 164). In sum, MT in the CAT tool would benefit if:

- TM and MT segment matches were more aligned (similar rating scores). MT matches could have a benchmark like fuzzy matches in the TM. Fuzzy matches are compared with previous TUs and the differences are highlighted and rated in percentages.
- MT matches could be compared with a potential and good reference translation and the difference (edit distance) could be shown in percentages.
- Differences between MT search engines could be overcome by an integration of MT systems on a single platform.

Advances seem to come from the CAT program manufacturers who have developed **adaptive MT** in CAT tools to leverage MT as a TEnT that learns from the TM. But before we discuss adaptive MT in CAT tools and translation management systems, we will discuss how MT search engines learn from TMs in the CAT tool.

Integration of machine translation **57**

Food for thought...

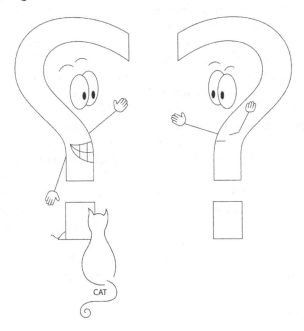

Why are many translators less enthusiastic about MT than the companies who make the engines?

3.5 Translation memories train machine translation engines

A custom or self-build MT engine learns from the data provided in the TM and Tmdb. The three databases are combined in a package where they are interactive and create a closed circuit. The MT engine observes the translator's input which is used to update MT suggestions. In a translation management system (TMS) (7.5), the translator interacts with the MT by accepting, rejecting, or editing suggested TM matches, thus refining MT while translating. The same happens in a CAT tool, if an API or plugin is used to access any of the standard MT engines. When the translator accepts or modifies an MT proposal, it is added to the TM and will present a prioritised TM match next time. The difference between integrated MT in a CAT tool and the closed-circuit TMS or self-build MT system is that an API or plugin in a CAT tool does not enable the translator to build or edit the MT search engine. In both systems, data are kept confidential, either in the closed circuit or through APIs and plugins that do not allow data to be kept or stored (6.4, 6.5).

Obviously, TM inconsistencies are replicated in the MT. If we maintain our TMs well, consistent TM data have a positive impact on the quality of MT output (Moorkens et al. 2013). Consistency is not only determined by output but also by input, by the source text. A study on 'data laundering' (Moorkens et al. 2013), the recycling of data, investigated if modified MT input in the TM would enhance consistency and results. It appeared that modifications were possible in either direction, and could have an upgrading or downgrading effect, the latter caused by repeated changed word order in the MT.

Quality and edits are the responsibilities of the user. Confirming unedited or poorly edited matches will have a negative impact on the TM and consequently on the MT, regardless of which database presented the match in the first place. The conclusion in the study was that TM data performed better than the baseline engine, which correlates with TAUS' findings (3.3).

A research group at the University of Trento Italy (Farajian et al. 2017) focused on MT input and discovered that the integration of NMT in a translator's workflow seemed to work reasonably well if source domains were controlled, but that quality deteriorated if there were multiple domains, large domains, and hence greater data diversity. They also found that NMT worked well when sentences were processed from domains close to the training data. Hence the success rate is likely to be higher when translators work in a limited number of domains, feed their own data into an integrated MT in their CAT tool, or build their own MT engines in translation management systems (7.5). Adaptive and self-build MT engines enable translators to influence, control, and edit MT content and quality before matches are confirmed and propagated.

3.6 Adaptive MT engines

Adaptive MT is a new category of artificial intelligence (AI). It learns from the translator's entries in real-time and customizes the data it finds in the TM via interchangeable TMX files. It can also learn from monolingual files. In addition, it learns from the translator's entries in the Tmdb and generates improved matches. As we discussed in 3.5, the TM stores the translator's TUs and offers perfect or fuzzy matches for reuse, based on similarity with previously translated content. The adaptive MT engine is smart and learns from our edits, our style, our terminology and syntax.

Modern MT★★(go to www.routledgetranslationstudiesportal.com/ – A Project-Based Approach to Translation Technology – link: adaptive MT engines), a three-year EU funded project (2015–17), was financially supported by the biggest EU Research and Innovation program, Horizon 2020, with nearly €80 billion of funding available over seven years (2014–20). ModernMT is a new open-source machine translation platform. The system did not make any changes to the baseline-engine but used a technology called 'example-based adaptive NMT', in which the adaptive part of the technology was new. A TM layer (or a very small TM) is the first to receive the translator's request. The NMT uses similar segments to generate a more suitable suggestion (Farajian et al 2017). The NMT adapts its engine on the fly. This kind of system removes the need to train an MT engine. The MT can be a large generic engine which then adapts the parameters of the translator's request while the translation is happening (Zetzsche 2019 (297th Journal)). It is a much more advanced method than the statistical MT LEGO brick building approach (3.2).

Adaptive MT engines are cloud based. In a translation platform system (7.3.4) the translator can access one controlled interface via a plugin or API and thus collaborate with other translators. The interface integrates the components MT, TM, and Tmdb and the engine provides the best suggestions based on the three components. It states the source of the proposed matches. The topic of adaptive MT engines is continued in translation management systems (7.5).

Food for thought...

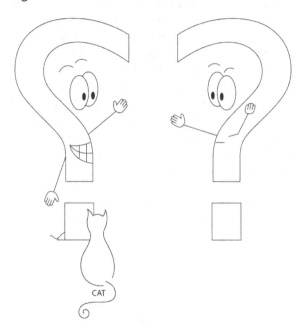

How do you see the benefits of MT as a TEnT when it is integrated in a CAT tool?

3.7 MT quality in the CAT tool

How can we define the quality of machine translation integrated in the CAT tool, where it is a shared quality with other databases? Quality itself is a relative concept, for example, the quality of a translation can be defined as being 'fit for purpose' or it can be measured against a benchmark, which presents an additional quality. A 'standard' with set boundaries is much more measurable. Hence, in the 1990s, the EAGLES working group (Experts Advisory Group on Language Engineering Standards) suggested the following purpose-based classification of translation qualities:

- Raw translation, which may contain minor grammatical or syntactic errors without impeding comprehension; to be used for large amounts of scientific material
- Regular quality translation, which transfers the information grammatically correctly but may be lacking in style correctness; to be used for technical manuals

60 Integration of machine translation

- Extra quality translation; both fluent and idiomatically and accurate, culturally correct in the target language; to be used for advertisements and literature
- Adaptation, which is not a direct translation of an original text; to be used for press releases and advertising

EAGLES 1996

Statistical MT cannot be measured against standards, because its translation model relies on a fluid corpus and it is not rule-based like its predecessors. It lacks a framework which could facilitate standardisation. Instead it takes its data from bilingual texts in a phrase table. The target phrases can then be scored for the phrase with the highest score to be picked and proposed in the CAT tool as the best match. SMT uses a language model of monolingual target texts and compares the segment with the highest score with a segment in the monolingual text. This method confirms that the proposed segment is likely to be an error-free translation. Proposals are based on algorithms and probability and not on standards. Neural MT also relies on statistical data and does not offer scope for measured standards.

It is not easy to measure the quality of machine translation in the CAT tool. MT is neither outcome nor product, but a process. We want to find out how MT as an additional TEnT can help us improve quality. In the CAT tool, integrated MT matches are post-edited. In adaptive MT the generated output is corrected by the translator, and the MT system 'learns' the correction so that errors will not recur. If we were to measure the quality of proposed matches and the respective post-edit time of integrated MT versus adaptive MT, we would expect to see a marked difference in favour of adaptive MT. At present measuring the quality of MT in the CAT tool is still an area with work in progress, although we can adopt ISO standards (5.4), or standards set by the translation industry (TAUS, BLEU in 3.7.2). Only the latter standards are specifically designed for integrated MT.

3.7.1 Quality management

Since 2015, many LSPs adhere to the ISO standard for translation (5.4), which measures the quality of the translation process. The ISO standard does not apply to machine translated texts. Good practice expects any commissioned translation to be sent out with a translation brief, a job instruction to ensure that the translator has understood the requirements and the purpose of the translation. The term 'quality' in translation briefs is generally not detailed, if at all mentioned. The most common qualification is that the translation must be delivered 'error-free'. In the following example of a translation brief, the purpose of the translation is not mentioned, nor its quality. A CAT tool will automatically perform the suggested quality checks. Quality management is one of the most difficult aspects of a translation project, partly because our individual concepts of quality differ, and a project with multiple languages is managed by project managers who may have different language pairs and concepts. The following translation brief should not give rise to much disagreement, but whether it will automatically guarantee good translation quality is a different matter:

- The font used throughout the document is Helvetica Neue
- Please translate all text that appears in the main slides and the speaker notes panel
- Please translate the 'Section' headings that appear in the slide thumbnails panel
- Please do not translate words that are brand names or product names
- Where possible, please try not to adjust the width, height or position of the text boxes. If the translated text doesn't fit then please reduce the size of the text
- If your language does not display properly in the Helvetica Neue font then please substitute for Arial or a similar sans serif font

LSP translation brief 2015

Views on quality differ. Muzii (2012) draws an analogy between purchasing a car and buying a translation. He suggests that when we buy a car, we want to know what the vehicle can and cannot 'do'. In a new car, we expect a different quality to that of a second-hand car, yet both should be structurally sound and do the job. External imperfections in a showroom car will not affect its performance and can be addressed by the recipient. So why shouldn't translations be offered at different qualities and different prices? Educating the client about the quality of translation is often suggested as a way forward. Muzii suggests that translation providers should 'profitably' signal what they offer in such a way that the buyer can understand and will accept the price tag. Translation providers need to be clear about the translation's quality, its purpose (who is going to read the translation and for what purpose), and its price (if adapted to its purpose – the price should be lower for gist, higher for publication). Offering quality is fine, but not without a detailed understanding of the quality concept by both parties, providers and recipients (Mitchell-Schuitevoerder 2015). How high should we raise the bar for MT quality in the CAT tool? Instead of proposing a de facto level of perfection, maybe we could determine adaptive MT quality in accordance with its purpose (gist or quality), the level of difficulty in the source text and per domain.

And finally, how does the client relate to quality? The client who has commissioned the translation needs to stipulate to what level of quality a translation is to be made. Negotiations between translator and client (often through an LSP) are primarily about time and cost. But shouldn't translators or LSPs, as intercultural communication experts, advise the client which translation technology is available and what is best suited to the source text or the purpose of the target text? And shouldn't we discuss the client's preferred terminology, and our translation approach (which combination of MT / TM / PEMT / HT)? If we decide that MT needs to be enabled in the CAT tool (due to high volume and time constraints), collaboration between client and translator is needed. Shouldn't the client provide the sources and data which the MT engine needs to learn from? If translator and client work together and there is a better understanding of the applied technology, the translator and their TEnTs are more likely to deliver a better-quality translation.

Food for thought…

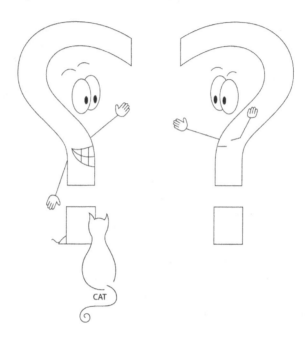

How would gisting quality impact the translator's work method?

3.7.2 How to evaluate machine translation

Despite continuous MT improvement, the developers, manufacturers, and organisations, such as TAUS, seem to focus on machine-led evaluation systems (Wilks 2008). Apparently, evaluation systems are currently perceived to be the key to improving quality and to reducing time spent on post-editing (3.7.3). Before we discuss quality estimation in detail, we will first determine if the translator can estimate MT quality in a CAT tool.

The evaluation of MT output is not straightforward. There are no absolute benchmarks, and it is multidimensional: MT is a TEnT designed to assist the translator in the three areas of quality, time, and efficiency, but none of them have clear boundaries. Moreover, evaluations and assessments are affected by the MT engine used, the evaluation model and metrics employed, the translator's proficiency, and PEMT, which is a subjective human-led activity. Furthermore, evaluation criteria for human translation, e.g. about style, are not transferable to the assessment of machine-translated text quality. Hence there is a shift in the current trend of MT evaluation towards automatic methods and metrics, which measure the quality of MT in relation to the quality of a similar

HT piece. Metrics are based on text similarities. The BiLingual Evaluation Understudy, BLEU (Papineni et al. 2001), was one of the first automatic MT metrics. It was an IBM research report that worked on the premise: the closer the MT output to HT output, the better. The analysis is based on n-grams, which in the field of computational linguistics and probability are a contiguous sequence of n-words in a piece of text: one word is a 1-gram, two words is a 2-gram, etc. The system looks at frequency of occurrence and assigns probability to an n-gram occurrence with other n-grams. Probability makes it possible to predict the next words and correct errors.

The automated approach to MT evaluation probably brings as many challenges as human evaluation. First, MT engines vary depending on the amount of data sets that have been used for engine training. Too much terminology data can give competing data which leads to output inconsistency. And data quality is also affected by the source of the input: TMs or glossaries. Second, MT cannot yet master style, such as a shift from formal to informal register within a sentence. Third, different search engines give different results: a generic engine (Google) is suitable for generic texts, whereas appropriate domain terminology is needed for specialised domains.

These challenges can to some extent be addressed by the user. The reliability of evaluation models is increased if the MT user checks the domain specificity of the MT engine. Domain-specific engines and open-source databases for self-build engines are available (Forcada 2015). Glossaries from clients for MT data training must also be checked: they require a high quality to give good quality results. Furthermore, expectation management should be part of the equation: if the client expects high results, they must provide domain-specific data. In return, the supplier of the translation must be able to estimate the anticipated quality level of the translation based on the input quality of data and source text. Data and ST management have become part of the translator's job. The responsibility to deliver good quality does, however, not only lie with client and translator, but also with the manufacturers of MT programs. The industry should be willing to align APIs and not make users pay for individual APIs. The type of error management set up by manufacturers and applied by the engines would benefit from uniformity across different MT engines.

In conclusion, evaluation models must give the translator clear indications of MT error levels in CAT tools, in line with TM match levels. An increased awareness of domain-specific terminology and a realisation that one engine does not fit all domains or texts would improve MT integration. Other points of importance for translators to note are that MT engines give different results for different language pairs. In fact, some language combinations use pivotal engines which means that automated translations between two languages run via another engine, e.g. Italian into Japanese may run via an English pivotal engine. A good understanding of MT engine output (and source of input) can greatly improve the quality process and the reliability of quality estimation and evaluation.

3.7.3 Evaluation models and metrics

The main goal of translation quality assurance (TQA) is to recognise a specific level of quality. **Automatic evaluation metrics (AEM)** are software programs that use

64 Integration of machine translation

a set of linguistic criteria for testing against a human reference translation. AEMs can make use of the information retrieval concepts *precision* and *recall* (Doherty 2017). **Precision** is the fraction of words in the MT output that is correct compared with the HT benchmark and **recall** is the total number of correct words (i.e. precision examples) produced by the MT. This is called **error typology**, whereas other AEMs measure the edit distance according to the minimum number of edits needed to match MT output to the reference HT. Of course, we could question the objectivity and reliability of the 'golden standard' human translation, which is used as the MT reference (Doherty 2017). Two translators will rarely generate identical target texts, and two reviewers will seldom produce the same review.

The following models, **LISA** (Localization Industry Standards Association) and TAUS, use metrics that are meaningful measurements and calculations to improve the engine and estimate the quality of the output. In this book we are not measuring pure MT but comparing MT and TM output in CAT tools in integrated and adaptive mode. Nonetheless, we can still apply the following metrics after we have generated a 'golden' benchmark translation in HT. The important feature is that the metrics are weighted. The LISA Quality Assurance (QA) model is used by companies or LSPs to structure feedback from reviewers on translation quality in the localisation industry. Errors are weighted with one point for a minor error, 5 for major and 10 for a critical error:

Weighting means that if we record two minor mistranslations, they will generate a score of 2. But if we record two critical mistranslations, they will generate a score of 20. Scores for all segments in the task are totalled to give a final score for the task. If the overall quality of the task falls below a predefined threshold, the task will fail the LISA check. It is important that scoring models are agreed to make sure that all reviewers score to the same standard.

The error typology template is used by LSPs to manage their quality program. TAUS has developed a Dynamic Quality Framework (DQF) which uses Multidimensional Quality Metrics to standardise translation evaluation. Their objective is that buyers and providers of translation can compare and benchmark MT productivity and quality. For translators it would be useful if we could apply metrics to a sample translation to give a client an estimate of quality, time, and cost. With the DQF plugin we can track our translation quality and productivity in a CAT tool. The plugin collects data from our CAT tools and sends a report to visualise our data.

TABLE 3.2 LISA model for quality assurance

	Minor	*Major*	*Critical*
Doc language			
Mistranslation	1	5	10
Accuracy	1	5	10
Terminology	1	5	10
Language	1	5	10
Style	1	5	10
Consistency	1	5	10

Integration of machine translation **65**

The new metrics are analytic metrics that try to explain why translations are good or bad, whereas holistic metrics merely state the quality level. In the DQF, TAUS sets new standards to define errors. It creates a taxonomy, a more accurate classification of translation errors, and a scoring method to produce numeric indications. A root cause analysis also refers to the source text and its quality. Its metrics require human intelligence, it is not a one-size-fits-all metric, it is not an automatic approach, nor a BLEU reference-based score. It renders a TQ qualification for any quality management system so that it is in accordance with ISO standards (5.4). It includes validity, verification, and reliability as properties of a metric.

The DQF-MQM (Dynamic Quality Framework-Multidimensional Quality Metrics) is an error typology used by TAUS like the LISA Quality Assessment. It is extensive:

The category Verity (Table 3.3) means that translations should be rendered according to locale conventions, for example, a copper wire in a product in one country might not be copper in another. The category Style tends to be subjective and is an area of disagreement among translators. The best rule is to aim for a minimal set of error types. In fact, it is best to avoid checking style if not relevant (e.g. in manuals or specifications).

The emphasis of metrics tends to be on error management and error repair. Good MT translator management should consist of domain-focused engine selection, TM data input and editing, and ST quality checks to enhance output quality. At the beginning of the chapter, MT was presented as a rigid, inflexible TEnT but we have discovered many ways of managing input, which should give us better results in integrated (adaptive) MT and reduce PE time within the CAT tool. The following project-based assignment gives us an opportunity to trial this aspect of translation tool management.

TABLE 3.3 TAUS (2019) Dynamic Quality Framework (DQF) uses Multidimensional Quality Metrics

Locale convention formats	Accuracy	Design	Verity	Terminology	Style	Other
Address	Addition	Length	Culture-specific references	Inconsistent with termbase	Awkward	
Date	Overtranslation	Local formatting		Inconsistent use of terminology	Company style	
Measurement	Undertranslation	Markup			Inconsistent	
Currency	Improper exact TM match	Missing text			Third-party style	
Shortcut key	Mistranslation	Truncation/ Text expansion			Unidiomatic	
Telephone	Omission Untranslated					

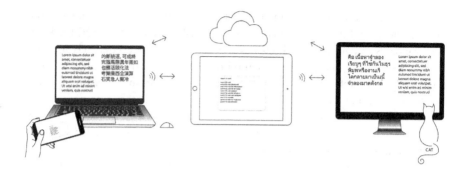

Project-based assignment

Objective:
Ability to estimate and assess output quality and efficiency of integrated TM and MT in a CAT tool

Assessment and outcome:
Team-based assessment of data collection after trialling integrated TM and MT procedures. You need to create a data presentation in a bar chart according to discussed metrics models

Method:
The assignment is designed for *project teams* with one language pair. A clear distribution of tasks is necessary to provide rich data for metrics; good data records will increase the reliability of results and restrict the impact of variable data

Tools:
CAT tool with integrated or adaptive MT; TMS system; APIs

Suggested resources:
Several source texts from different domains with high word counts to try different MT search engines

Language pairs and direction:
One language pair; both directions if TM is reversable

Assignment brief

The project assignment is about testing and assessing integrated MT in the CAT tool. You will need to set up a project team and appoint a project manager. As a team you prepare a quote for a 6000-word translation (a deadline of four workdays) which gives the client an estimate of the anticipated quality levels and cost of integrated MT, depending on the level of PEMT required. It is an analytical assignment, which can be performed by a project team or by an individual. You are trying to assess translation quality. The focus is on MT data in the translation project. There is less focus on team management, although task distribution within the team is important.

This project-based assignment provides the framework to assess quality and efficiency of integrated or adaptive MT and must be shaped by your team with a consideration of the following:

- The tools, CAT and MT (adaptive or integrated) + APIs available to you
- The selection of source texts and distribution within the team
- The procedures or combinations of TM/MT/PE/HT employed within the team and a special focus on PEMT
- The selected metrics model for evaluation
  - Choose and develop an evaluation model based on error typology or edit distance (3.7.3) (or a combination)
  - Create a metrics model before you start: your own or based on BLEU, LISA
- Selection and preparation of texts (see pitfalls): some should be highly suited to MT, and one should be less suitable. They should have similar word counts. MT suitability can be tested by running samples through freely available MT engines
- Allocation of integrated/adaptive TM/MT translation tasks with agreed deadlines. STs can be shared or split among team members. TMX files must be used
- Experience MT integration/adaptation in different domains
- Comparison of error typology and distance edit models
- Bar chart (s) (MS Excel) to illustrate MT/TM quality and/or efficiency
- A quote for the client based on edit distance and/or quality (Tables 3.1, 3.2, or 3.3).

Possible pitfalls

- TM(s) with little data
- Poor MT data
- Text suitability for MT: the evaluation may be less dependent on data than the suitability of the selected source texts. Test samples first

Concluding remarks

The objective of this chapter is to help you understand the processes used by MT engines and the conditions that make them work well in a CAT tool. We have explained how neural machine translation is a significant improvement after statistical machine translation, particularly in fluency, **syntax**, and word order, although not necessarily in terminology. You have had a chance to experience post-edits of MT matches in the assignment. PEMT will be discussed in more detail in Chapter 5. You have learned how CAT tools can integrate MT and give you access to the respective MT engines through APIs or plugins. We have examined how MT operates and provides matches from its own database or by learning from your TM databases while you are translating, which is called adaptive MT. We have reviewed how you can improve MT quality through good TM maintenance, by checking for high ST quality and matching generic and specialised MT search engines appropriately to ST domains. In addition, good management of integrated or adaptive MT gives you a powerful TEnT when you import client glossaries or external TMs, provided you apply regular TM edits. We have also seen how the industry has adopted a new approach to quality enhancement and typical MT error repair through models for error typology and edit distance. The models give an insight into the conditions that will give an acceptable to fair level of MT quality in the CAT tool and reduce our editing time for poor matches. Metrics help us produce estimates of quality and time investment in a potential translation project. All combined, you should now have an idea how MT, as a TEnT, can give translation work added value. The project team in the project-based assignment is a vehicle to experience how large translation projects incorporate MT. The assignment is not so much about managing team members and their operations. It is more about delivering the required level of quality through integrated or adaptive MT in a CAT tool.

Further reading

Doherty, Stephen (2017). 'Issues in human and automatic translation quality assessment'. In: D. Kenny (ed.), *Human Issues in Translation Technology*, pp. 131–48. London, UK: Routledge.

Forcada, Mikel (2015). 'Open-source machine translation technology'. In: Chan Sin-Wai (ed.), *Encyclopedia of Translation Technology*, pp. 152–66. London and New York: Routledge.

Garcia, Ignacio (2015). 'Computer-aided translation'. In: Chan Sin-Wai (ed.), *The Routledge Encyclopedia of Translation Technology*, pp. 68–87. London and New York: Routledge.

Hutchins, John (2015). 'Machine translation. History of research and applications'. In: Chan Sin-Wai (ed.), *The Routledge Encyclopedia of Translation Technology*, pp. 120–36. London and New York: Routledge.

Kit, Chunyu and Billy Wong Tak-ming (2015). 'Evaluation in machine translation and computer-aided translation'. In: Chan Sin-Wai (ed.), *The Routledge Encyclopedia of Translation Technology*, pp. 213–36. London and New York: Routledge.

Moorkens, Joss, Stephen Doherty, Dorothy Kenny, and Sharon O'Brien (2013). 'A virtuous circle: laundering translation memory data using statistical machine translation'. In: *Perspective Studies in Translatology*. DOI: 10.1080/0907676X.2013.811275

TAUS (2019). *DQF BI Bulletin – Q1*

Wilks, Yorick (2008). *Machine Translation. Its Scope and Limits.* New York: Springer.

Zetzsche, Jost (2019). 'The 298th Tool Box Journal'. *The International Writers' Group.*

4

THE TERMINOLOGY DATABASE

Key concepts

- The terminology database is a comprehensive database in the CAT tool
- A terminology database is usually internal and integrated in the CAT tool (but linked to the CAT tool if external)
- The terminology database complements the TM, especially when morphological changes affect matches
- The quality of online terminology resources is variable
- Corpora and concordances are indispensable terminological resources

Introduction

The terminology database (Tmdb), also called termbase in some CAT tools, is one you build yourself within the CAT tool. A good Tmdb optimises, refines, and customises TM recall. When the TM does not give anticipated matches, the Tmdb can assist. Terminological pairs must be added manually. They are not stored automatically like TUs in the TM. We create or open a Tmdb at the start of a project and add new entries by highlighting the source and target term pairs or phrases. We access the 'add term' function on the menu with a right click, a shortcut code, or through an icon on the ribbon. To add metadata, such as parts of speech (POS), synonyms or definitions, we use a different shortcut code or click on full entry in the drop-down box. When the term recurs, matches appear in the Translation Results window. They are marked with different icons or colours to show that they are Tmdb results. The Translation Results window in Figure 4.1 (top left) shows from top to bottom: two red TM matches with red ticks (1–2), three blue Tmdb matches with green ticks (3–5), and four EuroTermBank results with their typical icon (6–9) (4.6).

70 The terminology database

Translators give a higher reliability rating to matches proposed by the Tmdb than TM or MT. Possible reasons could be the specificity and accuracy of Tmdb matches, because they are not part of an **auto-assembled string** (see subsegment matching in 2.2), or because they are part of added reference material supplied by client or LSP and compensate for what is not yet stored in the TM. When translators look for a suitable target term, the TM only recalls what has been entered and the Tmdb presents what has been added. Therefore, if they do not know the meaning or translation of a term, they may consult digital dictionaries, use search engines on the internet, or post queries on language or subject-specific translator network websites. The CAT Tmdb is often underused or not well filled. Many users are content with the sophisticated search options within the TM. Undeniably, the building and editing of a Tmdb requires considerable effort and time, but so do online terminology searches, and web hits need checking.

FIGURE 4.1 Translation Results window in memoQ 9.1

The terminology database **71**

In this chapter we will touch on the vast quantity of available terminology resources available to translators. We will explore good terminology work practice and show how to integrate terminology in the CAT tool to give it the prominent place it deserves beside the TM.

4.1 Terms and terminology

Translators are keen to receive reference materials from client or LSP; the latter will try to obtain suitable material not only to support their translators, but also to ensure terminological consistency. We will therefore discuss the resource qualities of the Tmdb first and then explore how the Tmdb and the TM can be reconciled to optimise the CAT tool. Whereas the TM is used to memorise content and assist the translation process with the required level of consistency, the Tmdb is a more specific guide to help translators deal with domain-related terminology in a translation project. If the translator has access to clearly defined translations of terms in the CAT Tmdb, it will improve quality, maintain consistency, and increase the CAT tool's efficiency, partly through fine-tuning the TM.

4.1.1 Glossary

A glossary can be defined as a language dictionary in one or more languages containing all the terminology of a domain usually preferred by an organisation. A vocabulary is a list of terms with synonyms and definitions (or explanations) in two or more languages, relating to a specific subject field, but not pertaining to the activities of a company or organisation like the glossary. A good example of an online glossary is 'Electropedia', which is produced for the International Electrotechnical Commission by the International Electrotechnical Vocabulary, a leading global organisation that prepares and publishes International Standards for Electrotechnology★★(go to www.routledgetranslationstudiesportal.com/ – A Project-Based Approach to Translation Technology – link:glossary). Electropedia is multilingual, currently offering terms in 14 languages, accessible to all. Another example of a glossary created by an organisation is the Online Glossary on Governance and Public Administration developed by the Division for Public Institutions and Digital Government (DPIDG), of the UN Department of Economic and Social Affairs in collaboration with CEPA★★(link: glossary), Classification of Environmental Protection Activities:

> The purpose of the Glossary is to provide United Nations Member States, and all other interested parties, with a *common definition of the basic terms and concepts* related to governance and public administration used in United Nations documents, and DPIDG. In particular, the Glossary aims at improving the clarity of the intergovernmental deliberations of the United Nations itself; and at assisting Member States to better implement United Nations resolutions by providing a more unified understanding of governance and public administration terminology. This Glossary contains non-legally binding definitions

of terms most frequently used in governance and public administration in (a) United Nations documents and (b) in the work of DPI.

https://publicadministration.un.org/en/About-Us/UN-Glossary

The UN glossary is monolingual and contains definitions only, specifically designed to set terminology standards which will be recognised by all member states. The multilingual standardisation of terms is important to the translator to prevent the random use of terminology (see ISO standards in Termbanks 4.6 and 5.4). Definitions are needed to define a concept in clear words. For example, 'domain' is a technical term (and not a personal field or area) with different meanings in the fields of computing, physics or biochemistry. Definitions should be part of our personalised CAT Tmdbs and customised per client. Manufacturers have preferences: what may be called an 'item' by one, is called a 'product' by another. Such refinements can be added to the Tmdb, but not to the TM.

Food for thought...

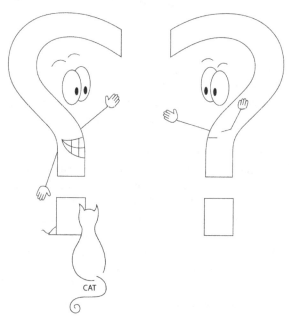

Why is a glossary, a potential source for a CAT Tmdb, more suitable than a vocabulary?

4.1.2 Term extraction

Term extraction is the process of extracting domain-relevant terms from a corpus, a body of texts or words. Imagine we are sent mono or bilingual reference material for a translation project; then searching for relevant terms, adding definitions and target terms, or pairing terms in a bilingual text can be time-consuming. After the search, we need to identify the terms and create a corpus, such as a bilingual glossary, in which to store them. Creating the glossary in a suitable file format (txt, csv) means that it can be imported in the Tmdb.

Before we extract terms, we should at least know how to identify and categorise them. A term is a word (simple term) or a multiword expression (complex term) of a concept within a specialist subject (domain). A concept is an idea that corresponds to its essential features. It will cover many varieties, such as pencil, piece of chalk, pen, all products of the same concept, the writing tool. The terminology of a subject is the set of special words and expressions used in connection with it (Cobuild). LSPs generally ask a translator about their 'specialisms', meaning terminological expertise, before they contract them. Terms behave in a distinct manner and have relatively fixed contextual surroundings (4.4). In the English language these are typically noun phrases, such as 'adapter socket wrench manufacturer directory', or verb phrases, such as 'to be in/out', which in cricket terminology refers to whether the players are batting or not. They are difficult to translate. Other features may be typographical, e.g. italics for scientific names, an acronym, such as WYSIWYG (What You See Is What You Get) or initialisms, for example, UN (United Nations, but known as UN), or the official title of a position (CEO – chief executive officer), organisation (FC – football club), department (DS – department of state) or unit (ARMAD – Armoured and Mechanised Unit Air Defence).

In a CAT tool, we can extract term pairs by highlighting and adding them to Tmdb on the fly. Several CAT tools★★(link: Term Extraction) offer monolingual term extraction as a regular part of the translation process or as a separate feature to build up glossaries or Tmdbs (Zetzsche 2003–2017). **Term extract** is a very useful but often underused feature. It extracts important words and expressions in a new source text or a corpus of existing translations. The selection is data-driven and uses algorithms. Consequently, a term list may contain a quite a few false positives, which are irrelevant results due to multiple meanings. An extracted term list, however, enables a translator to research important terms before translating the text and to include them in a Tmdb if they appear to be correct and consistent.

The CAT tool with an external Tmdb (SDL Trados Multiterm) uses existing translated documents saved in the CAT tool and checks the frequency of terms at subsegment level to create a term list. In CAT programs with an integrated term extraction editor, we can run term extraction each time we add new files. It will simultaneously search our Tmdbs. It is advisable to edit and maintain the lists constructed by the CAT, because they are created as proposals and may need some reconfiguration. Filtering (2.5.1) is also recommended to prevent the extraction of syntactic words without terminological significance, such as articles (the, a/n). Before we apply the useful function of term extraction, we need to understand how to create a reliable and usable Tmdb. The CAT tool can do the job, but it works better if we add metadata. They operate as a filter and reduce the number of useless matches.

74 The terminology database

4.1.3 Metadata

If we compare the translation memory with the terminology database, there is a significant difference in the amount and type of metadata either can store, and our control over them. Metadata in the TM tell us when and by whom a segment was translated or edited. This can be useful when comparing previously translated versions, which are all stored in the TM. When we set up the project, we can state the domain, client, and deadline. The Tmdb, in contrast, is filed manually and metadata are added by the translator: SL/TL variant(s), fields of application, **part of speech** (**POS**), definitions, sources, usage, and context (2.2, 4.4). When a Tmdb match appears in the Translation Results window, we can open a dialog with a right click to view added metadata. If the Tmdb is well filled and edited we call it a 'high-end termbase' (Melby 2012). This means that the concept entries have been checked (not taken from the web without quality control), and are accompanied by equally checked information, the metadata. These data help the translator choose appropriately if there are several target options for the source term. This work practice has a positive impact on the quality of the TM and reduces TM edit time if appropriate terms are selected immediately and consistently. Table 4.1 shows how a comprehensive terminological entry in the database removes ambiguities and supports terminological consistency in a translation project. It gives an example of a definition of a special breed of cat in the Tmdb of a 20,000-word-encyclopaedia-on-cats translation project:

The window 'Create term base entry' (memoQ 9.2) in Figure 4.2 opens after you have highlighted a source and target term pair in the translation editor and clicked on 'Add term'. It has entered the following metadata:

Termbase(s)	*en-nl-nl*
Term entry	*supplied* (duplicates 3)
Languages	*English Dutch*

TABLE 4.1 Example of term definition in SL

SL term	*Calico cat*
SL contextual definition	Sunnyvale: Rare male *calico cat* turns up at shelter. [...]
	Calicos are not a breed; their name comes from the animal's unique multi-coloured coat.
SL source	www....
Concept	Type of coat/ fur
TL term	....
TL contextual definition	....
TL source	www....
Translation equivalent (full or partial)	....

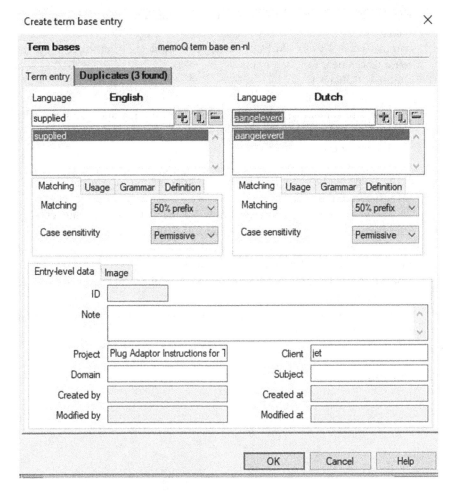

FIGURE 4.2 Term entry in memoQ 9.1

The translator completes the following:

- entry – source term(s): [+] for additional terms, [|] for change, and [-] for removal
- matching:
  - matching '50% prefix': morphological changes (4.5) such as verbal prefixes or endings are not immediately identified as matches by the TM. The '50% prefix' is the default setting. In this case, the Tmdb will look for 'supplies' and 'supplied' but not for 'supplying'. The default can be changed to fuzzy, exact, or custom
  - case sensitivity: this can be set to 'yes' or 'no', if you would like a term to contain small letters or caps or both.

- usage enables us to add forbidden terms, meaning how a term should *not* be translated
- grammar enables us to add POS, gender, and number. For example, the term 'research' can be a verb or a noun
- definition (Table 4.1)

Definitions are sometimes needed to clarify the meaning and standardise the term (4.1.4, 5.4), particularly in technical texts. A good and helpful definition will meet the following criteria:

- Predictability – the definition inserts the concept into a concept system: a carrot is a vegetable
- Simplicity – the definition is clear and concise and no longer than one sentence
- Affirmativeness – the definition states what the concept is
- Non-circularity – the definition does not begin with the term and does not use words which are dependent on the concept
- Absence of tautology – the definition is not a paraphrase of the term, but gives a description of the semantic features
- Part of speech – the definition begins with the same part of speech as the term you are describing

Pavel Terminology Tutorial★★(link: term definitions)

Food for thought...

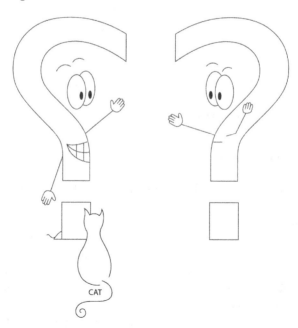

Which metadata would the translator find helpful in a TBX file provided by the LSP to assist a translation on fuel converters? Rank them in order of importance.

4.1.4 Standardisation and quality assurance

Consistency of term translation is enhanced if the Tmdb is managed well. It is best to follow agreed terminology standards and to perform regular terminology maintenance. We have discussed term definition criteria (4.1.3) which need to be met, although they do not guarantee agreement among the users. The industry relies on technical specifications and criteria, rules and guidelines to ensure that materials and products are interconnected and interoperable. This is called **standardisation**. We need to apply similar standards to terminology so that we agree which technical terms will be accepted as standard. Terminology standards for preferred terms and definitions ensure a common understanding of the key concepts. In other words, the standard definition of a 'tree' should be such that it is understood to be a tree anywhere in the world regardless of size, appearance or characteristics.

ISO standards★★(link: ISO terminology) can be applied to multilingual or bilingual terminology databases (5.4) and termbanks (4.6). But how are ISO standards of terms determined? Terms need to pass a reliability assessment; they should be able to cope with emerging knowledge and not be obsolete on the day they are standardised. Acronyms and names of school examinations, for example, are often reviewed, modified, or replaced. Our CAT terminology databases need to be maintained and kept up to date accordingly.

There are terminology management tools available to help us check consistency and relevance. They also provide quality assurance and a certain level of terminology management ★★(link: terminology management). We can import bilingual CAT formats, such as TMX, XLIFF in the terminology management tool that will then run checks for completeness, consistency, number, and tags. Results are presented in a common results window. The tool can also perform Quality (QA) checks in the CAT tool. Chapter 5 gives more details on the quality assurance (QA) function in CAT tools and its reliability.

4.2 Web searches

In their terminology searches, translators make prolific use of online mono/bilingual dictionaries, specialised glossaries, comparable and parallel corpora (4.3), MT, social networking and cloud technology (Wang and Lim 2017). Junior translators are the most frequent users of web resources and their search techniques are more sophisticated compared to senior translators when researching the translation of difficult terms. In their study, Wang and Lim (2017) found that senior translators rely more on experience and memory and have a more **linear** and **syntagmatic** approach to reading the ST. The senior translators read from beginning to end, compared to junior translators who are more **paradigmatic** and focus on the segment and its alternatives. The paradigmatic approach is more likely to lead to misinterpretations, which supports Pym's negative views (2008) on the impact of technology on human translation (segmentation 2.11). These findings also highlight the importance of good

78 The terminology database

search techniques and validity checks of our web hits. When we add a target term retrieved from the internet to the Tmdb, we must be sure of its validity and accuracy. Furthermore, the insertion of target terms in the CAT editor needs to be based on our understanding of the entire source text, and our translation benefits from a linear, syntagmatic approach.

4.2.1 Search techniques

The **World Wide Web (WWW)** is open source, it can be accessed free of charge, it can be modified, censored, and manipulated by users. A translator who needs to know the term of a consumer product in the target language and cannot find it in a bilingual dictionary will search the web. However, the internet was not designed for terminology searches. Hence our online term searches must be sophisticated. Web searches for terminology can be enhanced if we choose appropriate search engines best suited for our term searches. There are many search engines, but the main categories are threefold:

- *(General-purpose) search engines* are software applications that help search for websites in WWW and then access and display them. Each search engine has its own special features which also vary per country
- *Specialised search engines* show index pages for special topics only, which may not be shown in general-purpose search engines
- *Meta-search engines* are search tools that operate as aggregators and use other search engines' data to produce their own results★★(link: meta-SE)

Our search techniques can be made more term specific by using the operators AND, AND.NOT in the search box of the search engine. These operators are called **Boolean logic.** Its use has distinct advantages and immediate results:

- AND narrows the search by retrieving only documents that contain the keywords we enter, e.g. 'tea AND coffee' excludes 'tea and chocolate',
- OR expands the search by returning findings with either or both keywords, for example, 'nursery OR day care centre', and NOT limits the search to the first keyword only, for example 'coffee AND.NOT tea'.

The validity and accuracy of our term hits on the web are important. Boolean logic is a good filter and makes hits more specific. Another filtering method is to check the source and only accept term hits from reliable URL website addresses. The URLs presented to us by the search engine tell us about the origin of the website and help us determine a level of reliability. A **domain suffix**★★(link: domain suffix) is the last part of a domain and defines the type of website we may be about to access. 'Com' domains are commercial websites, whereas 'org' domains are used by organisations, and 'co.uk' means that the business is run in and from the UK. Domain suffixes are not entirely reliable and the actual website must be checked to be sure that it was not hijacked by a less trustworthy body for their own purposes. The quality of the website does not necessarily guarantee the quality of its terminology and linguistic checks are necessary. We can check the quality and usage of term hits by inserting them in linguistic corpora and concordances.

4.3 Corpora

'Corpora' (plural form of 'corpus') are large structured sets of texts or words. A terminology database in a CAT tool is a corpus of words, like a dictionary; the TM is a corpus of phrases or sentences. Aligned texts and reference files constitute corpora in a CAT tool (Alignment 2.3.1 and Reference files 2.3.2). Digital corpora can be external or integrated in the CAT tool. In the following sections we will examine some external corpora and their TEnT qualities. Glossaries and external terminology databases (interchangeable TBX files) can be imported in the Tmdb.

4.3.1 Digital dictionaries

Dictionaries are corpora. Printed dictionaries have always been associated with standards. Standards, however, vary and are closely linked to name, tradition, reputation, or price. A reputable dictionary will 'sample' a term before it is entered, which means that the **lexicographers** will look at one or more screenfuls of relative citations to see how the term behaves grammatically and lexically before it is entered or after an existing entry has been revised. With the vast rise of digital dictionaries, unpublished and free of charge, we cannot be sure that similar sampling procedures are applied, and consequently the quality of many digital dictionaries must be determined by the user.

With never-ending and ever-changing data available on the web, digital dictionaries offer new and excellent opportunities for lexicographers to compile corpus-based dictionaries (Müller-Spitzer and Koplenig 2014). They can be updated online without printing costs, the entries can be linked to collections of texts (4.4) and multimedia, such as audio files, graphs, and images. In addition, there is the new aspect of collaboration, the entire internet community can contribute, with Wikipedia as an example. Wikipedia has become a popular website, used as an immediate source of information. However, its open-source character, meaning that anybody can add, remove, and modify content without any validation or control, makes its content unstable, if not unreliable. The study by Müller-Spitzer and Koplenig (2014) showed that the following criteria were considered important in digital dictionaries by their respondents: reliability of content, up to date, and to a lesser degree, accessibility and clarity. Reliability of content means that all details represent actual language usage and that all details

80 The terminology database

are sampled and validated on a corpus. Maintenance by a well-known publisher or well-known institution was only given an importance rating of 8% (Müller-Spitzer and Koplenig 2014).

In conclusion, the quality of a digital dictionary is difficult to assess. Digital dictionaries are like websites: we can determine their source and origin by checking their URL, but without an ISO standard, they do not have a quality label. If bilingual dictionaries are machine translated, they are even less likely to have been validated. If we want to import their glossaries in a CAT Tmdb, we will find that digital dictionaries are generally protected and it is not possible to download and import them in the CAT tool. They must be treated as independent TEnTs. Only glossaries downloadable as text (rtf) or XML files can be imported as reference material in some CAT tools and will propose matches during the translation process.

4.3.2 Multilingual data corpora

Many large organisations make their multilingual corpora available online for general use and sharing, which means that users can upload and download terminology to and from the websites. There are some very impressive data sources available on the web, which we can use as TEnTs. The programs use web crawlers to search for translated content online, including e.g. EU multilingual data and then match it with web-based dictionaries**(link: multilingual corpora). In Figure 4.3 we see the results if we enter a source term or an entire phrase in the tool: it displays a vast amount of complete target segment matches. Some matches have warning symbols, such as 'this translation can be wrong'. The website of the source is listed below the match. The tool also states if translation pairs have not yet been reviewed.

Multilingual corpora with a more reliable quality are provided by TAUS. Its Data cloud**(link: multilingual corpora) is an extensive collection of translation memory data from large translation buyers predominantly in software and IT industries (Zetzsche 2003–17). It is a neutral and secure repository platform and gives translators, language service providers, developers, researchers, and stakeholders access to a number of services, such as Search, Upload (your own data for sharing), Discover & Download (only if you have uploaded, and acquired credits), Account History, My Data, and Feedback. Its collaborative plan gives you credit points if you upload data and you gain credits in return which enable you to download. The Data cloud is accessed through the web or API, and accessibility depends on a membership plan. Once corpora are created, they are offered as 'libraries' to other potential purchasers. The TAUS Data search engine in Figure 4.4 has produced 100 entries plus translations for the term 'unilateral'. These occur in compounds and phrases, ranging from 'Unilateral effects' to 'Anencephaly and unilateral anophthalmia' and 'Unilateral leg pain, and/or swelling'. The i (information) icon after the

FIGURE 4.3 Bilingual data corpora in Linguee stating that 'external sources are not yet reviewed'

first entry in Figure 4.4 gives information on industry (Legal Services), type (Standards, Statutes, and Regulations), Data owner (European Parliament), Data Provider (TAUS).

Google offers us multilingual data corpora by letting us search the web in the requested language. It gives a random set of links to the search term in context. Other kinds of open source multilingual corpora programs**(link: multilingual corpora) contain words and phrases which are too new or too rare to appear in a dictionary or standard corpus. Similar to TAUS Data cloud, they operate as a concordance in Key Word In Context (KWIC) style (4.4). There are many other free downloadable parallel corpora of texts (for alignment) and terms available to fill your tools, but this does not guarantee the quality of your translations (Zetzsche 2003–2017). Their web mining for material is done automatically and

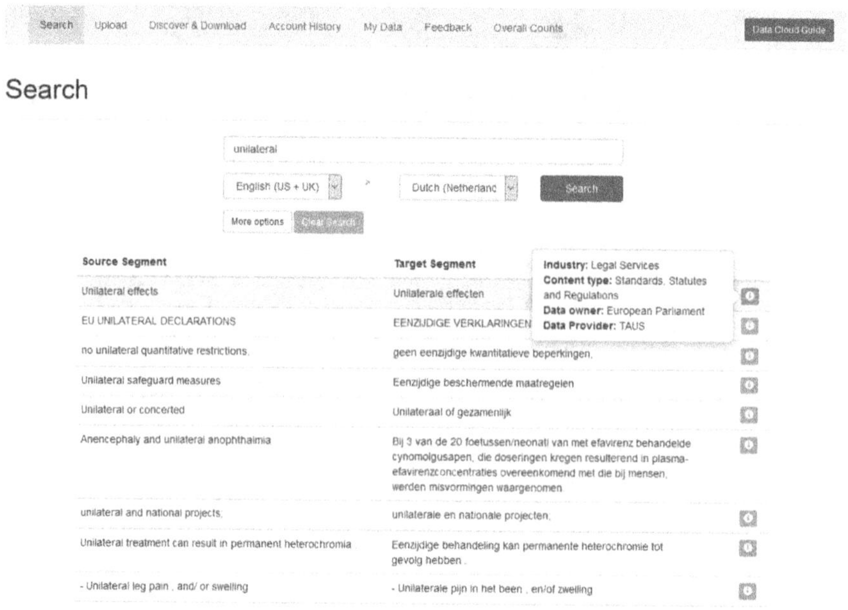

82 The terminology database

FIGURE 4.4 TAUS data cloud

manual corrections are not necessarily carried out.★★(link: multilingual corpora) Downloadable data deserve a thorough check before we use them: is the source reputable or is it a DIY corpus; is it bootstrapped, i.e. a glossary based on and derived from another glossary?

This brings us to the conclusion that the quality of online multilingual data does not necessarily meet guaranteed standards or required criteria. It does not mean that we cannot use them, but it implies that we must have a system in place to check their usage and accuracy. In the following section we will have a brief look at how corpora are built and how we can potentially build our own prior to importing it in the CAT tool.

4.3.3 The creation of corpora

An established dictionary published online may have a history of 200 years.★★(link: online dictionaries). It can then draw on a wealth of reliable, tested, and informative material. Its lexicographers will use language databases, i.e. corpora, in multiple languages to extract terms and try and test usage. The corpora ensure that language in the dictionary is authentic and accurate. New data is fed regularly from spoken or written material, from television, radio, websites, newspapers, journals, and books. The Bank of English is part of a larger corpus with approximately 650 million words. The full corpus★★(online corpora) contains 4.5 billion words from all English-speaking countries. If we want to create our own corpora to build our own terminology databases, we can extract terms from reference materials by 'bootstrapping' our corpora onto existing and available web corpora. For this there is the webBootCaT technology and there are BootCaT tools**(link: creating corpora for Tmdb). The designers (Baroni and Bernardini 2004) of the webBootCaT built a tool that does not need downloading but can be created by using the Google search engine. The basis method is that you first select a few **seed terms** (keywords), then send queries with the seed terms to Google and then collect the pages in Google's hits. The vocabulary in your created corpus of texts can be extracted automatically in the tool. The webserver of the designers will hold the corpus and load it into a **corpus query** tool, such as Sketch Engine** (link: corpus building) where it is investigated and analysed. The terminology database you have created must be converted to suitable formats (CSV) to import them in CAT tools. The corpus query language in the term extracting tool is a special language that looks for complex grammatical or lexical patterns to establish suitable search criteria. We can see the outcome of its searches in the concordance, where our queries are presented in context.

In the following section about the concordance feature we return to the parameters of the CAT tool which can give us more control over quality in our databases.

Food for thought...

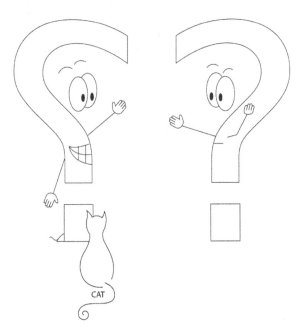

How could standards and quality in multilingual data corpora be made more transparent?

4.4 CAT concordance

The concordance feature in the CAT tool is very useful. It is intended for term or phrase searches and is often seen as a substitute or an alternative for the Tmdb. It allows you to access the TM when searching for individual terms or phrases within strings. It may explain why some translators prefer its convenience and the opportunity to search the TM rather than having to build a Tmdb. The CAT concordance retrieves all the entries of a specific word or phrase from the TM and displays them bilingually so that context-based information can be given of source and target segments. In the CAT concordance we must take account of subtle differences due to segmentation or morphological changes which affect what is retrieved by the TM (4.5). The CAT concordance is not only bilingual but also parallel as it gives multiple translations for one source term or phrase (Zanettin in Chan 2015). A concordance does not give any definitions, but it recalls nuances, and different shades of meaning in context. This is helpful to the translator when having to decide on a good match. If the Translation Results window does not propose any matches, the translator can retrieve term pairs through the concordance function. If the term pair is embedded in a string that is different to a previously confirmed string, the TM does not propose a match. The concordance function, however, ignores the string and focuses on the term pair (Figures 2.3 and 4.5).

The limitation of the CAT concordance is that it can only recall what has been entered in the TM. If the Tmdb presents matches from imported reference files, which have not yet been confirmed and entered in the TM, the concordance will not offer any results. External concordances are useful TEnTs to help the translator determine accuracy and usage of terms or phrases in context.

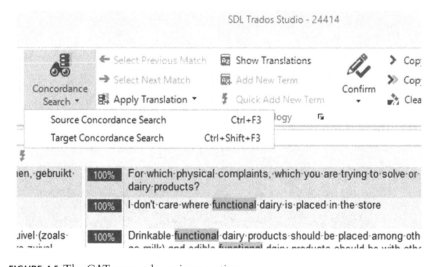

FIGURE 4.5 The CAT concordance in operation

4.4.1 External concordances

There are two types of external concordance: those which enable us to create a concordance through reference files, and comprehensive web concordances that we may use to check our target terms.

The World Wide Web has become indispensable to the translator, but it has its drawbacks. As we pointed out in our discussion of corpora in 4.3, mined terminology on WWW is uncontrolled, it lacks background, testing, quality assurance, and agreed standards. Nevertheless, it is an unrivalled source of corpora for specialist terminology and Tmdbs. Source texts with specialist terminology require two different kinds of source material, i.e. linguistic reference material to understand concepts and meanings, and a confirmation that we have selected appropriate target terminology, if retrieved from e-dictionaries or the web. Concordances or KWIC (Key Word in Context) tools provide solutions to both.

An external concordance**(link: external concordance) can automate the process of finding specific reference texts on the web and collate them in one corpus (Olohan 2004). The process is as follows: first the user provides a list of key terms and phrases in the program, which then sends them as queries to a search engine that returns a list of potential URLs. The user selects suitable URLs, and the program retrieves the webpages and converts them to plain text or saves them in 'txt' format. Some CAT tools accept the text files as reference materials, and they will then be incorporated in CAT concordance searches. The external concordance can retrieve and process many texts in a short period of time which makes it a very useful TEnT. Its external nature may have an additional advantage. Reference materials may not need keeping. They are useful to understand the ST or find translations for the TT as a one-off. TUs are then entered in the TM, which makes new terminology entries retrievable in the CAT concordance without having to store the reference material. The CAT term extraction editor (4.1.2) can add them to the Tmdb.

Digital dictionaries**(link: e-dictionaries) contain billions of words. If we search high-frequency words like 'make', the British National Corpus (BNC) (latest edition 2007 and no longer used for new dictionary material) may give hundreds of millions of results (known as 'citations'). If translators want to know more about actual usage, they can use online corpus search software which displays the searched term or phrase in combination with other words, called **collocates**, and the software gives the frequency of the collocations. A good external concordance can assist a translator in the following ways: show the most typical combinations of the word (or phrase), show synonyms (thesaurus), compare with another word and find examples of usage. In a parallel concordance we will find examples of alternative translations. We can apply filters to the tool, so that it customises and collates our searches. Because sources are provided for each citation, we can tell the program which sources are preferred. In sum, a concordance TEnT helps us select and control our web hits through its examples of usage.

86 The terminology database

4.5 Morphology and the terminology database

It can be frustrating when neither TM nor Tmdb recognises a term due to an added prefix or suffix, while you are convinced you have previously translated and confirmed it in one or both databases. This is a TM problem related to morphology, i.e. the form, shape, or structure of the word. If a derivative is not recognised, translators can try to resolve this by using filters (2.5.1) or highlighting the core of the word without the prefix or suffix and search in the concordance feature. Zetzsche (2019 (268th Journal)) made a study of TEnTs and their morphology support, i.e. the ability of the underlying technology to recognise that different forms of a word belong to one root version. TEnT manufacturers have created different solutions to prevent TM non-recognition associated with morphological change. A translation management system (7.5) uses AI to discern morphological changes in words. Some CAT tools require the user's application of an asterisk or pipe character to tell the tool that following characters should not exclude possible matches, such as 'support*/|' must include 'supported', 'supporter'. A CAT program with an external terminology database has incorporated morphology for a range of languages. The manufacturer decided not to use the external Tmdb but moved the process into the cloud where it is combined with the program's MT service**(link: morphological change). The user can select an existing web-based Tmdb and add new term pairs. Searches in the Tmdb differentiate between linguistic and character-based fuzzy searches. The former is based on the morphological core of the term and the latter is based on searches of three letters or more, comparable with asterisk and pipe-based searches. Especially interesting is the manufacturer's use of third-party tools, i.e. an existing web-based 'morphology engine', instead of developing their own engine. It should be noted that if the web-based Tmdb is shared, it could impact confidentiality (6.5).

Zetzsche (2019 (268th Journal)) stresses the need for morphological support in all CAT tools. Particularly languages such as German, with compound words would benefit from improved recognition. It would also increase the accurate verification of terms in the quality assurance (QA) function (5.2.1). The CAT tool may flag up false positives during a QA check and mark morphological changes as supposed inconsistencies or false matches. Until all CAT programs support morphological changes, we have the option to use the filters and change fuzziness settings. Although it is not advisable to lower the percentage of fuzzy matches, it could be useful in the read-only mode during a revision as it is more likely to include some morphological changes. Obviously, this is a second-best approach until the software developers find solutions in the CAT tool. It may well be an AI solution, as part of translation management systems.

4.6 Termbanks

Large external terminology databases are often referred to as termbanks**(link: termbanks). They have different modes of operation within or outside the CAT tool. If an integrated termbank in a CAT tool presents termbank information, or matches, in a results window while we are translating, it is called a 'push approach', whereas if we use the concordance or consult external terminological material, it is called the 'pull' approach (Warburton in Chan 2015: 656). One CAT tool performs push lookups through the EuroTermBank online terminology service, which is a databank with more than 600,000 entries of more than 1,500,000 terms. Figure 4.6 shows how a click on the Quick Access tab displays the Term Lookup icon in the CAT program. Because the Euro TermBank is integrated in the tool, the user can toggle between 'Search memoQ term bases' and 'Search Euro TermBank'. One unsuitable result for 'power' is shown in the Lookup term dialog. The Translation Results pane does not give a Tmdb result and the remaining option is to click on the Online Lookup in the Lookup term dialog. The subject field was not selected, which accounts for an inappropriate result found in the subject field of 'Communications and Education'. The TM, however, gives an acceptable 101% context match. The different features complement each other well, depending on the smart use of the translator.

External termbanks can be accumulated and aggregated on behalf of governments, multinational organisations, or international umbrella organisations, such as the UN, which rely on ISO standards. It is possible for registered users to download, but not to upload or share, terms in contrast to many online corpora run by web-based companies which make a profit through sharing and advertising. TERMIUM Plus®, for example, is maintained by a translation bureau under the auspices of the Canadian government. It is one of the largest termbanks in the world and it gives access to millions of terms in English, French, Spanish, and Portuguese**(link:Termium). It complies with ISO standards on Terminology (5.4). The majority of the termbanks are independent standalone tools not integrated in CAT tools.

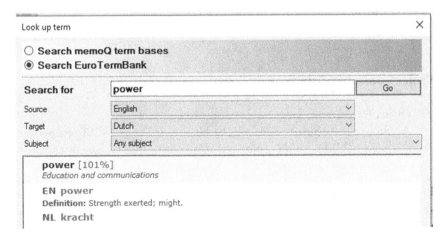

FIGURE 4.6 Termbank and lookup term in CAT tool (memoQ 9.1)

88 The terminology database

Termbanks are valuable components for us to use as terminological resources. Several CAT tools have the Term Extraction editor feature (4.1.2). Unfortunately, many termbanks and other terminology resources lack integration in the translator's workflow and the translator will need more than one screen to open several windows simultaneously. Standalone term extraction tools remove this problem and may suit translators who are keen to tap into as many resources as possible and build their own customised Tmdbs. The process of term extraction tools is explained in 4.1.2. There are several on the market which differ in the amount of metadata that can be added**(link: term extraction). Once terminology is extracted from the files you have uploaded into the tool, the term list can be imported in the CAT tool in an interchangeable format. One extraction tool, set up as part of an EU-funded project, runs the extracted term list against any of the following resources to query and check term pairs: your own CAT Tmdb, EuroTermBank, IATE (EU terminology database), TAUS corpus, and a statistical database of aligned web terminology (Zetzsche 2003–2017). Once the query process is completed, matches are displayed in the Results dialog of the CAT tool. Today's translator cannot complain that they are short of terminology resources. Our content and quality control over the TM are determined by quality and quantity in our Tmdbs, more than we realize. But we must first create and build terminology databases.

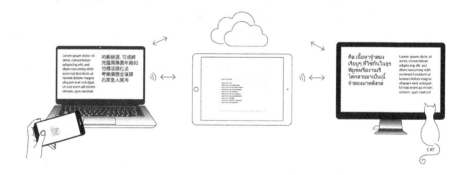

Project-based assignment

> Objective:
> A hands-on experience of creating, building and sharing a CAT terminology database (TBX) in a translation project to ensure quality and consistency in all translations across the project
>
> Assessment and outcome:
> Self- and peer-assessment of the impact of TBX on consistency in a shared translation project:

The terminology database **89**

- Assessment of quality and consistency in the revised project translation in comparison to your collaboratively agreed benchmark translation
- A file which lists all terminology resources used and consulted by team members and contracted translators (the checklist needs to be created for all, completed and returned)
- Checklists are shared and compared among the teams for assessment

Method:

The assignment is designed for:

- A *project* team with several terminologists, revisers and a project manager who create a TBX for sharing. You translate the text in-house. A revised translation on completion of the project will provide the basis for your assessment
- A *project management* team with terminologists, revisers and project managers who split the source text between multiple contracted translators and provide them with a TBX and monolingual/bilingual reference texts
- Collaboration between individuals to create a TBX prior to or during the translation of a shared source text

Tools:

CAT-tool (a server version is not necessary), access to online concordances, termbanks, WWW and other terminology supporting TEnTs discussed in the chapter

Suggested resources:

One digital source text with domain-specific terminology which can be split between multiple translators in a CAT tool. Consult your instructor.

Language pairs and direction:

One language pair; both directions if the TM is reversable

Assignment brief

A client requires the translation of a text in a highly specialised domain. They contact a language service provider (LSP) and ask for a quote and best turnaround time. The source text has an approximate word count of 500 words per available translator. The client cannot produce a glossary. The source text is split between translators. Teamwork is necessary to test the outcome of a shared translation supported by good terminology resources. The following minimum requirements for resource/reference materials and TBX apply:

90 The terminology database

- The TBX file for translators contains extracted terminology from mined sources
- The TBX file includes metadata if you use a CAT tool with an integrated Tmdb
- Reference files (mono/bilingual) are supplied to translators for alignment in the CAT tool

Possible pitfalls

- Inferior quality of mined terminology. If ISO standards are not associated with the resources, how do you check quality?
- If TEnTs are not available or require a subscription/licence, use available resources, glossaries and dictionaries and create your own quality Tmdb/TBX file
- Incompatibility of file formats of reference files/glossaries. Txt files or Excel files (saved as CSV) can be imported in most CAT tools or Tmdbs

Concluding remarks

Translation without terminological support would at times be impossible. We have seen that terminology occupies a database in the CAT tool in which term pairs must be added manually, unlike the TM database which accepts all confirmed TUs automatically. One CAT tool comes with an external Tmdb which gives the impression that terminology is a separate entity outside the CAT tool. The objective of this chapter is to demonstrate that the two databases are inseparable. The Tmdb is a benign, clever, supportive, and indispensable friend of the TM. Where the TM fails to present a match, despite subsegmentation, the Tmdb can do so, with data support from many other TEnTs, either in the cloud or through digital terminological resources. The volume of multilingual corpora we can draw from is infinite, ranging from digital dictionaries and WWW term searches to databanks. Our TEnT findings can be added to the CAT Tmdb. When they become confirmed TUs in the TM, they can be checked for consistency and usage in a CAT concordance or external concordance. Various CAT programs accept and integrate terminological reference materials to varying degrees, but one aspect stands out: a high-end terminological database greatly assists the operation of the TM. The translator is accountable for the quality of the CAT Tmdb, which is determined by our working practice and standards.

Further reading

Müller-Spitzer, Carolin and Alexander Koplenig (2014). 'Online dictionaries: expectations and demands'. In: *Ebook Package Linguistics*, pp. 144–88. Berlin: De Gruyter, ZDB-23-DSP.

Olohan, Maeve (2004). *Introducing Corpora in Translation Studies*. Oxon: Routledge.

Pavel Terminology Tutorial, https://termcoord.eu/wp-content/uploads/2018/04/Pavel_Silvia_and_Nolet_Diane_Handbook_of_Terminology-002.pdf.

Warburton, Kara (2015). 'Terminology management'. In: Chan Sin-Wai (ed.), *The Routledge Encyclopedia of Translation Technology*, pp. 644–61. London and New York: Routledge.

Zanettin, Federico (2015). 'Concordancing'. In: Chan Sin-Wai (ed.), *The Routledge Encyclopedia of Translation Technology*, pp. 437–49. London and New York: Routledge.

5

HUMAN AND TECHNOLOGICAL QUALITY ASSURANCE

Key concepts

- Translation technology tools offer quality assurance; translators offer revision, evaluation, or assessment of translations
- Translation quality assurance in the CAT tool and revision are complementary
- The final quality check is performed by the user of the CAT tool
- ISO standards apply to the translation process rather than the translation
- A post-editor's task is complex and deserves more recognition

Introduction

In the previous chapters we presented translation environment tools (TEnT) as invaluable to the translator for 'better quality, more efficiency and productivity, and higher profit'. Ultimately, improved quality, productivity, and profit is determined by our efficient management of the tools. In this chapter we will try to discern a balance between human assessment and its technological counterpart, which is referred to as translation quality assurance (TQA), quality assurance (QA), or language quality assurance (LQA) respectively, depending on the CAT tool program. QA does not only mean quality assurance but can also mean quality assessment. There is a difference:

- **Quality assurance** is the function we use when we enable the CAT tool to resolve errors or flag up warnings to prevent errors. QA in the CAT refers to the checking of terms, spelling, grammar, **non-translatables**, omissions, tags. The process, also called 'verification', uses default specifications, such as the spellchecker, terminology verifier based on our Tmdb, and tag verification to check that tags have not been moved or omitted. Verification already happens on the fly while we translate and can be requested again on completion. It will then list all identified 'errors' in a separate window.

- **Quality assessment** (sometimes called 'quality evaluation') measures the extent to which a product complies with quality specifications. Because of its analytical nature, it is something a linguist may be asked to do; it is beyond the scope of the CAT tool.

In our discussion of translation quality, we will include ISO quality standards, which are external requirements. It is important that we examine how CAT tool and translator work together, recognising that the final decision must always be delivered by the latter.

5.1 Quality and standards

Quality in relation to human and automated translations was defined in 3.7.1 and standards were discussed in 4.1.4. In translation, neither quality nor standards can be absolute, they are fluid: translation quality is related to its purpose and rated by the user, and translation standards are benchmark translations by which other translations are assessed or evaluated. But what makes a translation a benchmark translation, and who was/is the creator? We currently have ISO standards for translation (5.4), agreements which bring translation close to agreed standards. They do not lead to standardisation, in contrast to consumer products that rely on technical specifications and criteria, rules and guidelines. These will ensure that materials and products are consistent and exchangeable, regardless of source or manufacturer. In Europe, where you can drive through several countries in one day, traffic signs and notices are standardised: red and round signs prohibit, triangular signs are warnings, and rectangular signs give information. The designs may vary, but they are recognised by all road users. TMX and XLIFF files are good examples of standardisation in CAT tools: they make files exchangeable and operable in different CAT programs. The standardisation of translations may not be possible, or desirable, because it would prevent the translator from dipping into the beauty, variety, and richness of language. Standards, however, and quality can certainly be agreed and achieved. In the following sections we will try to clarify the differences between quality assurance and quality assessment in TEnTs and the role of the translator in quality control.

5.1.1 Quality assurance and assessment

Quality assurance (QA) is a useful function in the CAT tool and many LSPs make QA a mandatory requirement prior to the translator's delivery of a

94 Human and technological quality assurance

translation. QA employs the TM database and checks, using statistical grounds and algorithms (Munday 2012). A translator's quality assessment is based on evaluative criteria, but it also uses emotions and intuitions to make selective choices as to what is right or wrong. Our emotions emerge from our response to the ST or TT (Munday 2012), which affects the assessment in a subjective way. None of this is to be found in the CAT QA, which systematically checks the accuracy of the translation process. QA cannot check the product; it is a technological assurance of quality of the translation process. We could say it checks the quality of the TM and its operator (you) but leaves it to the translator or reviser to perform a quality assessment of the final product according to agreed quality standards.

Organisations and companies work with goals, objectives, and values to assure quality in procedures and assess quality in products. Their criteria are measurable, they use KPIs (Key Performance Indicators) and their business goals are SMART: Specific, Measurable, Achievable, Relevant and Time-bound. Consumers can file claims if they do not receive the anticipated quality or standard in the products. Employees attend annual appraisals, which are reviews of their performance against agreed objectives. In academic organisations students are accustomed to scores, percentages, and grades, with set criteria and descriptors that express grades in words.

Can we apply such forms of evaluation to translation work? And if so, do we? All parties involved in a translation project recognise that translation errors are made but there is not much agreement on the criteria used to categorise and rate translation errors. Sometimes there is disagreement on whether an error is in fact an error. Most LSPs in the UK will choose to meet ISO standards, which require revision by a third person. Nonetheless, freelance translators are advised and sometimes required to take out an **indemnity insurance**, which protects them against claims by the client for faulty or substandard translations.

Although assessments and error correction seem to be preferred methods to deliver improved translation quality, it appears that more effort is made to protect against defects than to set measurable translation standards. LSPs guarantee translation quality assurance to the client by confirming that they will meet ISO standards. The processes of quality assessment vary between LSPs: self-revision and assessment or third-party revision and assessment. If it is a self-assessment, the translator will confirm that self-revision (often incorrectly called proofreading) has been carried out, including a check of *all* pre-translated text and CAT tool verification; that specifications have been followed; that queries have been raised with a project manager and subsequently resolved. If it is revision of a TT, a third-party linguist will return the revised TT with a completed assessment form.

Self-assessment and revision statements are sent to translators for signing. They do not guarantee that the translation is error-free. They only confirm that revision and assessment have been carried out.

Ideally, we need a basic revision model like translation job model contracts, which are made available to translators by professional organisations (7.3.1), with reference to technological tools and methods that can assist good translation quality. The revision model should include guidelines for self and third-party revision, but also for full use of the QA function available in CAT tools. Quality assurance and quality assessment are essential parts of the revision process. Revision is a critical stage in the translation project.

5.2 Quality in different TEnTs

Quality assurance is easier to understand if we accept it as a CAT tool function: default error checks against confirmed entries in the databases. The following sections are about quality assurance (QA) of the bilingual document in and by the CAT tool and our quality assessment of MT and localisation as translation tools.

5.2.1 Quality assurance in CAT tools

The QA function in CAT tools is an active feature that checks the quality of the translation in progress and at any time when it is enabled by the translator. It cannot provide a human evaluation. It does not analyse target sentences or consider linguistic context; it measures against data in the database. It is corpus-based, phrase-based, and statistical: if the match is not 100% correct, some CAT tools place error warnings, and spelling errors are marked with a red underscore. Omissions are flagged up as inconsistencies by means of warning symbols. In a final check the QA lists all 'inconsistencies' in a separate window for the translator to edit or ignore.

QA was designed in the CAT tool to support the translator. Boring jobs, repetitions, numbers are notorious for typos and errors. QA checks that your numbers are correct, that you have not typed two spaces, that you have used your client's preferred terminology in a custom Tmdb, that you have been consistent, that you did not miss or misplace tags. And if the warning error is inappropriate, you can tick an ignore box. QA should be used for its good qualities. LSPs often make it a requirement to perform a QA check before delivering the target file. The use of regex and filter functions (2.5.1 and 2.5.2) can reduce error warnings significantly.

QA can be carried out at any time and repeatedly during the translation process. Human revision can unfortunately generate new typos or inconsistencies and it is recommended to run a QA as a final check before exporting the file. The function in the CAT tool is not a revision feature; it is an error spotter. As such, it is an indispensable tool for a revising translator and fulfils revision parameters much better than we perhaps realise. QA can have some pedantic and irritating habits (if repetitive, use the filter!), but its value should not be underestimated.

5.2.2 Quality assessment of MT technology

We recognise that MT is not 100% reliable; errors are obvious in the target language. Neural machine translation (NMT), however, delivers correct syntax and linguistically correct phrases in the TL, but this does not guarantee correct equivalence between SL and TL. Its apparent linguistic correctness in the TL makes it more difficult to spot errors.

Poor MT quality has been addressed by manufacturers, with varying degrees of success. ISO standards exclude machine translated texts. Other standards are needed. MT services have opted for a standard-based approach that sets a **reference translation** (human-produced) as a benchmark. Originally, the reference translation was a human translation used to test the quality of speech recognition. The human translation has been adopted in the machine translation industry as a benchmark to assess machine translated output and is called the reference translation. The industry has set an absolute quality standard for MT based on TQA metrics (3.7.2, 3.7.3) with **BLEU scores** (Hernandez-Morin et al. 2017), and we call this error typology. The question we may ask ourselves is whether any reference translation is a quality benchmark or an evaluation standard.

There are many ways of addressing the quality problem in translation. TAUS defines two levels of quality: 'good enough' or 'near human'. This is very much the industry's approach that compares MT with HT. The industry would like both to have equal quality instead of HT, the reference translation, always being the accepted benchmark. Academic researchers and manufacturers approach MT quality differently. Academic studies focus on user tolerance of MT output, in other words, what the user finds acceptable determines the quality (Bowker 2007). Doherty and O'Brien (2014), however, take a different view and assess MT as a tool. '**Usability**' is their quality criterion, which means that the evaluation is based on how well the MT translation can be used to achieve a goal. Apparently, manufacturers use acceptability and usability tests to determine a standard (Hernandez-Morin et al. 2017). These tests consist of yes/no questions put to the user. Here we might wish to question the level of objectivity.

A more subtle typology approach to the assessment process consists of two steps: first we assess the 'acceptability' of the target text and then the 'usability' of the TT in relation to the ST (Daems, Macken, and Vandepitte 2013). Gouadec's view (Daems et al. 2013) is that translation errors have different effects on the user, and they also have different levels of criticality. Any form of human assessment is bound to be subjective compared to automated assessments. We must, however, bear in mind that automated assessments have been set up by humans. Therefore, it is worth stepping back and assessing the automated quality assessment in CAT tools not from a right or wrong perspective, but rather in degrees of helpfulness to the translator who ultimately determines the quality.

Food for thought...

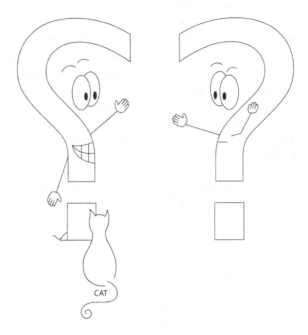

Discuss the reliability of a reference translation as a quality benchmark.

5.2.3 Web localisation and quality

Web localisation constitutes such a substantial part of translation technology that it must be mentioned. LISA (Localization Industry Standard Association) gave a clear definition of localisation:

> Localisation involves taking a product and making it linguistically and culturally appropriate to the target locale (country/region and language) where it will be used and sold.
>
> *LISA 2013*

Web *localisation* (often written as **l10n** = 10 letters including first and final letters) requires a different take on translation quality. Hypertexts can be presented in the tool in a nonlinear fashion, which means that what the translator sees is quite different to how it will be read by users. The content is often split and shared among translators and it is difficult to adopt a holistic approach to the text (Jiménez-Crespo 2013: 30). It is even more important that the localising translator has a greater awareness of digital genres, so that they know what kind of localisation is required, particularly if the topic is not immediately clear from the segmented text.

Compliance with local norms and conventions will make or break the quality of the translation in the eyes of the reader.

We use special localisation tools to localise websites**(go to www.routledgetra nslationstudiesportal.com/ – A Project-Based Approach to Translation Technology – link: localisation tools). They are like CAT tools and have a TM. Their filters are prepared for the most common types of files found in software and websites. They separate text segments (called 'strings') from the source code so that the coding is not visible to the translator. It makes translation more straightforward and the codes are not exposed to unintended changes that could damage the product. Another important feature of localisation is that files are 'internationalised' (internationalisation – **i18n**), an intermediary stage in which the source file has been delocalised. The ST has had linguistic and culturally specific features removed so that translators can start their localisation from a neutral file (Jiménez-Crespo 2013). Figure 5.1 illustrates how a UK clock, which shows 10 o'clock at night-time, is internationalised and localised to a 24-hour clock, used in many other countries.

Localisation is a growing industry which should not be ignored by any translator. Dedicated localisation tools, some of which can be integrated in the CAT tool, may be better suited to digital material. Web content is becoming so heavily coded that even CAT tools struggle. Localisation requires the translator to have a good understanding of metalanguage and adaptation. The client may internationalise web texts before they are sent out for translation, simply to standardise the process and standardise strings in future updates.

Quality management in localisation is comprehensive. The industry's approach is to use QA procedures to guarantee that quality requirements are met. It uses quality control (QC) procedures from ST to TT delivery to check the quality of product or service (Jiménez-Crespo 2013: 104). QA procedures include the localisation of links and images hidden in the website structure.

Quality in web localisation is of interest because of its fluid nature and diversity. One-size quality cannot fit all localised texts. In this respect the 'corpus-assisted approach to quality evaluation' (Bowker 2001) deserves mentioning. We have seen how many methods despite metrics are subjective such as the human reference

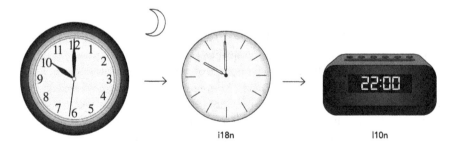

FIGURE 5.1 From i18n (internationalisation) to l10n (localisation)

translation. Localised text with much metalanguage cannot be assessed according to a reference text. Bowker suggests that the corpus-based approach is useful at an earlier stage in the localisation process because it can identify quantifiable data in strings and recurrent patterns. The relationship between the linguist and localisation is an interesting one. Localisation tools can automate web texts to the extreme, but there is always the point where quality comes into the equation and human input is needed. We will return to localisation when we discuss digital platforms in Chapter 7.

5.3   Revision in CAT tools

The best-known parameters of revision are accuracy and completeness. They are checked specifically by the CAT QA: new matches are compared against confirmed matches in the database. Spelling and formatting errors are identified through the spellchecker and against matches found in the database. If the ST contains 'hidden text' that is not visible, it appears in the source segments of the translation editor. It cannot be overlooked by the translator. 'Hidden text' is a feature in MS Word, which includes not only footnotes, or tracked changes, but also text from any other document inserted by the creator. The CAT tool eye does not miss anything during the conversion phase when importing the document. Other revision parameters are logic, facts, customisation, terminology, mechanics, layout, and typography (Mossop 2014). The CAT QA can accommodate them in different and unexpected ways:

- Logic – The translator is expected to deliver a coherent target text, in language and content. This is the parameter of logic. The QA cannot check content logic but it can highlight inconsistencies in the TT, and even in the ST. If there are terminological inconsistencies in the ST, such as item, article, product, and you decide to be consistent in the TT and use one term, QA will alert you to this perceived inconsistency. Source texts often contain errors, which is why some CAT programs allow edits in the source segments to prevent TM corruption. Coherence is part of logic: sequences must be logical. Numbers (plural/singular) and tenses must match. This kind of linguistic error is picked up in a QA and classified as an inconsistency. It is matched against correct pairs in the database.
- Fact – QA checks texts for factual errors: its observance of number matches is important.
- **Customisation** and terminology – We have discussed the importance of customised terminology when creating TMs (2.1): customisation of phrases and terms in line with, for example, client glossaries is checked carefully against the Tmdb in QA.
- Parameters of mechanics, layout and typography – They are catered for by tags containing formatting instructions and make sure that the target text

is delivered in an identical format. QA flags up error warnings when it detects typographical errors, such as different font, missing punctuation or capitals.

What the QA does not check is smoothness or cohesion which relate to style and a smooth flow of words. We already explained (4.2) how segmentation can interrupt the translation process if the translator does not take a linear approach to the whole text. If segmentation affects the TT in spite of precautions, the final monolingual revision of the TT must address style parameters.

5.3.1 CAT revision of bilingual and monolingual files

Self-revision can be performed in the editor of the CAT tool, in an exported bilingual rtf file or in the final monolingual target file. Third-party revision can be carried out in an exported XLIFF file, in an exported bilingual (review) file, and of course in the final clean target file, using track changes. Third-party revision is preferable in XLIFF or bilingual docx/rtf files because the reviewed file can be re-imported in the translator's or LSP's CAT tool to update the TM.

From a technological and a human perspective, there is a difference between revising XLIFF and bilingual docx/rtf files. Revision in either type of file enables updates of the databases. There are advantages and disadvantages to revision in either file format. Layout and formating are best checked in XLIFF files where you can insert and check format tags. In bilingual rtf/docx files, tags might be inadvertently moved. Tags should always be checked in a final QA in the CAT editor. Technological features, such as glossaries or term matches are not accessible in bilingual files. However, from a human perspective, a bilingual file offers more clarity with less information and fewer windows to distract the eye. Table 5.1 compares the positive or negative impact of several features in XLIFF and bilingual files on self-revision. Changes made in bilingual files must be updated in the TM and Tmdb after re-importation. It is good practice if the translator receives a third-party revised file to accept and reject changes in the editor of their CAT tool, so that databases are updated. Time constraints sometimes prevent LSPs from returning revised files to the translator.

What stands out in Table 5.1 is that 'clarity' in the bilingual file features positively. We all know how easy it is 'to see yet not to see'. We can be selective in what we see. Segments in both types of file seem to function as boundaries and restrict what the eye sees and the mind takes in. Hence it is understandable that translators like to do the final revision, a monolingual read, in a clean target text. This mode is not suitable for revisers who need to see S and T segments side by side. A revised clean target file can be re-imported in the CAT tool to update the TM.

Human and technological quality assurance **101**

TABLE 5.1 Positive and negative sides to revision in XLIFF or bilingual files

	XLIFF file	Bilingual doc file	Comments
TM checks	+	–	TM not accessible in bilingual files
Tmdb checks	+	–	Tmdb not accessible in bilingual files
Clarity	–	+	Only one view
Tags	+	+/–	In bilingual files tags are reduced in number and quality, which can be visual gain but detrimental to formatting
Additional CAT features, such as concordance	+	–	Not accessible in bilingual files
Clarity of revision comments	–	+	Bubbles in XLIFF; text in bilingual

A final comment about monolingual revisions: after hours of revising your own work (it is estimated we can revise approximately 1000 words per hour), we become tired. We read but can no longer take in what we read. Other than leaving the desktop and taking the dog for a walk or making a non-essential trip to the supermarket, there are a couple of tricks that can wake us up and renew our critical faculties, for example, changing the background colour of your file, or reading white letters on a dark grey background. The other trick is to make yourself alert by moving to a different place, such as taking the laptop to another room or even sitting on the stairs. The latter may well be uncomfortable and will make you want to get the job done!

5.4 ISO standards

Third-party revision in addition to personal checks is required to meet ISO standards. The CAT tool's features for revision (Quality Assurance 5.1.1) are not sufficient. The International Organisation for Standardisation, ISO (with over 160 member countries) is an independent, non-governmental international organisation with a membership of national standard bodies. Through its members it brings together experts to share knowledge and develop voluntary, consensus-based, market relevant international standards, also called benchmarks★★(link: ISO). ISO 17100:2015 is the internationally recognised standard for translation services and was created in 2015 to respond to the market need for a universally accepted benchmark. It is a process standard and does not define the quality of completed work; it sets quality standards for the translation process. The standard does not apply to interpreters, nor does it include machine-translated work.

ISO 17100:2015 is an ISO norm for translation services. It includes several pertinent recommendations. These affect not only the translation service provider (TSP) but also the client's specifications (Mitchell-Schuitevoerder 2015):

ISO 17100:2015 provides requirements for the core processes, resources, and other aspects necessary for the delivery of a quality translation service that

102 Human and technological quality assurance

meets applicable specifications. Application of ISO 17100:2015 also provides the means by which a translation service provider (TSP) can demonstrate conformity of specified translation services to ISO 17100:2015 and the capability of its processes and resources to deliver a translation service that will meet the client's and other applicable specifications. Applicable specifications can include those of the client, of the TSP itself, and of any relevant industry codes, best-practice guides, or legislation. The use of raw output from machine translation plus post-editing is outside the scope of ISO 17100:2015. ISO 17100:2015 does not apply to interpreting service.

www.iso.org/iso/catalogue_detail.htm?csnumber=59149:2015

In other words, the ISO 17100:2015 standard specifies translation steps such as:

- Translation (including a translation check by the translator themselves)
- Revision by a third party
- Review (an optional step, designed in order to assess the suitability of the translation against the agreed purpose, domain, and the recommended corrective measures)
- Proofreading (an optional pre-publication check) of the monolingual final target text
- Final verification

The following definitions taken from the Oxford English Dictionary (2019) and Merriam-Webster (2019) give us an accurate definition of the above terms used in the revision process:

- evaluation   the determination of the quality of something; assessment
- assessment   the process or means of evaluating academic work; an examination or test
- proofread   to read (text, esp. in proof) in order to find and mark errors for correction
- spot check   a check or inspection made on a random or representative sample of a group, or one conducted without warning
- revision   critical or careful examination with a view to making corrections, amendments, or improvements
- review   the action of looking (again) over something, as a book, text, etc., with a view to its correction or improvement; revision; an example of this
- edit   to prepare (written material) for publication by correcting, condensing, or otherwise modifying it; change (text) on a computer

ISO 17100 Translation Services Management Standard has superseded the old European quality standard BS EN 15038 for language service providers that was set up by the European Committee for Standardisation in 2006. The former BS EN standard continues to be embraced by many language service providers as a stamp of approval, which indicates that their products are delivered with an acceptable quality. The translation industry's initial enthusiasm for the BS EN 'fit for purpose' standard may be due to a lack of consensus within the industry (Gouadec 2007; Pym 2010a) as to what a standard should be. One of the differences between ISO 17100:2015 and the earlier BS EN 15038:2006 'fit for purpose' standard is that the ISO now has an additional competence requirement which means that the translator must be able to translate into the target language using appropriate style and terminology (Mitchell-Schuitevoerder 2015). Another key difference is that there is a greater focus on the customer:

- identification of key customer requirements prior to production
- handling and processing of customer feedback and
- the delivery of the service as a whole

Furthermore, this International Standard applies to LSPs without internal translators but with freelance contracted translators, LSPs with employed in-house translators, but also to individual translators who collaborate with other translators.

The reliance on revisers by LSPs does not necessarily guarantee good practice. The translator needs to take full responsibility for the quality of their work in accordance with reasonable and agreed standards. Furthermore, the translation industry requires good, recognisable standards, which should be negotiated between client and translator in a spirit of fair play. Too often the ball is kicked into the translator's court. And finally, as the use of raw output from machine translation plus post-editing is outside the scope of ISO, the question arises who will set and agree MT standards, especially when the target text emerging from a CAT tool is likely to be a product of machine and human combined (Mitchell-Schuitevoerder 2015).

Food for thought...

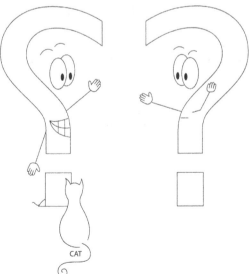

Create three sets of revision standards: for human translation, for CAT translation, and machine translation. Are there any major differences?

5.5 Revision and evaluation

In practice, there does not appear to be much agreement on descriptors used for third-party evaluation to meet ISO standards. 'Proofread' is a common term used in the translation industry: 'Please *proofread* the translation according to listed criteria. Use a score from 1 (lowest) to 5 (highest) in the supplied *evaluation* statement' (LSP 2019). The LSP expected the reviser to revise (not proofread) a translation and score an evaluation of the translation based on error correction in the target text. Table 5.2 contains a random selection of third-party revision descriptors used by LSPs. The first column shows the most frequently used descriptors and the third column lists those that were only found once. The fourth column gives two scoring systems. It was found that if a scoring system is used, it is generally numerical and not weighted.

The descriptors in Table 5.2 suggest that the reviser is expected to revise and correct: 'proofread' is generally a misnomer for translation revision and is more appropriate for desktop publishing services when checking the final proofs. The term 'proofread', often used by LSPs, is the least applicable to translation evaluations because it only requires the marking of errors for correction. If the revision process is managed well, a translation is sent to a third-party reviser and returned by the LSP to the translator who can accept or reject track changes in the file. **EU/DGT****(link: quality control) distinguishes two types of quality control: revision is a *bilingual* examination of target language content against source language content according to its suitability for the agreed purpose, and review means *monolingual* examination of target language for its suitability for the agreed purpose.

In the translation industry, evaluation and revision are performed seemingly without any clear or universal model. Translators may be asked to do tests before they are entered in the LSP database. Yet they may be asked to revise peer translations or evaluate peer tests without specific qualifications. They are unlikely to be tested on revision or assessment competences and skills, contrary to translation skills, which are frequently assessed by LSPs. Revision now is an ISO requirement, but there needs to be an acceptance that a translator is not necessarily a competent third-party reviser.

TABLE 5.2 Random selection of criteria found in LSP evaluation statements (2019)

Assessment criteria (most frequently)	Assessment criteria (frequently)	Assessment criteria (infrequently)	Scoring systems
accuracy	lexis	cohesion	score 1–5 (1=low 5= high)
comprehension	syntax	coherence	seriousness of mistake:
grammar	register	organisation of work	1. very serious
punctuation		orthography	2. serious
spelling		accentuation	3. not too serious
		TT fluency	
		terminology	

Agreed criteria for revision are crucial. Third-party revision and self-revision require different mindsets: third-party revision is best performed with circumspection and respect for the translator who has undoubtedly translated to the best of their ability. We do not know the circumstances under which the translation was carried out, for example, was there time pressure? What was the quality of the original ST? Were reference files sent to the translator? Was it a shared translation? A reviser should check a translation without comparing or modifying according to personal preferences. It is better to query when there is doubt and leave it to the translator to review their own choices and decisions, especially if they are not evident errors (Mossop 2019). He suggests revisers should ask themselves the following questions after completing their revisions:

- Was each change I made needed? If so, did it adequately correct the problem?
- If the change was adequate, how would I justify it (does it fit the checklist supplied by the LSP)?
- Have I missed any errors?
- Have I introduced new errors?

Mossop 2019: 205

In heavily revised translations it is not unusual to find that the reviser has unintentionally introduced new errors. If Track Changes is used, it is best to hide the red lines during the revision process to keep the text readable.

Revisions and evaluations require skill, competence and experience. They are potentially subjective: they should be carried out according to appropriate criteria and returned to the translator for acceptance or rejection, ideally in the CAT tool to update the TM (and Tmdb).

5.5.1 Human evaluation

From a study it appeared that there was a significant divergence between different reviewers (Guerberof 2017). They generally agreed on poor and good translations, but not on the classification of errors. CAT tool data were taken into the equation and there was more agreement on the number of no match errors than on Fuzzy and MT matches. The grid in 5.3 is based on LISA QA (see 3.7.3) and the error typology is applied to translations performed in CAT tools.

Overcorrection in the grid is an interesting but often ignored feature that consists of revision or post-edits performed by the translator that were unnecessary and may have led to incorrect renditions. The findings (Guerberof 2017) showed that different linguists who reviewed the same translations confirmed a trend in which the no match category showed the highest number of errors and that Language and Style were the grey areas where nobody agreed. LSPs are keen to use the category Language, but they do not make a clear distinction between Grammar and Syntax. Style is often not included in an evaluation statement, because it can be too subjective. Furthermore, terminology errors were low in MT matches and style errors were low in fuzzy matches. From other studies it appears that the initial MT quality is important, and not the amount of post-editing. PEMT has a superior quality compared to translation from scratch (Nunes Vieira 2017).

Revision and translation assessment, or evaluation, are closely related to quality and standards. Dynamic quality evaluation models for translation (Table 5.3) break with the standard error typology, in line with the fit-for-purpose principle commonly used by LSPs. Error typology is used as a quality safeguard (O'Brien 2012). Quality is closely linked with customer opinion and yet its evaluation is based on static evaluation models (O'Brien 2012). Existing models may be a form of security, because LSPs apply them to large volumes of translation generated by large numbers of freelance translators in their HR database, all with different levels of translation competence and skills. The LSP must meet ISO requirements: each translation must be reviewed by a linguist other than the translator. The main concern of the LSP is cost and time. Quality is measured according to the number of errors, and action is taken if the number of errors is considered too great. Action may consist of not giving the translator further work (O'Brien 2012). In a worst-case scenario, the translator will not be paid.

What can a translator do to improve quality? How should a translator practise self-revision? A translation should not be delivered containing grammatical errors, inaccuracies, term inconsistencies, or omissions (Lawrence 2018). The translator needs to know what level of quality is required. Commercial translations (advertising) have an optimisation problem: either you make the translation as good as you can in a fixed amount of time, or you decide how good it needs to be and get it to the required standard as quickly as possible (Lawrence 2018). It does not mean that you should cut corners. Instead, think of your work method. When do you do your research? Do you skim read the ST

TABLE 5.3 Error typology grid applied to a CAT tool with integrated MT

Type of error	No match	MT match	Fuzzy match	Totals
Mistranslation				
Accuracy				
Terminology				
Language				
Consistency				
Country				
Format				
Style				
Over-correction				
Totals				

Source: Guerberof 2017: 201

before you start and mark your problem areas, or do you begin without reading the ST and stop and start each time you come across an unfamiliar term? Do you confirm each segment, or do you send segments to the TM in draft mode? What is your best method and what is your quickest way to revise? How is your CAT tool set when you re-import revised bilingual documents? Does it import the file with Track Changes enabled, which means the translator must review each modification before confirming? If time is short, is it acceptable to skip some steps by, for example, not checking the revisions in the editor but simply clicking on accept and confirm all. After all, the CAT file history function records all your changes: you can compare them after you have confirmed them, if there is any doubt. Your work method has a significant impact on your time and productivity, as well as its quality.

5.6 The post-edit of wholly or partly machine translated texts

Post-editing refers to the correction of machine generated translations by humans. The edit consists of the removal of major errors and the improvement of fluency (linguistic quality) in machine translated texts. Our focus is on MT engines used in CAT tools, preferably in adaptive and integrated mode (3.4, 3.5, 3.6). It automatically lifts the quality and expectations and virtually removes a PEMT requirement if the editing is performed on the fly, i.e. while the translator translates in the CAT tool and modifies proposed MT matches. This type of PEMT on the fly is a fine example of human and technological revision combined. The results are good.

We therefore need to define the difference between the act of translating and post-editing and recognise where they overlap. First, the post-editor is not only post-editing but also translating. It is not possible to modify a target sentence without generating a translation in your mind. How can the post-editor make choices and changes without knowing what they should be? Thus, the post-editor is not only an editor but also a translator. The editing process is not simple. It can be broken down into four actions: deleting, inserting, replacing, and moving words (Zetzsche 2019 (298th Journal)). Replacing is paradigmatic, i.e. you take out the wrong word and replace it. The other actions are syntagmatic, i.e. you upset the sentence structure by deleting, inserting and moving words, and must then repair it (Zetzsche 2019 (298th Journal)). And because the MT engine does not understand metaphors or metalanguage, the resulting errors add to the post-editor's cognitive load. The post-editor's cognitive effort is undervalued (also financially) if we consider the many thought patterns needed while post-editing.

A typical PEMT difficulty created by neural machine translation is that NMT tends to be fluent and it is difficult to spot errors in the machine translated text without a thorough scrutiny and comparison of ST and TT sentences (Zetzsche 2019 (298th Journal)). This also adds to the post-editor's cognitive burden, and the overall tendency to reduce word fees by more than 50% for post-editing does not recognise or reward the post-editor's effort.

108 Human and technological quality assurance

Food for thought…

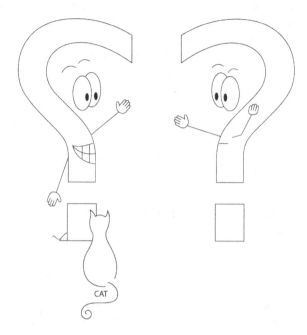

Can you agree on the editorial corrections needed in a machine translated paragraph and a suitable financial reward on an hourly or a word basis? Discuss and offer suggestions.

5.6.1 PEMT quality

The quality of a post-edited product is best understood if it is expressed in terms of fluency (linguistic quality) and adequacy (translation accuracy) (Nunes Vieira 2017). Both are closely related to the quality of the MT product that is delivered to the reviser. Fluency and linguistic quality especially, smoothness and readability, suffer if the edit requires many corrections. There is a clear link between the human editing process and the quality of the edited MT product. The quality depends on the amount of temporal, technological and cognitive effort made by the reviser (Nunes Vieira 2017). The three types of effort are closely related, for example, the more thinking effort, the longer the editing time. The technological effort refers to the technological operations that need to be performed in the CAT tool. These efforts require time and consideration. They also apply to the revision of human translation in a CAT tool where the final linguistic quality shows less improvement when the number of errors is high.

Recent versions of major CAT tools measure the edit distance, either PEMT or self-/peer-revision in the CAT tool. The so-called Levenshtein distance used in the CAT tool is an algorithm and it measures the minimum number of single-character edits (insertions, deletions, or substitutions) needed to change one word to another. Here is an example in which the edit distance is 3:

bitten > bittin (1 change); bittin > bitin (2nd change); bitin > biting (3rd change)

Three-digit changes have been made. In PEMT, the edit distance can be used to measure the post-editing effort: fewer edits indicate less effort on the post-editor's part – and payment will be less as the post-editor is only paid for changes made. If this approach is taken, many aspects of PEMT that are in fact similar to translating from scratch in a CAT tool, such as job preparation, reading and comparing of source and target segments, topic research and checking supplied glossaries or style guides, final QA and delivery and administration, are overlooked.

The differences between MT post-editing and HT revision are largely determined by the purpose of the translations. For example, if an MT text is not for publication and only for gist, there is less emphasis on high quality and time and cognitive effort will decrease. Another difference relates to the predictability of errors in MT, such as terminology inconsistency, lack of cohesion in grammatical number, gender, or punctuation. These typical errors make post-edits easier and quicker, whereas errors in HT are less predictable: they vary from translator to translator. It is difficult to predict how remuneration and fees will continue to be calculated. It is to be expected that time and effort in PEMT are put under pressure depending on the purpose of the translation and that quality may not be the main priority. On the positive side, adaptive MT in the CAT tool allows us to make corrections to proposed matches before they are confirmed in the TM. This should automatically reduce the need for PEMT and improve quality levels.

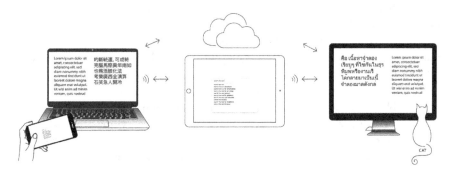

Project-based assignment

Objective:
To measure efficiency (post-edit time) and quality during the revision process and after revision or post-edit

110 Human and technological quality assurance

Assessment and outcome:
Self-/peer-assessment through revision and QA procedures with special focus on the use of appropriate translation quality criteria

Method:
The assignment is designed for a project management team but collaboration within a project team or between individuals is possible

Tools:
CAT tool (a server version is not necessary but would facilitate collaboration between contracted linguists and team members)

Suggested resources:
One digital source text of approximately 1000 words

Language pairs and direction:
Multiple language pairs and/or directions but there must be multiple users of each pair or direction

Assignment brief

The assignment incorporates steps discussed in previous chapters and requires you to manage them through collaboration: ranging from the recruitment of required linguists to the sending out of Purchase Orders (PO) (1.7.2) and translation briefs (3.7.1), the distribution of files for translation and revision, and the receipt of invoices from contracted linguists. The new component is human revision combined with QA features in the CAT tool. In your team you must agree on revision and assessment criteria. You arrange the translation of your source document and third-party revision.

The project-based assignment provides the framework to manage and assess translation quality and must be shaped by your team with due consideration of the following:

- Establish separate sets of revision and evaluation (scoring) criteria for your contracted revisers, which are appropriate for your chosen digital source text
- Create and send a clear job description, requesting QA from translators before they return target files
- Create and send personalised POs to translators and revisers with agreed fees
- Fees may vary per linguist (concerning language pairs), provided the total cost does not exceed the budget agreed by the team
    - Fees for post-editing may be calculated according to the edit-distance function in the CAT tool

Human and technological quality assurance **111**

- Manipulate your source text and send out different versions to translators or revisers, as appropriate, for example:
  - prepare and send a clean ST to translators
  - prepare and send a clean ST with a TBX or glossary to translators
  - pre-translate the ST with MT in the CAT tool and send to revisers
  - pre-translate the ST with MT but clear 50% of the target segments and send to translators
- Prepare files for revisers in the following formats: XLIFF, bilingual doc or clean target files
- Return revised files to the translators for rejection/acceptance
- An accounts PM manages incoming invoices and creates a spreadsheet
- Compare and discuss revisions and evaluation statements; compare the quality of target files translated and revised through different methods; discuss and compare the target quality of manipulated source files after revision. Show your findings in tables or diagrams

Possible pitfalls

- Quality – too many criteria will make it difficult to measure your objectives
- Time – the time factor plays a significant role in revision and editing. If the revision of a 1000-word file exceeds one hour, the reviser should be given the option to return the file to the PM, who will then contact the translator and request self-revision. In PEMT files with reduced fees (lower than translation), post-editors should be advised about the time allowed and the quality required
- Profit and fees – in this assignment fees are important and must be negotiated with the different parties including the client. Fees can be variable according to the type of service required but the PM team must stay within a budget when contracting their linguists. The budget is decided after the price of the translation service charged to the client is set.

Concluding remarks

This chapter discusses translation standards and quality, evaluation or assessment and review, revision and edits without the requirement for a benchmark translation. Standards are necessary, but they cannot be standardised, nor should we say that we are fully in control of translation quality. The arrival of the internet and TEnTs have accelerated the time to complete and deliver translations. Reduced time will not necessarily improve translation quality, but if the end user is content, maybe we should accept that the quality must suit the purpose. It is time for us to reconsider our ideas of standards and quality benchmark translations. ISO 17100:2015 fails to set standards for the translation product but sets them for the translation process. We must accept that boundaries are shifting (Jiménez-Crespo 2013:112–13), for example, between professional and non-professional translations (in crowdsourcing

112 Human and technological quality assurance

7.3.6). There is bound to be a noticeable difference between human and machine translation. PEMT blurs the boundaries between MT and HT. Quality is partly inconsistent due to the fragmentation of source texts: the translator no longer receives complete and coherent texts, but updates; or the ST arrives partly pre-translated; STs are often split and shared among multiple translators.

The best standards are those which are agreed by all parties in the translation process: the client, the translator the reviser, the terminologist, and other linguists. LSPs can play a major role in this process. Their best tool is transparency as to what is required from all parties, and the level or integration of human and technological input in the translation. The interaction between TEnTs and the translator is quite striking: in some cases, the final intervention comes from the translator (in PEMT) and in reverse, technology provides the final touch through a QA. We must recognise the level of interdependence between humans and technology in the field of revision and accept that quality is often determined by the purpose of the translation.

Further reading

Cronin, Michael (2003). *Translation and Globalization*. London and New York: Routledge.

European Commission. Directorate-General for Translation (2015). DGT Translation Quality Guidelines. Brussels/Luxembourg. [Online] https://ec.europa.eu/translation/maltese/guidelines/documents/dgt_translation_quality_guidelines_en.pdf [accessed October 2019].

Jiménez-Crespo, Miguel A. (2013). *Translation and Web Localization*. London and New York: Routledge.

Mossop, Brian (2014; 2019). *Revising and Editing for Translators*. Manchester: St Jerome Publishing.

Nord, Christiane (1991). *Text Analysis in Translation*. Amsterdam-Atlanta: Rodopi.

Nunes Vieira, Lucas (2017). 'From process to product: links between post-editing effort and post-edited quality'. In: Arnt Lykke Jakobsen and Bartolomé Mesa-Lao (eds), *Translation in Transition. Between Cognition, Computing and Technology*, pp. 161–86. Amsterdam/Philadelphia: John Benjamins Publishing Company.

O'Brien, Sharon (2012). 'Towards a dynamic quality evaluation model for translation', *The Journal of Specialised Translation*, 17. [Online] www.jostrans.org/issue17/art_obrien.pdf [accessed May 2014].

6

DIGITAL ETHICS AND RISK MANAGEMENT

Key concepts

- Intellectual property rights of translations need a clear definition about ownership
- Confidentiality is at risk when web-based TMs and terminology databases are shared
- Collaborative translation environments challenge digital ethics
- Non-disclosure agreements could potentially put the translator at risk
- Security and risk in the translation project are the responsibility of all parties

Introduction

This chapter is about our consideration of ethics in the digital translation industry, where terms of business should govern the ways in which translators, LSPs, and the client collaborate. The contractor trusts that good work will be delivered and the contractee expects that it will be remunerated fully and in time. Purchase orders (POs) can give both parties some legal standing. POs carry agreements between LSP and contracted linguists. Invoices from linguists will include their terms and conditions about payments.

Digital ethics relate to digital materials: how we store them, protect them, what we do with them and what happens to them once they are in the cloud. Published and printed materials are copyrighted. They are protected and cannot be sold for profit, wholly or partly, without permission from the owner, the author, and publisher. We must now ask ourselves how we can protect our translations in digital format against modification and other forms of violation, which could impact the quality and consequently our reputation. And the second question is: how can we

114 Digital ethics and risk management

practise confidentiality of translated contents, either imported or exported? TMX files are shared and our databases can be used to feed machine translation engines. How do we keep sensitive materials out of the public domain?

As translators we may wish to check if LSPs have drawn up ethical policies for their collaboration with contractees, but we should first raise our own awareness of privacy and intellectual property rights in relation to our translation work. The chapter also discusses questions about risk management and our response to risk, whether we are project management teams or freelance linguists.

6.1 Intellectual property rights (IP) and ownership

Intellectual property (IP) is a broad term used to protect your ideas (for example, patents) and intellectual creation (such as design). A patent is a licence to protect your idea or product for a set period. It gives you the sole right to make it, use it or sell it. IP can be split into six main categories: patents, copyright, database rights, know-how, for example, specialist technical knowledge, designs and trademarks of established products or brands. Database rights are like copyrights: any electronic database is protected for 15 years from the moment of its creation. It does not need to be registered. Our TMs, TMX, and TBX files are arranged methodically and systematically, they are accessible electronically and therefore meet the criteria to be copyright-protected. When our digital files are shared with a client or LSP, it is within a translator's right either to restrict usage or to charge a fee. IP ownership is not straightforward. If the work is collaborative, the LSP may have a valid claim to your database. The LSP could argue that e-files are part of the translation job and that they are included in the agreed fee. Copyrights are rarely discussed. LSPs send agreements to be signed by the contracted linguist, and the translator must sign in order to be given the go-ahead and start the translation. Many agreements are biased and weighted in favour of the client and LSP. The copyrights of the translator are barely mentioned if at all (Figure 6.1). Our signatures are not unlike Faustus' signature when he sells his body and soul without recall. A signature can make the signee (the translator) accountable if confidentiality is breached or a poor translation causes damage to the client. But should all the blame be ascribed to one person only?

Collaborative translation environments and complex translation projects are challenging because they involve shared resources and materials. Considerations of confidentiality, ownership, copyright, **authoring rights**, associated legal matters, costs, trust, quality, and reliability (Drugan and Babych 2010), all deserve more attention. Unthinking signatures under terms and conditions without recognition of IP rights, or realising that copyright should be attributed to multiple parties, or that copyrights may have to be shared, could put all parties involved in a translation project (client, linguist, and LSP) at risk.

6.2 Confidentiality and non-disclosure agreements

It is indisputable that confidentiality in digital files must be respected. The client and LSP will require guarantees that confidential details in the source text are kept secure. Any translation service involves the submission of potentially sensitive material to other parties and transfers between computers. The client and the LSP will aim to protect the content of ST/TT files from distribution and exposure to other parties. They will therefore ask the linguists involved in the translation service to sign a **confidential disclosure agreement (CDA)/non-disclosure agreement (NDA)**. If the translator breaches the agreement, the commissioning party could seek financial compensation from the translator. Therefore, linguists are encouraged to take out an indemnity insurance to protect themselves against potential claims.

There has been a shift in translation ethics, the focus seems to have moved from the translation to translators and linguists (Chesterman 2001, 2018; Baker 2018). It means that we view translation ethics from the translator's perspective, the translator and ethics, rather than the traditional view of the translation and ethics, which was about the way in which we could best translate sensitive material. The questions now are more likely to be: 'Is it safe for me to translate this?' and 'What happens to my work after I have delivered it?' The range of sensitive material is extremely broad and includes product promotion prior to the launch, minutes and agendas of business meetings, surveys, police reports. There is very little material that is not sensitive other than what has already been published in the public domain.

LSPs are most certainly aware of risks to confidentiality and take appropriate measures. Confidentiality does not only apply to, for example, financial or legal texts, but also to commercial products. Because the launch of a new product is prepared well in advance, promotion material needs to be localised prior to the launch and the client is keen to keep the information secret from their competitors. It is the responsibility of the LSP to prevent a leak of data in the ST/TT. They therefore ask their contracted linguists to sign a Non-Disclosure Agreement, which may contain some of the following conditions:

1. Audio-visual material for translation may not be shown or used for any other purpose than translation
2. The linguist promises to take measures to protect confidentiality by preventing digital copies from being passed on
3. The linguist promises not to discuss the client or the product or mention that they work for the client
4. The linguist must sign that all files and materials will be deleted, removed, or destroyed after completion and delivery of the translation
5. Logos, ideas, designs, notes, etc. shall not be used by the linguist

The second condition is intended for the linguist, but is it also signed by the LSP and any project manager dealing with the digital files? And how does this condition

116 Digital ethics and risk management

relate to TM databases, or TMX files, or TMs on servers, or TMs linked to adaptive MT? The fourth condition does not specifically mention the translation memory database(s) used by the linguist.

Terms and conditions in NDAs are legally binding once signed and offer little protection to the translator. If there is an unintentional leak of data, for example by posting a query on a platform or forum, it is important that the translator can prove that all conditions have been met. In practice it may be a difficult thing to do. It is important to be aware of the potential consequences of NDAs before signing them, and to ask questions about the retention of your TM databases.

6.3 Business terms and conditions in relation to confidentiality and digital security

The NDA is a client's/LSP's safeguard against potential risk (6.6.2). LSPs increasingly send their terms and conditions to contractees. Translators are advised by their professional organisations to submit their own terms and conditions (T&C)★★(go to www.routledgetranslationstudiesportal.com/ – A Project-Based Approach to Translation Technology – link: T&C of professional organisations). Table 6.1 gives a selection of terms and conditions relating to digital security and confidentiality only. What stands out in the T&Cs of either party (LSP and translators) is that the conditions of the two parties do not add up. The two parties claim copyright but do not include provisions for shared copyrights, which is likely to be the case in a translation project with an author and a translator. Owner rights of digital files, such as terminology and TM databases, are defined by the professional organisations. The deletion of files ordered by LSPs does not allow the translator to retain proof of their work if it were to be violated. There is little mention of digital distribution through file transfers between the different parties, or uploads and downloads through web-based tools. Electronic transfers of materials between different parties are numerous; the translator is only one party in the process and should not be held solely accountable if there were to be breach of confidence.

T&Cs manifest in diversity. Some streamlining would be beneficial to all parties. The starting point could be a basic model that concentrates on the ownership and copyright of the source text. This might require or encourage the client to take ownership and responsibility for the whole process from translation to final version in print or on the web. The client could thus take control of deletions and modifications to the TT for layout purposes, without causing any damage to the translator. The translator can claim copyrights for TM and terminology databases, but if the client wishes to have ownership after completions to protect confidentiality, this can be agreed with the translator in exchange for a fee. And finally, there is much existing legislation that gives mutual copyright protection when multiple parties are involved. The wheel does not need to be reinvented for the translation industry.

Table 6.1 does not display a harmonised approach to terms and conditions There is hardly any mention of the translator's intellectual property rights. There

TABLE 6.1 Selected terms and conditions for translation services

TRANSLATOR ORGANISATION Confidentiality	LSP Confidentiality	TRANSLATOR ORGANISATION Digital security	LSP Digital security
The translation remains the property of the translator unless agreed otherwise in writing.	The translator guarantees to give the contracting LSP all intellectual property rights associated with their services.		The translator shall do their best not to use or store confidential information in an externally accessible computer or electronic information retrieval system without security software and shall prevent unlawful access by third parties.
Copyright must be ensured by the client before the source material is given to the translator.	The translator gives the LSP all copyrights and other intellectual property rights.		Confidential information requires the use of software to protect confidential information and the translator must ensure it is updated regularly.
The parties agree that a third party may be consulted over specific translation terminology.	In normal circumstances the translator shall not pass confidential information to others or use it for their own benefit, even after the contract has ended.	If a translation memory is used, the translator licenses the use of the translation for this purpose.	All data transmitted for the translation and particularly translation memories remain the LSP's property. They must not be used for any other job.
		Confidentiality should not apply to the following: - Information that is or becomes available to the general public,	

Continued

TABLE 6.1 Cont.

118   Digital ethics and risk management

TRANSLATOR ORGANISATION *Confidentiality*	LSP *Confidentiality*	TRANSLATOR ORGANISATION *Digital security*	LSP *Digital security*
		– and terminological glossary entries compiled by the translator for and during the translation service(s). Unless the client and translator agree in writing that the glossaries become the client's property after payment to the translator. The conditions of confidentiality will then apply.	
The client's documents are only considered confidential if this was stated by the client.	All clients' texts and translations are confidential and should not be transmitted to unauthorised third parties.		The translator must ensure updated antivirus software is used so that files are returned virus-free.

Source: ITI, ATA and global LSPs 2016–19

Digital ethics and risk management 119

is an urgent need for guidelines as to who owns the TM before, during and after the job is completed, the client or the translator (Berthaud 2019). In our digital work environment, confidentiality is challenged in source texts, target texts, file transfers, interchangeable file formats, CAT tools with or without MT, and many other cloud-based tools. T&Cs are meant to protect the client or the translator, but there needs to be more specific information as to who and what are being protected and where. Confidentiality is a broad concept and a statement like 'the client's documents are only considered confidential if this was stated by the client' (Table 6.1) is an obvious starting point. The same applies to copyright and ownership which can and should be defined in an initial agreement. A good point of departure would be for the translator to inform the client which digital tool is used and the level of security practised.

Food for thought…

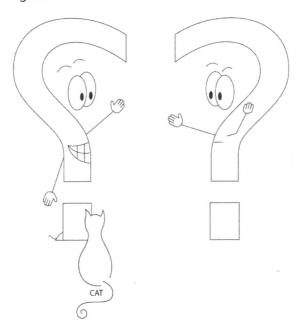

Discuss and create a workable set of terms of business for translators in relation to their translation memory databases.

6.4 Data sharing and data protection

We continually share data, on our phones, laptops, and tablets. How much thought do we give to confidentiality and the protection of information? General Data Protection Regulation (2018) is an EU law on data protection and privacy for all individual citizens of the European Union and the European Economic Area. It also

120 Digital ethics and risk management

addresses the transfer of personal data outside the EU and EEA areas. It not only affects the way in which we communicate digitally, it regulates how businesses should handle and process data. LSPs have become keen to show that they are GDPR compliant and ask their contractees to sign that they agree. GDPR has given a significant boost to uniformity in work practice within the EU/**EEA** area and beyond.

Large global organisations outside the EU/EEA area need to be GDPR compliant because the legislation affects their business to and from the EU/EEA area. TAUS, the independent data collection and sharing network, collects language data, metadata, and personal data. Language data include source and target texts, metadata are associated data, including language pairs, data about industry sector and content type; personal data include information that will identify the person (name, email address, IP address). Since GDPR, TAUS has introduced a different method for selecting data, it removes all metadata, including, for example, company names. It is important for companies to know that their company name is no longer attached to any of their language data uploads.

GDPR has affected LSP work practice in several ways. LSPs store a large amount of personal data, such as bank details of their contractees. They must assure that such details are stored safely and that they have permission to store them. Group emails must not show names other than that of the addressee. LSPs now ask their contractees to take precautions regarding the materials they store on their devices, and may ask for encryption of files and emails, or password protection. There is a growing awareness on all sides that it is essential to treat all transferable data associated with translation projects with great care.

6.4.1 Google and GDPR

Google, a large global company, well known for its MT engine, is developing fast and its developers are aware of security and confidentiality issues. They claim Google is GDPR compliant:

> Google has been certified compliant with ISO 27018 for G Suite and Google cloud Platform ISO 27018 (cloud Privacy). ISO 27018 is an international standard of practice for protection of personally identifiable information (PII) in Public cloud Services.
>
> Google does not claim any ownership in any of the content (including text and labels) that you transmit to the cloud Translation API.
>
> *Google 2019*

Google Cloud Translation, contrary to Google Translate which stores data for training, claims their **API** (7.1) is secure and that data uploaded to their MT engine will not be stored and reused:

> When you send text to Cloud Translation API, we must store that text for a short period of time in order to perform the translation and return the

results to you. The stored text is typically deleted after a few days, although occasionally we will retain it for longer while we perform debugging and other testing. Google also temporarily logs some metadata about your Cloud Translation API requests (such as the time the request was received and the size of the request) to improve our service and combat abuse.

Google 2019

Clients and LSPs are concerned about the insertion of 'we must store that text for a short period of time in order to perform the translation and return the results to you', and in their terms and conditions LSPs may prohibit use of the MT engine. The difference in GDPR compliance between open-source Google Translate and API-controlled Google Cloud Translation is not always recognised by all parties in the translation industry. In LSP terms of business (ToB) MT engines may be listed as 'third parties' that have unauthorised access to content. Furthermore, the difference between CAT tools with secure integrated close-circuit MT engines, and CAT tools with secure APIs, or APIs to open-source MT engines deserves more delineation in job descriptions. In her study, Berthaud (2019) discovered an unwillingness to engage with digital ethics relating to MT. Some of her responding LSPs did not know or want to know whether their translators use MT. This kind of ignorance creates ethical issues. LSPs must know which tools their contractees use and know the level of security and GDPR compliance necessary to deliver subcontracted translations to clients with confidence. The impact of MT on translation quality is recognised and a much more graduated view of quality in machine translated translation is growing. The digital ethics of Google Cloud Translation deserve a closer examination rather than an unqualified decree by LSPs that MT should not be used by their contracted translators.

6.5   Digital ethics of shared TM and MT databases

Statistical machine translation databases would not exist without our uploads. When we download, we use shared data – source, authenticity and quality unknown. Hence, the condition in a professional organisation's ToB that 'copyright must be ensured by the client before the source material is given to the translator' is pertinent. The translator has a right to know who owns the copyright of the source text before starting the translation process and potentially uploading and sharing (Drugan and Babych 2010). When you translate on a server with a shared TM, how do you know if the proposed match is an original match? How many edits were performed on the TM content before it reached your desktop? Should we query the authenticity of an ST or a shared TM before we become party to the translation project? A code of ethics to guide us from the moment we are commissioned to the point of delivery and subsequent payment is essential to prevent the translation project from becoming a thick pea soup in which no party can claim copyright or ensure confidentiality.

122 Digital ethics and risk management

TMs and MT are merging in CAT tools and may soon be inseparable. Adaptive machine translation (3.2) learns from our entries in the CAT tool. Programmers and manufacturers insist that all data belong to us and are kept safe, in other words not shared with other users. Neural Machine Translation uses **encryption.** Data centres and all operations are ISO 27001:2013 certified, which means that they will not use our translation for training purposes★★(link: adaptive MT confidentiality). Any content uploaded by users to the NMT engine, new or edited, is not shared. Once or twice a year the NMT engine will, however, use our data together with multi-billion-word corpora to improve the performance of their engine. Apparently, it does not impact confidentiality or security because it is not possible to reconstruct authentic sentences from NMT training data. Zetzsche (2019 (297th Journal)) queries whether this process does not raise a digital ethics issue considering that other major MT systems decided not to use data for training purposes after the introduction of GDPR legislation, if APIs★★(link: adaptive MT confidentiality) are used. If there is concern about confidentiality, an organisation can use a model based on their server to give the utmost privacy. Translators do not have this option and must trust that their entries in the MT corpus cannot be used by third parties.

Whatever our feelings about the digital ethics of integrated and adaptive MT support in CAT tools, the NMT engine needs our TM entries before it can produce and generate matches. If there might be a confidentiality requirement in the ST, we can disable the MT function in the CAT tool. The programmers and manufacturers claim that MT has been trained on legally acquired data, wherefore it is safe to use without breaches of confidence. If we accept commissions with an awareness of ethical risks in shared digital sources and resources, and we make our commissioning LSPs and clients aware of our and their **authoring rights**, combined efforts will be a step in the right direction. Confidentiality in digital materials is just as important as our intellectual property rights.

6.6   Risk management

Risk is part of any translation project run by a team: perhaps the contractees do not appear to be up to the job, or the responsible project manager has left the team and the client is threatening action because the deadline has not been met. Translators experience risk by not meeting the deadline due to hardware failure, problems relating to ST, incompatible file issues … and if the source of the problems does not even lie with the translator, they will feel aggrieved if their earnings are disappointing in relation to their time and effort expended. We need to identify risk, learn from past experiences and find strategies to prevent harmful risk. Gouadec (2007) suggests that detailed job descriptions supplied by the LSP could reduce risk to both parties. Pym (2010a) builds on Gouadec's proposed job description and suggests the following workable job description:

- list of materials (ST and reference files),
- function information (readership and quality profile),

Digital ethics and risk management **123**

- task information (deadlines, fees, format/CAT tool, terms of payment), and
- agreement on translator options (in/formal address, spelling, cultural adaptation).

Pym questions Gouadec's opinion that job descriptions may lead to risk reduction, and suggests that high-risk jobs may benefit, but low-risk jobs could be left to the discretion of the translator. Undoubtedly, translation projects requiring NDAs need detailed job descriptions, but in real time, the focus tends to be on quick recruitment and prompt agreement between LSP and contractees and on a smooth transfer of digital files between users. Important details about readership and target audience of the translation job in hand are often *only* supplied on request. The LSP is not always informed by the client.

There seems to be an unspoken gentleman's agreement that a good collaboration between LSPs and linguists depends on trust, communication, and understanding. Clients cannot be part of this relationship, if they do not know enough about translation to draft a translation job description. Our conclusion must be that in the digital era a gentleman's agreement can be a risky agreement. All parties need to increase their awareness of security risks and breaches that could adversely affect translation work, file storage and transfers.

6.6.1 Our security and intellectual property rights in translation projects

Breach of security and risk factors often pass unnoticed until the damage is done. Translations move around in electronic transfers, uploads, and downloads 24/7. Files may be sent to an incorrect email address. Confirmations of receipt are not always sent. LSPs may request that delivered translation be deleted from our devices to secure content entrusted to them by the client. Security requires appropriate software against threats, malware, computer viruses, hacking, and more, on all our devices. Lack of security may affect the content of ST/TT.

We need to ask ourselves if intellectual property rights will protect our translations against misuse? Are our rights in translated material regulated by law? Does translation carry property rights (Wong in Chan 2015: 249)? Copyright gives the creator the sole legal right to print and publish literary, artistic, or musical material. But who is the creator: the author of the source text or the translator of the target text? Are only literary translations protected (Wong in Chan 2015: 249)? Translations are protected on paper and in electronic publications, but what happens to the translator's property rights when they are uploaded to the web? What are the legal regulations when we share files and databases? Property rights can be shared but they must be discussed and negotiated. Risks can have a negative impact on content. They should be identified before we start work so we can take suitable measures. We can do this as individuals, but ideally in collaboration with other parties involved in a translation project.

Food for thought...

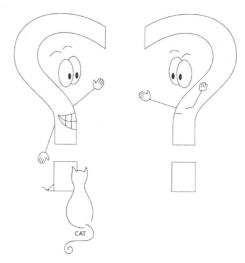

We take risks even if we also see a positive outcome. What kind of digital risks would an LSP be prepared to take which might affect a translation positively or negatively?

6.6.2 Risk factors

Risk management is more than risk response, it includes risk avoidance. Risks are not always predictable, but it is possible to recognise their potential and take steps to reduce the possible impact. Common risks are the incompatibility of hardware or software, loss of a file, the use of computers in public buildings with shared hardware. In public buildings it is advisable to save files in a generic interchangeable format, such as TMX and TBX, and store them in different locations, in the cloud, on a USB device for immediate transfer, or temporarily in the Inbox of a personal email account.

Risks need triggers to make them happen and they need circumstances in which to occur (Lammers in Dunne 2011: 211–32). We may not be able to anticipate or control circumstances, but we do recognise triggers. If a translation is shared among several translators, and one or more translators miss the deadline, the final translation cannot be delivered to the client on time. In response, the LSP could investigate what caused a translator to miss the deadline, rather than penalise the translator, financially or by refusing to offer future work. Other questions the LSP could ask are: 'Was the deadline reasonable?' 'Did the translators' expertise match the type of ST sent to them?'

Typical management risks (Figure 6.1) that may impact a translation project are technical and project-management related (Lammers in Dunne 2011: 211–32). In response, we can apply some of the categories in the **Risk Breakdown Structure** (RBS) proposed by the Project Management Institute (US) to translation project

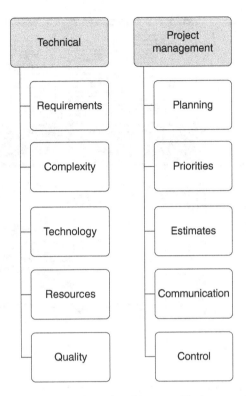

FIGURE 6.1 Classification of technological and human risks in a translation project
Source: PMI Risk Breakdown Structure (PMI 2004)

management. Although we will consider it from a project management team perspective, the risk categories are just as pertinent to the individual translator as they are to the organising team.

Technical challenges (RBS) for translation projects (PMI 2004) are:

- Requirements and complexity
  Clients invest much time in their websites or design of products and packaging and expect the translation to be delivered in an identical format ready for print. Source files come with text wrap around the images. Cartons with instructions and illustrations are provided as PDF files. A PDF of a carton contains much small print, some of the text appearing upside down. The CAT tool conversion could impact text chronology (Figure 6.2).
- Technology
  Hardware and software (in)compatibility, inadequate IT skills, incomplete or corrupted file transfers, power failure – the list is infinite. Can the translator or the LSP manage automated workflows on platforms, servers with multiple agents with different equipment and in different time zones? The following email contains a job offer to a translator which consists of a

126 Digital ethics and risk management

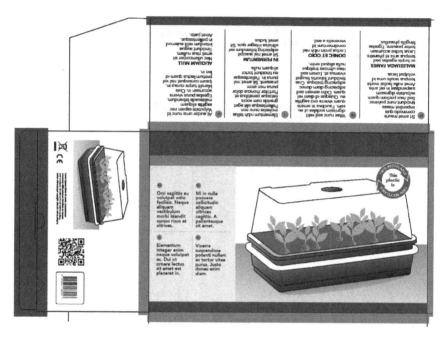

FIGURE 6.2 PDF of three sides of a carton with text sideways and upside down

graphics file that cannot be processed in a CAT tool and requires specialist tools for conversion:

> Dear translator,
>
> Would you be available to translate a brochure? The source texts are EPS files and we would require the translations to be supplied as EPS files so that we can place them into the artwork for printing.
>
> *Email from language service provider, 2018*

Should the job offer have been sent to the translator? The translator may take it on without realising that the files are incompatible with their CAT tool…. It is interesting to read threads on translator mailing lists and forums. Quite possibly the technical Q&A threads outnumber terminology queries.

- Resources
  Good resources include reference files, glossaries, and more, but also appropriate human resources (specialised translators) with appropriate tools. How do LSPs prepare translators for collaboration in a shared translation project?
- Quality
  The translation brief must state the purpose of machine and human translated texts, target audience, locale (for example, GB or US English), etc. What does the translation brief state about quality? Is the application of QA in the CAT tool adequate?

6.6.3 Risk response

Challenges for translation project management (PMI 2004) from the LSP perspective:

- **Planning, prioritising, and estimates:** Planning related risks are primarily linked to the time schedule, which in turn depends on prioritising tasks. For example, is it wise to book a reviser when a translator has not yet been found? The other major risk is cost and time estimations: how do you cost a translation project when the client keeps returning with additions or modifications? How do you cost a revision that takes much longer than expected? How do you reward linguists when their cost is taking you over budget and you risk losing the client?
- **Communication:** Emails are a common method to contact translators and to respond to queries. Some are automated, others are not personalised (they start with 'Hi' and are sent to many translators at the same time), and some direct the translator to a portal where they can find information about a potential translation job. The risks are that contacted linguists do not respond to non-personal emails or invitations to view jobs on (password-controlled) portals (7.3.7); the risks are that project managers lose the plot due to the volume of incoming emails from linguists with queries and attachments; confusion of job numbers and contracted linguists.
- **Control:** The selection of risk factors suggested above relate to quality, scope, efficiency, and profit. They affect agents and tools. The question always is how can a project management team stay in control of large translation projects? How well are they informed by their client and how well do they inform their contractees?

Once risk and identified risk factors are understood, course of action can be as follows (Figure 6.3): it can be decided to avoid certain situations at all costs and take preventative

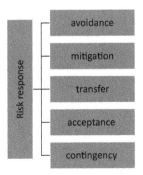

FIGURE 6.3 Risk response
Source: PMI 2004

measures, or it is decided that risks are acceptable, either because their impact is low and not worth the investment of time and effort, or because the risk is worth taking. Alternatively, potential serious risks can be mitigated by introducing some measures that are not too demanding on time and effort, or there is a transfer of risks by using, for example, a different translator. If risks are taken seriously, it is wise to design contingency plans so that if plan A does not work, a quick transfer to plan B can be made.

Risk management is indispensable and should be practised by anyone involved in the translation business. Understanding risks is the first step, but the implementation of appropriate measures can also be a risk. Very often a balance is needed between the investment of time and resources to mitigate or avoid risks and the potential gain if those investments are made (Lammers in Dunne 2011: 211–32). In other words, the translation provider, LSP, or translator, must prioritise risks and make choices. Risks are not always negative; they can have a positive outcome and be worth taking. The other much-needed balance is between the client's expectations and the actual role of the translator. Technology has made translators and other linguists easily accessible, which is good news. The downside is that working hours are not and cannot be respected if collaboration takes place across time zones. The accessibility of MT engines and translators on the web carries the risk that translators and MT are juxtaposed and perceived as equal but different modes. Furthermore, translation technology is considered to lighten the translator's load, without any realisation that the opposite can be true: time pressure due to increased volume, shared projects with fluctuations in consistency and quality, and breaches in confidentiality arising from poorly regulated electronic transfer, storage and sharing of databases. These are problems that need to be dealt with by freelance linguists and LSP teams. Raised awareness and transparency as to what constitutes breaches or risks would be a step in the right direction.

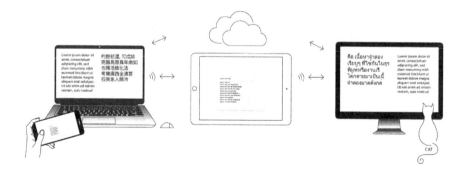

Project-based assignment

Objective:
Identifying digital risk and taking appropriate measures to prevent breach of confidentiality in project-based digital translation

Assessment and outcome:
Peer and team assessment of risk management in a translation project

Method:
The assignment is designed for a project management team but collaboration within a project team or between individuals is possible

Tools:
CAT-tool, and MT engine in the CAT tool (a server version would facilitate an examination of security breaches and/or risk in web-based shared databases and files)

Suggested resources:
One manipulated digital source text (you may have to artificially create confidential issues) of approximately 1000 words; a (manipulated) TMX and TBX file. The ST must contain confidential issues to check the suitability of your safeguarding measures

Language pairs and direction:
Multiple language pairs and/or directions

Assignment brief

Call your project managers and other team members together to discuss a previous translation project: you have received a serious complaint from the client who has discerned a breach of confidentiality. Alternatively, the press release you were asked to translate has been leaked and consequently a competitor has announced their imminent launch of a similar product. Some of the terminology that was provided to you by the client was leaked – intentionally or unintentionally. The client has threatened legislative action.

- You must now identify the risk factors that may have caused breach of confidence, e.g.:
  - Inadequate Terms of Business on all sides
  - Your human resources database does not tell you what TEnTs your freelance translators use; whether they use MT in their CAT tools
  - You did not ask your contractees to return XLIFF files, which contain much metadata (e.g. about possible use of MT)
  - Other risk factors
- Identify and discuss your risk responses to prevent recurrence
- Set up a new translation project, apply your preventative measures and check to what level you have managed to avoid potential breaches or risks that were experienced in the previous project

130 Digital ethics and risk management

- Conclude with a debrief for your team and discuss how well your contractees responded to your new set of requirements and how well you managed risks

Possible pitfalls

- Too many potential risks – it is not possible to prevent and avoid risk entirely. The identification of too many risks may cause you to lose focus, become demotivated to keep agreements and cost too much time and effort
- Being too risk adverse or too risk tolerant. Try to find a workable balance
- GDPR begins in the way you communicate with your contracted linguists and adherence must be stressed in the job description sent to your contractees

Concluding remarks

In this chapter we have discussed the digital ethics of intellectual property, copyright in digital materials, in TM databases and in translated digital files. We know the risks surrounding digital ethics, we can identify the problems, but the solutions are not always apparent. We see conflicting Terms of Business sent by LSPs and translators. If there is an issue, the parties may prefer not to look for answers because it requires too much effort, and blame goes to the party that signed. It is not easy to define confidentiality, but we could accept that material is confidential only if the client or LSP state its confidentiality. We could also check the security of the digital sources and resources we have received. If we are likely to receive confidential material, our TEnTs require security software and strong passwords to prevent unauthorised access.

Our reputation could be damaged if the target text or TM is modified by a third party and no longer matches the authentic source text which is under the client's copyright. Copyright also applies to attachments in emails. Copyright is difficult to define in shared tools: the materials can be uploaded or downloaded innumerable times, modified, edited, revised. We must be aware of potential risks when sharing files.

Digital ethics affect the working practice of all parties involved in a translation workflow: client, LSP, and contracted linguists. It may be appropriate to sign a non-disclosure agreement. However, conditions that remove the rights of the translator to their translations, should be questioned. All parties must know which TEnTs have been used and there needs to be multilateral agreement on TEnT usage. A global recognition of GDPR would be a solid step forward towards a working code that is understood by all.

Further reading

Chesterman, Andrew (2018). 'Translation ethics'. In: Lieven d'Hulst and Yves Gambier (eds), *A History of Modern Translation Knowledge. Sources, Concepts, Effects*, pp. 443–8. Amsterdam: Benjamins.

Drugan, Jo and Bogdan Babych (2010). 'Shared resources, shared values? Ethical implications of sharing translation resources.' In: Ventsislav Zhechev (ed.), *Proceedings of the Second Joint EM+/CNGL Workshop. Bringing MT to the User: Research on Integrating MT in the Translation Industry.* Available from: https://pdfs.semanticscholar.org/4acd/2c229ef9dfa3f a903911ed7447e62f726edc.pdf.

Kenny, Dorothy (2010). 'The ethics of machine translation'. *Proceedings XI NZSTI National Conference.*

Lammers, Mark (2011). 'Risk management in localization'. In: Keiran J. Dunne and Elena S. Dunne (eds), *Translation and Localization Project Management,* pp. 211–32. Amsterdam and Philadelphia: John Benjamins.

Moorkens, Joss (2019). 'Uses and limits of machine translation'. In: *Ethics and Machines in an Era of New Technologies.* ITI research e-book.

Project Management Institute (2004). *A Guide to the Project Management Body of Knowledge. (PMBOK® Guide).* 3rd ed. Newtown Square, PA: PMI Press.

7

WEB-BASED TRANSLATION ENVIRONMENT TOOLS

Key concepts

- Translation environment tools move into the cloud
- Collaborative translation projects can be managed centrally when using servers and translation management systems
- Digital platforms offer opportunities for translators and LSPs to collaborate, to recruit linguists or source jobs and exchange knowledge
- Translation must adapt to different reading techniques of web-based material
- LSPs and translators have different views on the impact of web-based translation technology on quality, efficiency and profit

Introduction

This chapter is about the interaction between the translator and web-based tools. It describes new trends in translation technology and examines the technologies that may be helpful in our work. The TEnT market evolves, new tools come and go. Translation management systems, for example, incorporate CAT features and are gaining popularity among LSPs, because the comprehensive system enables them to manage the workflow in the translation project from beginning to end. LSPs expect contractees to work online in their translation management system. The translator's challenge is to be up to date with any web-based TEnTs we may be required to use. We will also visit several **digital platforms** to find out what is on offer there. Digital platforms are virtual meeting places where vendors and buyers of translation can discuss matters, ask for support, look for answers, translate, localise, offer or bid for translation jobs. They are gaining popularity among freelance translators as a virtual meeting place where jobs are advertised, or as a resource centre and knowledge base.

The ownership of translation tools is changing too. New trends show that it is unnecessary to invest in an expensive CAT tool with its annual maintenance fees

Web-based translation environment tools **133**

paid to the manufacturer. There is the option to subscribe to web-based CAT tools or machine-assisted translation systems★★(go to www.routledgetranslationstudies-portal.com/ – A Project-Based Approach to Translation Technology – link: machine-assisted translation systems) with integrated CAT functions. You are not tied into a subscription but can opt out when required. If, however, you feel comfortable with your CAT tool and gain much benefit from your TM and terminology databases, it is worth considering APIs and plugins which give access to many web-based tools. In the project-based assignment you will be given an opportunity to test translation project workflow in different web-based tools. The objective is that your experiences with a variety of TEnTs give you the skills and competence to try new ones and to be ready for changing trends.

7.1 Integrated translation environment

Translators have free online access to huge databases. In 2.3.3 we discussed the downloadable TMX file with a collection of translation memories from the European Union and United Nations. The database is managed, curated, picked, and produced by a commercial company★★(link: online TMX database). Database integration is possible in several CAT tools★★(link: CAT tools with TMX integration). It would also be useful to have integrated access to our preferred glossaries and e-dictionaries. Switching from the CAT tool editor to open glossaries or dictionaries in other windows on our screen(s) is inconvenient. The manufacturers, however, like to keep control of what can be linked to their CAT programs. Dictionaries, for example, are limited to the ones they make available on their open servers. If we want to integrate our own glossaries, we must convert and save them in a suitable format (CSV spreadsheet format in Excel) and import them in our Tmdb.

Meanwhile, the range of APIs and plugins in CAT tools, which gives us access to other web-based TEnTs, is growing rapidly. The range varies greatly between programs. API (Application Programming Interface) is a piece of software that allows other programs to use its functions. To integrate an MT engine in a CAT tool, you will need an API to access the MT engine you would like to use. The API itself is free but the user is charged on a monthly basis for the number of digits generated by the requests to the MT engine. In CAT tools we can choose from a range of MT engines to suggest matches while we translate in the translation editor. We pay the MT engine provider for usage, not the CAT tool manufacturer who offers the convenience to integrate the MT engine in their CAT tool, unless they have developed their own baseline (generic) engine and adaptive MT model★★(link: integrated adaptive MT model).

APIs are independent connectors between different programs, whereas plugins are offered by the CAT tool manufacturer for integration of other software in their own programs★★(link: plugin to external TMs). A plugin is a small component in a larger piece of software and performs a specific task. The API is an external program that can be used for access within different CAT tools or other programs, whereas a plugin is meant for usage in a specific CAT tool and is usually made available by the developer. MT plugins may come with an API. A wide range of different plugins

134 Web-based translation environment tools

can be downloaded free of charge. The following list of plugins shows a selection which are provided for and by a variety of CAT tools:

A range of CAT tool plugins

File filter	for complex file formats
Glossary converter	to convert a glossary into a Tmdb or vice versa
Invoices and quotes	for price calculation, quoting, invoicing, with a built-in time tracker
Lookup	performs web or **local search**es for terminology
Match bleeper	gives audio hints for available matches for visually impaired users
MT	plugins for major CAT tools
Resource lookup	to receive matches from the CAT tool's server TM (API needed)
Sketch Engine	Concordance integration in the interface
Terminology	to access external terminology portals, e.g. EuroTermBank
TM finder	searches in the TMs of another CAT tool on your computer or a range of public TMs★★(link: plugin to external TMs)

In sum, plugins are developed to enhance the CAT tool by integrating external programs. APIs, sometimes called connectors, are a convenient way of integrating tools into your CAT tool but require a fee to be paid to the provider. Plugins appear to be under-used by translators (Nunes Viera and Alonso 2018). Lack of awareness may explain why translators tend to export their translations for a spell and grammar check outside the CAT tool (most CAT QAs include spellchecks, not all include grammar checks★★(link: CAT grammar check). The plugin was not initially designed for the translation market but has found a new niche in the translation industry and we will undoubtedly see the range increase. It is good to 'shop around' because quality varies greatly, and so does cost. Some plugins are free, others require a licence or API. Several CAT tools now have the microphone icon for **speech recognition** (SR). It is not a new TEnT but it is to CAT tools. It may require the use of a smartphone as a microphone★★(link: CAT tool with ASR).

7.1.1 Speech recognition

Speech recognition started as a dictation tool and has become sophisticated speech technology. Automatic speech recognition (**ASR**) now is a cloud-based AI speech technology, which is available in speech-to-text (**STT**) and text-to-speech (**TTS**) software. Both types are useful to the translator: STT generates a translation when you speak your translation in the microphone. There is no direct need for a keyboard while you are speaking your translation if you make use of spoken commands to make the STT do what you want it to do, such as 'move down' to the next segment. A wireless microphone means that you do not have to sit down and stare at your screen. Sight translation (also practised by interpreters) can be done from your ST on a piece of paper while walking around, if you wish. TTS allows you to listen to your translation read by an artificial voice. TTS presents an alternative and very different way of revising your translation. It also invalidates the criticism that segmentation in CAT tools reduces translation quality, because TTS helps you 'see and hear' your translations in context. The TT is presented to you as a coherent text. TTS helps you assess the level of fluency in your translation (Ciobanu 2019).

ASR, STT, and TTS are forms of weak AI, they do not operate like NMT, they are not creative, they cannot produce novel utterances, but rely on historical data, i.e. the exact data previously entered by the speaker. ASR can however be trained by you, they can be corrected on the fly, and they can learn shortcut codes for functions, which you would normally type on your keyboard. Of course, ASR becomes strong AI when it is combined with NMT: a speaker at a conference who uses ASR will see machine translated speech-to-text appear on the audience's tablets without time delay. NMT uses the ASR generated data to generate the target text.

A good quality ASR program can achieve a very high level of perfection and can be used in the CAT tool. It needs to be told and trained how to move from one segment to the next and how to open your frequently used functions such as concordance, lookups, find, etc. If you spot an error while you are translating, you can correct it in real time or leave it and do an ASR or manual keyboard revision later. Some translators claim that they can increase their translation speed by 500% (Ciobanu 2019). This increase can only be achieved if the translator does terminology research in advance, if speech recognition errors are few, if the text has a smooth narrative with full sentences to facilitate recognition, and if the translator can 'sight translate'. Pauses and incomplete sentences or phrases hinder the tool from recognising speech matches in the corpus. A paid SR program can recognise over 86 languages, including character languages. Free online SR programs recognise around 30 languages.

In the CAT tool it is possible to combine STT and the keyboard without conflict. If you want to increase your productivity, the ASR tool needs to be taught commands. Your tone of voice is important for the ASR to recognise when it is a command and not a phrase for translation. There are a few CAT tools with integrated STT**(link: CAT tools with ASR). They call the function 'dictation', and it can be enabled with or without an app.

There is still much scope for CAT tool developers to improve the audio feature, but also for translators to understand the benefits of ASR. Adaptive technology should help ASR work with other integrated tools. For example, MT and ASR do not yet speak to each other, in other words, give each other priority. Consequently, it causes conflicts when both are used simultaneously. Integrated audio data in our tools would also offer opportunities for different kinds of immediate communication

FIGURE 7.1 Speech-to-text and text-to-speech software

between collaborating linguists. The potential benefits of automatic speech recognition for translators are numerous.

7.2 Servers and web-based CAT tools

Major CAT tools now have server versions, which are designed to integrate all the translation stages for a smooth workflow. LSPs manage complex translation projects on servers or in translation management systems (TMS) (7.5). A CAT tool server is often referred to as TMS. The difference between a server and TMS is that the server remains a CAT tool without additional TMS features, such as administration and accounting. TMS is part CAT tool but places more emphasis on MT and integration of the other tools.

When users connect to cloud-based apps, servers, and TMS, these are also called **software as a service (**SaaS**)**. It means that the apps or programs are accessed and not owned by the user. LSPs use servers as a web-based CAT tool to facilitate collaboration between project managers and contractees, the workflow in the translation process, apportioned files, pre-translation, the locking or hiding of segments (to prevent revision or modification), and the sharing of TMX or TBX files. The translator and reviser can download and upload their files from and to the server or perform their tasks on the server, which is the usual method, and they will not retain the translation after it is completed. Servers, run by LSPs, are desktop-based CAT tools or cloud-based programs. Both types of server, desktop (purchased) and cloud-based (leased), come with an agreed pool of licences for LSPs to supply to contracted linguists for the duration of the translation project. Licences are not required for contractees who have their own CAT tool. They are given password access to the server. Alternatively, LSPs sometimes email project packages to the contractees: they contain XLIFF and TMX files compatible with most major CAT programs. The translator or reviser returns the files in a 'return package'.

The server gives the LSP many advantages: it keeps the translation project together, makes smooth collaboration possible, and prevents the misdirection or loss of emails with file attachments. The LSP's TM will absorb entries from many translators. The downside is that a huge TM becomes unmanageable or slow and in need of much editing. TM management is a significant task.

The advantages of the server for the contracted translator are significant too. The translation process on the server is shorter and quicker because the document files are ready for translation without the need to save, store, and import into the CAT tool. They do not need exporting either. If collaboration between multiple translators in a translation project is well organised, the TM and Tmdb will update in real time and support consistency. The translator can see what colleagues have entered in the database. Well-edited and customised TMs and Tmdbs, plus reference material, are great resources for the translator. A temporary LSP licence supplied to the translator means that there is no direct need for the translator to purchase a CAT tool. If the translator would prefer to pay monthly for a licence rather than buy a CAT tool, it is possible to lease a web-based CAT tool★★(link: web-based CAT tool).

There are, of course, disadvantages to translating on a server or web-based CAT tool for the translator, such as potential unfamiliarity with the CAT program, an inability to link or integrate your usual TEnTs, such as dictionaries, your TM and Tmdb databases, or MT API. If the web-based CAT tool has an offline editor, the file can be downloaded as an XLIFF file from the cloud and translated in the off-line editor. This allows you to work beyond a wifi signal. It is possible to download the file from the editor into your own CAT tool before returning it to the web-based tool via the offline editor★★(link: web-based CAT tool link to personal CAT tool). This procedure does not allow you to benefit from matches in the web-based TM: they are only accessible online. When translating in the offline editor, matches can be checked once the translation is uploaded to the web-based CAT tool. It is not a straightforward method for the translator, whereas the LSP enjoys an automated workflow without having to manage attachments in emails. Working on the server raises two questions: whose are the property rights associated with the translation and TM entries, and how can the translator make convenient good use of their own resources?

Web-based CAT tools are becoming more sophisticated: as translation management systems and in portals or on platforms. At this level of sophistication, the main market consists of companies, organisations, and LSPs. The translator risks becoming a confused user with the reins taken from them. These developments are important and in the following sections we will discuss various aspects of working in the cloud.

7.3 Digital platforms

A **digital platform** is a technology-enabled business model which facilitates exchanges between multiple parties, such as clients, agents, and linguists in the translation industry, who do not necessarily know each other. The parties either offer or require services that need to be managed efficiently and offer quality. They are typically easily accessible to all. In everyday life, we are familiar with platforms for advertising, marketplace, media, social media, knowledge, and crowdsourcing. Translation platforms are similar but have different faces depending on their purpose and user groups. We will concentrate on two types: the business platform (and portal) for translation and crowdsourcing where translations are produced and the platform where translators meet, which can be a mix of advertising, marketplace, social media or be knowledge based.

7.3.1 Translator platform

When paper or digital resources do not provide the required term translation, freelance translators frequently turn to human resources. Their requests need not only be about terminology but also for information about LSPs, such as their payment reliability, CAT tool problems, etc. Translator platforms have emerged on social media, as web groups and through professional translator organisations★★(link: professional translator organisations). There are specialist web groups and mailing lists where translators with the same language pairs, CAT tools or specialisms can post their queries and receive or find answers.

Professional translator and interpreter organisations in all countries aim to promote not only high standards in the translation industry, but also to support their members in many different ways: with advice (practical, legal, etc.), training and career development, professional examinations and qualifications, information, regional, language, and specialist support groups. Their websites may act as an interface between those who need and those who offer translations. Translators must apply for membership, which will be granted if they meet the required standards. Full membership may require the candidate to pass a translation examination set by the organisation and to demonstrate experience as a practising translator. Members will then have their contact details, working languages, and specialisms added to a website which can be accessed by any individual or organisation that wishes to commission a translation. To safeguard standards and quality, the organisations may ask their members to record their **CPD (continuing professional development)** activities, which consist of training in any format, for example, by attending professional webinars or conferences, by authoring features in journals, organising translator events, etc. Increasingly, LSPs are requesting their contractees to send them a list of recent CPD activities.

Translator platforms are primarily supportive and intuitive digital platforms without financial support or top-down organisation. A different kind of translator platform is Translators without Borders (TWB), which is a non-profit organisation that offers language and translation support for humanitarian and development agencies and non-profit organisations on a global scale. Their work is supported by volunteers, grant funders, donors, and sponsors. They provide language services as one of the components where an emergency has arisen. They work with volunteer translators worldwide who may provide translations or train translators in the crisis area to deal with the situation themselves. The organisation runs predominantly on a platform★★(link: non-profit translator platform) with only three offices across the globe.

7.3.2 Marketplace platform

A very different kind of digital platform is the marketplace. It is a platform that can be used by translation buyers to post translation jobs or browse a translator's directory and it is a platform where translators can apply for jobs or bid for them. It is called a marketplace platform because its main purpose is offering and buying translation services. Buyers may choose to use the platform to attract multiple translators for one job. It enables them to select the most suitable translator in terms of pricing, availability, and specialism. This kind of platform (generally password protected) can ask competing translators registered with the agency to bid for the job, and the buyer, an LSP, can select the translator with the lowest bid, which gives the LSP more profit. It is distinctly different compared to the previous platforms because of its financial and business/marketing aspects.

The first marketplace digital platform was set up in 1999. It has seen a succession of other marketplace platforms**(link: marketplace platforms). They have gradually become more than a commercial marketplace and are now virtual translator communities. They offer a wide range of TEnTs that can be purchased (with or without discounts): conversion tools, EU TMX files and TBX files with specialist glossaries, software downloads, and more. Translators appreciate the discussion forums and the online glossaries. Membership is graded, either free or paid. The platform operates according to a reputation system: the more recommendations a party receives from agents or linguists, the more stars they have, the better their perceived reputation. Like any marketplace, vendors and buyers can be good, bad, and indifferent. On the platforms it is recommended that you check the status of any organisation or individual requesting a translation service and that you do not post personal details or CVs without protection against identity theft. It is a problem when translators post their CV on the platform to find that their data, including their professional qualifications, are stolen and to see them offered in fake profiles by an unprofessional translator (a scammer), usually to win bids. Fraud can also be committed by individuals who present themselves to the translator as an LSP, for the translator to find that their translation is accepted without any hope of payment or recall because the contact details are fake. These situations can be prevented by checking 'blacklists' (often on the platform) and testing all details and website data about the buyer, prior to accepting a commission.

7.3.3 Localisation platform

Web localisation and quality were discussed in 5.2.3. Tools for localisation can be linked to the translator's CAT tool (or integrated), but the platform takes the automation process one step further. On a localisation platform source content and translations are automatically synced to a global content database that can be accessed by users at any time. Different teams can work and communicate directly on the platform with translators and project managers. It is an open and connected platform which integrates into a translation project managed by an LSP. The platform is a business model that offers on the fly localisation so that translators

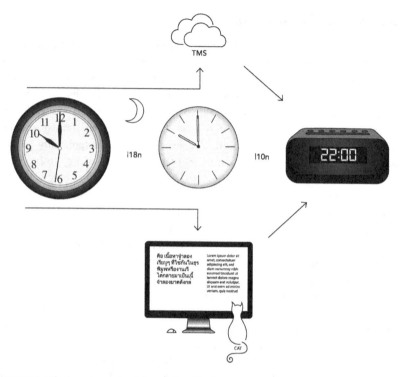

FIGURE 7.2 File-based or cloud-based localisation

working on live content in the development cycle, can keep up with language updates. The translator can either push content for translation, i.e. upload files to the platform, where localisation will be performed, or use the pull approach (4.6) and consult the platform database.

When localising website material, the choice is between a file-based solution or a cloud-based solution. Figure 7.2 shows potential workflows in a simple localisation activity. Analogue twelve-hour clocks as used in the UK must be localised to digital 24-hour clocks. The manufacturer may deliver the ST in an i18n version and the translator can perform l10n in a CAT tool (file-based) by using an API. Alternatively, the process can happen in the cloud (cloud-based) in TMS (7.5).

A cloud-based platform requires an API to obtain access, and payment is based on usage**(link: localisation platform). In this case, the localisation function is automatically integrated in translation management systems (7.5).

7.3.4 Translation platform

A translation platform is a fully automated platform without translators. Translation platforms rely heavily on MT to be fully automated. Web-based CAT tools are offered as a translation platform to companies and businesses whose websites need localising. The web-based CAT tool on the platform can pre-translate documents with NMT and the client can then turn to an LSP, or directly to a translator, for PEMT and/or translation of any segments beyond the scope of the tool★★(link: online open source adaptive NMT platforms).

7.3.5 Knowledge platform

A knowledge platform is a platform that enables an organisation, such as CAT tool developers to manage formal learning and to share knowledge in a single location. The exchange of knowledge may also be between users of a CAT tool if the owner of the platform has enabled the posting of messages in a **Q&A** section. Whereas manuals and Help features were the way to help users understand and learn how to use CAT tools in the early years, the Help function in the CAT tool is now more likely to take you to the manufacturer's 'Knowledge base', where you can find answers, watch supporting videos, and where you are led to the appropriate Help section that offers solutions in response to your query. If you have signed up to the CAT tool, you may be sent invitations to attend webinars to learn more about new features in the tool. Many digital platforms have a knowledge-sharing aspect on their platform, which is a helpful development for CAT tool users.

7.3.6 Crowdsourcing platform

Cronin (2012) makes the following observation about crowdsourcing: it is a consumer-oriented translation activity in which the consumer becomes the pro-sumer (producer+consumer). This style of translation activity upsets the traditional norms in which the LSP is productivity oriented. Crowdsourcing happens when an individual or an organisation use a platform to appeal to crowds for free or low-cost translation submissions. Instead of asking traditional service providers, they encourage the online community to deliver translations. The platform makes it possible. Facebook was launched in 2008 and two years later their website was available in 75 languages (Drugan 2013: 174). The best way to describe this phenomenon is that an online community of friends decided to produce the Facebook translations for the benefit of the community. Their act of translation was selfless and not for financial gain. In 7.3.1 we saw how an **NGO** uses a platform for a good cause, which would not be possible without the willingness of translators to translate free of charge. It is a type of crowdsourcing that is called cause-driven (Jiménez-Crespo 2013: 193–7). Although the main difference between translator and crowdsourcing platforms seems to be that crowdsourcing involves non-professionals, there are now commercial companies that have embraced crowdsourcing. One company with major LSPs introduced a paid crowdsourcing platform in 2013★★(link: paid crowdsourcing platforms), which is called 'outsourced crowdsourcing' (Jiménez-Crespo 2013: 193–7) or 'people-powered'. The company uses a crowdsourcing platform which operates in a similar way to the marketplace platform, the main difference being that responding translators need to be registered with the crowdsourcing company. The company claims that it delivers 'high quality results'. It does not give details to confirm that it is ISO certified, including QA and third-party revision. The emphasis is on convenience and speed.

Crowdsourced material is predominantly web-based. Readers have a different approach to reading webpages, it is nonlinear, superficial (skimming), and accelerated (Pym 2010b). Sometimes the reader is looking for keywords and a 'gist translation' is all that is needed. Quality does not matter. Interestingly, the collaborative aspect of crowdsourcing does in fact improve the quality of lay translation through collaborative correction (Pym 2010b). It would be wrong to say that a crowdsourcing platform is inferior and for amateurs only. Although crowdsourcing on a commercial basis is growing, it does not receive much attention from academics (O'Hagan in Kenny 2017), whereas the collaborative workflow with translation and revision is resourceful and supports quality in such a way that even the professional should consider the values of voluntary collaboration, such as peer revision.

7.3.7 The portal

The operations on a translator portal are like those on a platform. The main difference is that a portal is dedicated to a company or LSP. It is a website that provides access to, for example, an LSP and its functions. First you log in to a portal, create a password and complete a personal profile. The LSP will then warn you by email if there is a job available which you can accept (or reject) on the portal and download. When the translation is completed you will upload it to the portal. Invoicing has become an automated feature on the portal, and it is not necessary to create your own invoice. The portal is not a TEnT, it is an administrative tool. Large LSPs may even use their portals as marketplace platforms and ask you to bid for the offered job, as explained in 7.3.2. The styles of portal and their intent depend greatly on the ethics of the companies or agencies that run them. They are not regulated.

Food for thought...

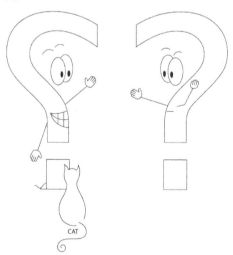

Discuss the different digital platforms and their benefits from the translator's perspective.

7.4 From content to translation management systems

Before we discuss the translation management system, which shares characteristics with the translation platform, we must consider what gave rise to its development. The volume of documents for translation continues to increase, and so does competition. It means that LSPs and clients want to manage volume efficiently and keep prices down. Digital content and volume begin with the **content management system (CMS),** usually managed by the client, which is a software application that allows users to collaborate in the creation, the authoring and editing of texts. It enables the production of digital content, such as webpages, websites, blog posts, etc. CMS is morphing into WCMS (web content management system): content no longer consists of hard-copy files but includes emails, mobile apps, social media, websites and more. Because of the complexity of its content, CMS (WCMS) has become a management system, which originally began as a business presentation system with PowerPoint files for product presentations. Today, the entire content is digital, including multimedia, and requires smart exposure on the web with **SEO (Search Engine Optimisation** (7.6)).

Translation happens in the TMS, which can be either connected to the WCMS or operate as an independent system. A marketing organisation will want to optimise successive communications in different formats for laptops, tablets, and smartphones and in many different languages, which can all be managed collectively in the TMS. Optimisation increases the number of hits on the web and the SEO requirement is an additional challenge for the translator, regardless of the system used.

It is understandable that clients prefer to outsource comprehensive content management, including translation and localisation, instead of managing it themselves. They move their entire digital presence to global CMS platforms. LSPs have jumped on the bandwagon and through API connectors they can align client content across multiple platforms globally in the relevant languages. Connector packs are sold as 'integration solutions' and they enable LSPs to manage the clients' CM systems in their translation management systems. Here is an internet advertisement for a TMS that can be connected to a CMS:

> **Request, manage, track, and view the progress of your translations**
>
> With the client portal you have on-demand access to SaaS tools and reports for requesting, managing, tracking, and viewing the progress of your translations.
>
> It's easy to use and navigate and provides enterprises with a portal they can share with internal teams for requesting translations and checking the status of translation projects. Includes API for custom system integration.
>
> *WWW advertisement of a translation management system 2019*

7.5 Translation management systems

A translation management system (TMS)★★(link: TMS systems) supports complex translation projects. Its main features are workflow management, translation memory and terminology database management, integrated machine translation (MT), and administrative functions. A TMS is more than a CMS, because of its translation feature. An update of a company's website content in the TMS can be assigned to LSPs or teams where the members are not necessarily located in the same office or even at the same location, but in different countries and time zones. Many TMS programs include APIs for a range of MT providers and use adaptive MT. Businesses can use TMS as a plugin in their CMS, which is useful if content needs to be localised. Localisation is highly automated in the TMS and will be done without linguists.

There are several types of TMS, but the two main types are desktop-based or software as a service (**SaaS**) cloud-based systems. SaaS is also known as **on-demand software** which provides the same or enhanced capabilities compared to in-house software. The main benefit is that companies pay a flat monthly fee for their use of the software and can leave the service any time. The provider selling the service is responsible for security, maintenance, and global accessibility. TMS functions are increasingly included in major CAT tools on their servers. They are language centric, with the typical functions needed by project managers, translators, and revisers. SaaS versions have the advantage of being totally cloud-based, available 24/7 with browser-based access. They do not need installing but offer a licence model where the user pays for usage (Shuttleworth in Chan 2015: 680–1).

The objective of a TMS is to automate the translation process. It makes a complex translation project more controllable and avoids repetitive tasks. A project manager can oversee multiple projects, multiple freelancers, check delivery times, check progress, and manage terminology requirements. If the TMS has an on-demand platform or a portal, the project manager can oversee progress because all tasks are automated. The TMS has many attractions for the LSP for a variety of reasons. Online systems do not require software installation, or licences for subcontracted translators. They are said to be intuitive and easy to manage by the user. The TMS is generally integrated with a global portal-like platform (7.3.7) which allows the translator to receive, perform, and deliver translation jobs irrespective of their location or software. Purchase orders and invoices are managed on the platform. TMs, glossaries, source files, and other project materials are readily available to the translator. Downloads, uploads, and emails are no longer necessary when working in the cloud. All materials are accessed on the platform. When you, as a contracted user, complete your translation or revision job, you simply change the status button from 'in progress' to 'completed' to inform the project manager that the job is done. You can then move on to the invoice tab and click on a ready-made invoice for you. With a click, your invoice is sent, and your translation is in the cloud.

The TMS has the following business functions to suit the project manager:

- project planning
- workflow management
- integration of TEnTs for large-scale translation activities
- coordination of all contributors within, outside and across organisations
- automation of repetitive tasks
- reduction in file management and transfer

- lower risk of errors
- huge data access
- smooth workflow in integrated system

Sargent and DePalma 2007; Chamsi in Dunne 2011: 61–2; Shuttleworth in Chan 2015: 550–62

The TMS has the following translation features to suit the translator:

- segments and terms entered by one translator can be reused by all
- it facilitates collaboration with colleagues
- translation platform systems centralise databases, maintenance, simplify and automate tasks
- it is an interface between the translator and adaptive MT
- it offers choice between CAT tool ownership and TMS subscription

Garcia in Chan 2015: 80

The main selling point of TMS is adaptive MT: whereas CAT tools offer MT access as a plugin, the primary TMS focus is on its access to an MT engine. The TM and Tmdb databases are integrated in the TMS. The TMS needs the two databases to make the MT adaptive. The MT engine learns from your entered TUs in the TM and adjusts as you translate. TMS developers believe that TMS tools will offer such high-quality MT that the user will not even have to post-edit (Zetzsche 2017 (281st Journal)). The translator edits on the fly, confirms and adds TUs to the TM, and the MT learns from the TM. The other major difference between CAT tools and TMS is the latter's inclusion of business management functions.

Food for thought...

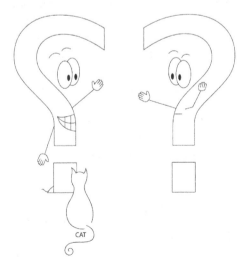

Discuss potential implications of the translation management system regarding cognitive ergonomics (1.6.3, 1.6.8).

146 Web-based translation environment tools

7.6 Localisation of webpages and search engine optimisation

The localisation of commercial webpages includes SEO (Search Engine Optimisation) in the target language (TL). SEO is a technique used to move websites to the top of search engine rankings by means of search words or keywords. Keywords, also called **seeds**, are the words the website visitor is likely to type in the search box. A seed list consists of baseline keywords and phrases most relevant to a domain. In US women's fashion, for example, the search volume of 'dresses' is 1,830.000, cocktail dresses rank 450.000 hits and plus size dresses rank 301.000 hits. In another country, the ranking order will be entirely different and 'cocktail dresses' may not be a term used. The localisation and translation of commercial websites do not only concentrate on keywords but also on metadata, which are the data about the webpage under the URL address. Metadata must also be optimised. Another point of consideration is that countries use specific search engines that rely on different algorithms to rank websites. For the translator, it is advisable to use the search engine in the target country/language to discover the ranking order of terms.

LSPs tend to list SEO skills under translator competencies. There are however many tools to assist the translator, ranging from translation management systems to plugins, Google's tools, and more. The objective of this book is not to cover the field of localisation and SEO, it is rather to give an understanding of the nature of webpage translation and an awareness of supportive tools.

When translating a webpage with SEO, the translator has two objectives: first, the keywords must be such that the search takes the visitor to the website, and second, the keywords must hold the visitor's interest and keep them reading and clicking. SEO translations require thorough keyword research, an understanding of marketing, in-depth SEO knowledge, and good **copywriting** skills. There are many keyword-research tools available on the web, some Google based. 'Google Analytics' is a tool that gives a better understanding of the customer's search behaviour. For example, readers of webpages generally stay less than 10 seconds on the page, their reading is nonlinear and has taken on a form of accelerated power browsing, with a strong visual component (Cronin 2012). The way readers approach web-based material is changing: skimming and scanning of web texts is becoming the norm. It affects the way texts are composed and subsequently translated. Reading for gist and less interest in text quality must be taken into consideration by author and translator.

SEO optimisation in Google is performed as follows:

- Google uses *crawlers,* programs that systematically search the World Wide Web to collect data. Based on those data, Google creates ranking algorithms
  - Algorithms determine the ranking order of a website: at the top of the page, at the bottom, or on pages 2, 3, etc. In order to push a website up the ranking order, visits can be influenced through suitable website content, appropriate length, relevance and keywords or keyword phrases

- The Google analytics tool checks the following:
  - how long and how many customers stay on the site
  - bounce rate (do customers look at one page or move on to other pages?)
  - metadata: the information put in and under the URL address
  - website security: the lock symbol confirms a secure website, [i] means insecure
  - backlinks to other websites and backlinks on those webpages to your website.

ITI webinar UK by David García Ruiz 2019

Although SEO based on a seed list is not a creative form of translation, the client who needs web translation may ask for transcreation rather than translation, including SEO. Transcreation (translation + creation) is a marketing term that refers to the adaptation of ST to localised TT. One LSP (2019) referred to transcreation as a 'creative and adaptive translation'. Another LSP (2019) described transcreation on their website as a 'hybrid of innovative, culturally adapted content and straightforward translation, in which the sense or feeling of the original must be retained in the target language'. The question worth asking is whether these features have not always been part of translation.

7.7 Translation technology and the users

The European Union of Association of Translation Companies (EUATEC) held a survey in 2019 about the expectations and concerns of the European language industry★★(link: 2019 Language Industry Survey report). They received 1404 responses from 55 countries, many outside Europe, from companies, LSPs and translators. The objective of the survey, which was also held in 2017 and 2018, is to gain a sense of mood among translators and LSPs and to identify trends and concerns. We will focus on findings that relate to the use of web-based TEnTs:

- What clients want
- Technology improvement wish list
- Technology investment plans
- Tool familiarity and usage
- CAT user rights and ownership

What do clients want? The designers, developers, and manufacturers of CAT tools believed their tools delivered the mantra of *less time, more profit, better quality*. LSPs and translators agreed that quality of service came first, followed by responsiveness, meaning prompt delivery, the quality of the translation, and flexibility. It is interesting that price, or rather low cost, was not considered a top priority for the customer by translation providers. LSPs and translators disagreed about the language focus which they thought was expected by the client: translators reported domain specialism, whereas the LSPs believed the client was looking for a broader spectrum of language services.

When it comes to technology improvement wishes vary. Translators would like more ease of use of their tools and a lower cost of ownership, whereas the LSPs would like to see better integration, better MT quality. They agreed on the cost of ownership of tools, which both parties considered too high.

The gap between LSPs and translators widened in terms of tool-investment plans: LSPs scored 62% for machine translation (cf. 16% for translators) and 52% for automated workflow (cf. 6% for translators). QA tools were not popular with translators, contrary to LSPs, which suggests that translators are not (yet) convinced that QA tools offer added value.

Tool familiarity was on a par across the board: MS Office, major CAT tool and Google Translate were among the top five. The difference between familiarity and usage, however, was significant. Google Translate dropped from high familiarity to 50% among LSP users and to 75% among translators as a frequently used tool. LSPs do not appear to recognise the different levels of confidentiality risks between open-source web-based MT engines (high risk) and API access with adaptive use (low risk). In the survey, concerns for breaches of confidentiality and inferior quality were high among LSPs. The following communication from the LSP to their contractees confirms these concerns:

Instructions to the translator:

… It is not permitted to copy or partly copy the source texts we send you and to enter any part into machine translation engines on the internet. Nor is it permitted to upload the source texts, wholly or in part, via MT functions in TM software to those machine translation engines. …

LSP communication to contracted translators 2019

Translators gave a higher rating to Linguee, a web concordance, compared to LSPs. The major CAT tools came first among both parties, LSPs and translators, in terms of usage. TMS tools were more frequently used by LSPs. They hardly featured as a frequently used tool among translators.

The 2019 survey results for CAT user rights and ownership in respect to transfer to the client had not changed compared to the two previous years. Translators objected to transfer, whereas the larger LSPs did not hesitate to pass TM rights on to their clients. The survey showed a sharp rise in the level of transfer of TM rights by LSPs. Among translators there was a consistent decline in the transfer level of TM user rights, followed by the transfer level of TM ownership. The transfer levels of terminology user rights and ownership showed a very slight increase among translators, whereas among LSPs, they showed a sharp decline. This finding is not entirely surprising: terminology databases remain potentially underused. The reliance on the TM and the concordance feature, and the effort required to build a terminology database or glossary, may be a root cause.

Two main points stood out in the survey: translators are not habitual users of TMS, and although translators covet their TMs, they are seemingly generous with their terminology databases. LSPs show remarkably little interest in ownership and transfer of terminology databases. Both points are closely related with ethics and property rights. Contracted translators that work in web-based tools, such as the TMS, do not have ownership of their work. The transfer of user rights is very much beyond the translator's control, especially if a contract agreement is signed in which the translator is requested to give away their rights. The seemingly involuntary transfer of ownership and user rights deserves a wakeup call among translators. They could lay claim on the industry's mantra and take ownership of translation quality, efficiency, and profit by informing the client and LSP what they can deliver within the given parameters.

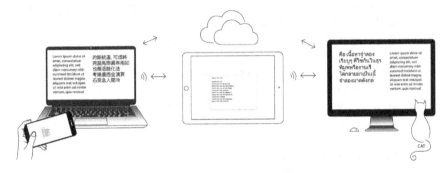

Project-based assignment

Objective:
Planning, implementation, and management of your own web-based translation project through teamwork and contracted translators with new cloud-based TEnTs

Assessment and outcome:
Team- and peer-assessment after completion of the project. Peer evaluation can be arranged on a platform where team assessments are posted. Responses can be social media style, such as threaded discussion, informal language. The primary team assessment is based on some or all web-based activities suggested below.

Method:
The assignment is designed for a project management team but collaboration within a project team or between individuals is possible

Tools:
Server or TMS; CAT tool with internet access; ASR

150 Web-based translation environment tools

Suggested resources:
HTML source text for localisation

Language pairs and direction:
As required

Assignment brief

In this assignment you must

- apply all your management skills, design your own team translation project and run it on a TMS or server. Alternatively, use a CAT tool but access digital platforms, or create your own (marketplace? crowdsourcing? portal?) platform. Your choice depends on what is available to you
- apply any new TEnTs available to you: TMS, CAT + server, plugins, APIs, speech recognition
- recruit translators and revisers in the cloud on existing platforms or on a self-created platform
- apply localisation skills (SEO) to the text through recruited translators, through localisation tools, or in your team.

Do not forget a plan and workflow at the beginning and the quality assessment of the translation at the end of this assignment.

Make sure that you can tick the following activities in your evaluation of your project management skills:

- Design and implementation of workflow in TMS (see 1.7.2)
- Assessment of shared TM/Tmdb benefits
- Assessment of integrated (adaptive) MT quality
- QA and third-party revision
- Use of digital platforms
- Crowdsourcing of (untrained) translators (from undergraduate language degree courses?)
- Quality control of recruited translators via platforms
- Digital ethics
- Administration and accounting
- Other TEnTs (ASR).

Possible pitfalls

- Impact on quality by unqualified translators
- Impact on quality as a result of incompetent usage of TEnTs or platforms
- Impact on product (translation) as a result of project manager incompetence

- Stagnation in the workflow if project management team members are not sure about their roles

Concluding remarks

How does the industry's mantra sit among freelance translators and LSPs? Data for this assessment are based on interviews in 2018 with translators and LSPs conducted by Lucas Nunes Vieira and Elisa Alonso (University of Bristol UK) in collaboration with the Institute of Translation and Interpreting (UK) and the Western Regional Group of the Institute of Translation (UK). The interview questions related to MT output. Bearing in mind that the translation management systems discussed in this chapter use MT as their primary tool, the answers in the survey are pertinent.

The mantra of quality was considered most important and yet also most problematic: the concept of quality needed defining and quality needed negotiating. LSPs would ask translators to post-edit within a given time. It was not a problem if MT output was good but detrimental to final quality if the output was poor. Translators felt that their sense of quality and their pride in delivering quality was under attack. We have seen that adaptive MT in TMS can resolve this problem if the translator can select and modify proposed MT matches on the fly rather than perform a post-edit. None of the interviewees stated that MT provided better quality.

The mantra of productivity saw an imbalance. LSPs did not see initial gain in productivity when the MT technology was introduced, but improvement after the arrival of NMT increased productivity by more than 100%, from 2000 words a day to 4000 to 5000 words. Translators commented that they saw little gain if MT output was poor. In this respect adaptive MT in TMS may not be a temporal improvement if the translator is faced with having to make too many match choices and too many edits. They are time-consuming.

The mantra of profit is closely related to the experiences described by LSPs and translators about MT quality. The LSPs appreciated the increased translated word rate, and the translators felt that post-edits were more profitable than translation if the quality was good. It was agreed that the pricing structure of word rates did not suit hybrid translation when MT was used. Translators were not happy with alternatives such as pricing according to edit distance because they felt it did not account for effort. Time spent on thinking was not part of the calculation.

A pertinent conclusion in the survey was that in large collaborative projects translators felt like a small cog in the wheel with little say, especially when they were expected to work within a given structure or procedure, such as TMS or platform/server. Translators stressed the human side of translation, which meant that they considered feedback important and that communication between all parties was of prime importance. They would like the industry to listen and respond to their concerns about TEnTs they want to use or are expected to use.

152 Web-based translation environment tools

Further reading

Cronin, Michael (2003). *Translation and Globalization*. London and New York: Routledge.

GALA (Globalization and Localization Association) www.gala-global.org/what-translation-management-system

Jiménez-Crespo, Miguel A. (2013). *Translation and Web Localization*, pp. 193–7. London and New York: Routledge.

Nunes Vieira, Lucas and Elisa Alonso (2018). 'The use of machine translation in human translation workflows. Practices, perceptions and knowledge exchange'. Milton Keynes: Institute of Translation and Interpreting.

O'Hagan (2017). 'Crowdsourcing and the Facebook initiative'. In: D. Kenny (ed.), *Human Issues in Translation Technology*, pp. 25–44. London, UK: Routledge.

Pym, Anthony (2010b). 'The Translation Crowd'. Tradumàtica 8. www.fti.uab.cat/tradumatica/revista/num8/sumari.htm# [accessed November 2019].

Shuttleworth, Mark (2015). 'Translation management systems'. In: Chan Sin-Wai (ed.), *The Routledge Encyclopedia of Translation Technology*, pp. 687–91. London and New York: Routledge.

BIBLIOGRAPHY

Anderson, Lorin W. and David R. Krathwohl (eds) (2001). *A Taxonomy for Learning, Teaching, and Assessing: A Revision of Bloom's Taxonomy of Educational Objectives*. New York: Addison Wesley Longman.

Austermühl, Frank (2001). *Electronic Tools for Translators*. Manchester: St Jerome Publishing.

Baker, Mona (2018). *In Other Words: A Coursebook on Translation*. London: Routledge.

Baker, Mona and Gabriela Saldanha (eds) (2009). *Routledge Encyclopedia of Translation Studies*. London: Routledge.

Baroni, Marco and Sylvia Bernardini (2004). BootCaT: Bootstrapping corpora and terms from the web. *Proceedings of LREC 2004*.

Berthaud, Sarah (2019). 'Ethical issues surrounding the use of technologies in the translation and interpreting market in the Republic of Ireland'. In: *Ethics and Machines in an Era of New Technologies*. ITI research e-book.

Bowker, Lynne (2001). 'Towards a methodology for a corpus-based approach to translation evaluation', *Meta*, 64: 345–64.

Bowker, Lynne (2002). *Computer-aided Translation Technology: A Practical Introduction*. Ottawa: University of Ottawa Press.

Bowker, Lynne (2005). Productivity vs quality? A pilot study on the impact of translation memory systems. *Localisation Focus*, 4(1): 13–20.

Bowker, Lynne (2015). 'Computer-aided translation. Translator training'. In: Chan Sin-Wai (ed.) *The Routledge Encyclopedia of Translation Technology*, pp. 88–119. London and New York: Routledge.

Byrne, Jody (2014). *Scientific and Technical Translation Explained: A Nuts and Bolts Guide for Beginners*. Hoboken: Taylor & Francis.

Chan, Sin-Wai (2015). *The Routledge Encyclopedia of Translation Technology*. London and New York: Routledge.

Chan, Sin-Wai (2017). *The Future of Translation Technology. Towards a World without Babel*. London and New York: Routledge.

Chaume, Frederic (2012). *Audiovisual Translation: Dubbing. Translation Practices Explained*. Manchester: St Jerome Publishing.

Chesterman, Andrew (2001). 'Proposal for a hieronymic oath'. In Anthony Pym (ed.), *The Return to Ethics*, special issue of *The Translator*, 7(2): 139–54.

154 Bibliography

Chesterman, Andrew (2018). 'Translation ethics'. In: Lieven d'Hulst and Yves Gambier (eds), *A History of Modern Translation Knowledge. Sources, Concepts, Effects*, pp. 443–8. Amsterdam: Benjamins.

Ciobanu, Dragoş (2019). 'Speech technologies: the latest word in AI-driven game-changing language technologies'. In: *Ethics and Machines in an Era of New Technologies*. ITI research e-book.

Cooper, Alan (2004). *The Inmates are Running the Asylum: Why Hi-Tech Products Drive Us Crazy and How to Restore the Sanity*. Indianapolis: Sams Publishing.

Cronin, Michael (2003). *Translation and Globalization*. London and New York: Routledge.

Cronin, Michael (2010). 'The translation crowd'. *Revista. Tradumàtica 08*. Catalonia: UAB.

Cronin, Michael (2012). *Translation in the Digital Age*. London: Routledge.

Daems, Joke, Lieve Macken, and Sonia Vandepitte (2013). 'Quality as the sum of its parts: a two-step approach for the identification of translation problems and translation quality assessment for HT and MT+PE'. In: Sharon O'Brien, Michel Simard, and Lucia Specia (eds), *MT Summit XIV Workshop on Post-editing Technology and Practice, Proceedings*, pp. 63–71. European Association for Machine Translation.

Doherty, Stephen (2017). 'Issues in human and automatic translation quality assessment'. In: D. Kenny (ed.), *Human Issues in Translation Technology*, pp. 131–48. London: Routledge.

Doherty, Stephen and Joss Moorkens (2013). 'Investigating the experience of translation technology labs: pedagogical implications'. *JoSTrans* 19. www.jostrans.org/issue19/art_doherty.pdf

Dragsted, Barbara (2005). 'Segmentation in translation. Differences across levels of expertise and difficulty'. *Target*, 17(1): 49–70. John Benjamins. https://doi.org/10.1075/target.17.1.04dra.

Drugan, Jo (2009). 'Intervention through computer-assisted translation: the case of the EU'. In: J. Munday (ed.), *Translation as Intervention*, pp. 118–37. London & New York: Continuum International Publishing Group.

Drugan, Jo (2013). *Quality in Professional Translation: Assessment and Improvements*. London/New York: Bloomsbury Academic.

Drugan, Jo and Bogdan Babych (2010). 'Shared resources, shared values? Ethical implications of sharing translation resources'. In Ventsislav Zhechev (ed.), *Proceedings of the second joint EM+/CNGL workshop. Bringing MT to the USER: Research on Integrating MT in the Translation Industry*. Available from: https://pdfs.semanticscholar.org/4acd/2c229ef9dfa3f a903911ed7447e62f726edc.pdf.

Dunne, Keiran J. and Elena S. Dunne (eds) (2011). *Translation and Localization Project Management*. Amsterdam and Philadelphia: John Benjamins.

EAGLES-EWG (1996). Eagles Evaluation of Natural Language Processing Systems, Final Report EAG-EWG-PR.2, Project LRE-61-100, Center for Sprogteknologi, Copenhagen, Denmark. [available at: www.issco.unige.ch/projects/ewg96/]

Ehrensberger-Dow, Maureen and Gary Massey (2014). 'Cognitive issues in professional translation'. In: John W. Schwieter and Aline Ferreira (eds), *The Development of Translation Competence; Theories and Methodologies from Psycholinguistics and Cognitive Science*, pp. 58–86. Cambridge: Cambridge Scholars Publishing.

Ehrensberger-Dow, Maureen and Sharon O'Brien (2014). 'Ergonomics of the translation workplace: potential for cognitive friction'. In: Deborah A. Folaron, Gregory M. Shreve, and Ricardo Muñoz Martin (eds), *Translation Spaces*, 4(1): 98–118. Amsterdam and Philadelphia: John Benjamins.

European Commission. Directorate-General for Translation (2015). DGT Translation Quality Guidelines. Brussels/Luxembourg. [Online] https://ec.europa.eu/translation/maltese/guidelines/documents/dgt_translation_quality_guidelines_en.pdf [accessed October 2019].

Farajian, M. Amin, Marco Turchi, Matteo Negri, and Marcello Federico (2017). 'Multi-domain neural machine translation through unsupervised adaptation'. *Proceedings of the second conference on machine translation. Denmark, Copenhagen.* DOI: 10.18653/v1/W17-4713.

Flanagan, Kevin (2014). 'Subsegment recall in translation memory — perceptions, expectations and reality'. *JoSTrans* 23.

Forcada, Mikel L. (2015). 'Open-source machine translation technology'. In: Chan Sin-Wai (ed.), *The Routledge Encyclopedia of Translation Technology*, pp. 152–66. London and New York: Routledge.

Garcia, Ignacio (2015). 'Computer-aided translation'. In: Chan Sin-Wai (ed.), *The Routledge Encyclopedia of Translation Technology*, pp. 68–87. London and New York: Routledge.

Gintrowicz, Jacek and Jassem Krzysztof Jassem (2007). 'Using regular expressions in translation memories'. *Proceedings of the International Multiconference on Computer Science and Information Technology*, pp. 87–92.

Gouadec, Daniel (2007). *Translation as a Profession*. Amsterdam and Philadelphia: John Benjamins.

Guerberof, Ana (2017). 'Quality is in the eyes of the reviewer. A report on post-editing quality evaluation'. In: Arnt Lykke Jakobsen and Bartolomé Mesa-Lao (eds), *Translation in Transition. Between Cognition, Computing and Technology*, pp. 187–206. Amsterdam/Philadelphia: John Benjamins Publishing Company.

Hernandez-Morin, Katell, Frenck Barbin, Fabienne Moreau, Daniel Toudic, and Gaëlle Phuez-Favris (2017). 'Translation technology and learner performance: professionally-oriented translation quality assessment with three translation technologies'. In: Arnt Lykke Jakobsen and Bartolomé Mesa-Lao (eds), *Translation in Transition. Between Cognition, Computing and Technology*, pp. 207–34. Amsterdam/Philadelphia: John Benjamins Publishing Company.

Holmes, James S. (1988a). *Translated! Papers on Literary Translation and Translation Studies*. Amsterdam: Rodopi.

Holmes, James S. (1988b/2004). 'The name and nature of translation studies'. In: Lawrence Venuti (ed.), *The Translation Studies Reader*, pp. 180–92. London and New York: Routledge.

Hutchins & Somers (1992). *An Introduction to Machine Translation*. London: Academic Press.

ISO 704:987 Principles and Methods of Terminology – http://lipas.uwasa.fi/termino/library.html [accessed 2019].

Jiménez-Crespo, Miguel A. (2013). *Translation and Web Localization*. London and New York: Routledge.

Jiménez-Crespo, Miguel A. (2015). 'Translation quality, use and dissemination in an internet era: using single-translation and multi-translation parallel corpora to research translation quality on the web'. *JoSTrans* 23.

Kenny, Dorothy (2010). 'The Ethics of Machine Translation'. Proceedings XI NZSTI National Conference.

Kenny, Dorothy (2011). 'The effect of translation memory tools in translated web texts: evidence from a comparative product-based study'. In: Walter Daelemans and Veronique Hoste (eds), *Evaluation of Translation Technology, series 8/2009 Linguistica antverpiensia. New Series – Themes in Translation Studies,* pp. 213–34. Antwerpen: Artesis Hogeschool Antwerpen. Departement Vertalers en Tolken.

Kenny, Dorothy (ed.) (2017). *Human Issue in Translation Technology*. London and New York: Routledge.

Kiraly, Donald C. (1995). *Pathways to Translation: Pedagogy and Process*. Kent, Ohio: Kent State University Press.

156 Bibliography

Kiraly, Donald C. (St. Jerome 2000/Routledge 2014). *A Social Constructivist Approach to Translator Education: Empowerment from Theory to Practice*. Manchester, UK and Northampton, MA.

Kiraly, Donald C. (2005). 'Project-based learning: a case for situated translation', *Meta: Translators' Journal*, 50/4:1098–1111.

Kiraly, Donald C. (2012). 'Growing a project-based translation pedagogy: a fractal perspective', *Meta: Translators' Journal*, 57/1: 82–95.

Kit Chunyu and Billy Wong Tak-ming (2015). 'Evaluation in machine translation and computer-aided translation'. In: Chan Sin-Wai (ed.), *The Routledge Encyclopedia of Translation Technology*, pp. 213–36. London and New York: Routledge.

Lammers, Mark (2011). 'Risk management in localization'. In: Keiran J. Dunne and Elena S. Dunne (eds), *Translation and Localization Project Management*, pp. 211–32. Amsterdam and Philadelphia: John Benjamins.

Land, Ray, and Meyer, Jan (eds) (2006). *Overcoming Barriers to Student Understanding: Threshold Concepts and Troublesome Knowledge*. London and New York: Routledge.

Lawrence, Oliver (2018). 'The finishing line', *ITI Bulletin. The Journal of the Institute of Translation and Interpreting*, Nov/Dec.

Martin, J.R. and P. White (2005). *The Language of Evaluation: Appraisal in English*. New York: Palgrave Macmillan.

Melby, Alan K. (2012). 'Terminology in the age of multilingual corpora', *The Journal of Specialised Translation*, 18. [Online] www.jostrans.org/issue18/art_melby.php [accessed December 2019].

Melby, Alan K. and Sue Ellen Wright (2015). 'Translation memory'. In: Chan Sin-Wai (ed.), *The Routledge Encyclopedia of Translation Technology*, pp. 662–77. London and New York: Routledge.

Mileto, Fiorenza and Muzii, Luigi (2010). 'Teaching computer-assisted translation and localisation: a project based approach'. In: Łukasz Bogucki (ed.), *Teaching Translation and Interpreting*, pp. 13–14. Newcastle: Cambridge Scholars Publishing.

Mitchell-Schuitevoerder, Rosemary (2013). 'A project-based methodology in translator training'. In: Catherine Way, Sonia Vandepitte, Reine Meylaerts, and Magdalena Bartłomiejczuk (eds), *Tracks and Treks in Translation Studies*, pp. 127–42. Amsterdam and Philadelphia: John Benjamins.

Mitchell-Schuitevoerder, Rosemary (2014). 'A project-based syllabus design' – Innovative Pedagogy in Translation Studies'. PhD thesis. Durham University.

Mitchell-Schuitevoerder, Rosemary (2015). 'A reconsideration of translation quality and standards'. *Journal of Siberian Federal University. Humanities & Social Sciences* 8(12): 2908–19.

Moorkens, Joss (2012). 'Measuring consistency in translation memories: a mixed-method case study'. Thesis. Dublin City University.

Moorkens, Joss (2019). 'Uses and limits of machine translation'. In: *Ethics and Machines in an Era of New Technologies*. ITI research e-book.

Moorkens, Joss, Stephen Doherty, Dorothy Kenny, and Sharon O'Brien (2013). 'A virtuous circle: laundering translation memory data using statistical machine translation'. In: *Perspective Studies in Translatology*. DOI: 10.1080/0907676X.2013.811275

Mossop, Brian (2014, 2019). *Revising and Editing for Translators*. Manchester, UK: St Jerome Publishing.

Mossop, Brian with Jungmin Hong and Carlos Texeira (2019). *Revising and Editing for Translators*. London and New York: Routledge.

Müller-Spitzer, Carolin and Alexander Koplenig (2014). 'Online dictionaries: expectations and demands'. In: *Ebook Package Linguistics*, pp. 144–88, Berlin: De Gruyter, ZDB-23-DSP.

Munday, Jeremy (2012). *Evaluation in Translation. Critical Points of Translator Decision-Making.* London and New York: Routledge.

Munday, Jeremy (2012; 2016). *Introducing Translation Studies: Theories and Applications.* London and New York: Routledge.

Muzii, Luigi (2012). *A Contrarian's View on Translation Standards.* [e-book], www.lulu.com.

Nord, Christiane (1991). *Text Analysis in Translation.* Amsterdam-Atlanta: Rodopi.

Nunes Vieira, Lucas (2017). 'From process to product: links between post-editing effort and post-edited quality'. In: Arnt Lykke Jakobsen and Bartolomé Mesa-Lao (eds), *Translation in Transition. Between Cognition, Computing and Technology*, pp. 161–86. Amsterdam/ Philadelphia: John Benjamins Publishing Company.

Nunes Vieira, Lucas (2018). 'Automation anxiety and translators', *Translation Studies.* London and New York: Routledge. DOI: 10.1080/14781700.2018.1543613

Nunes Vieira, Lucas and Elisa Alonso (2018). 'The use of machine translation in human translation workflows. Practices, perceptions and knowledge exchange'. Milton Keynes: Institute of Translation and Interpreting.

O'Brien, Sharon (2012). 'Towards a dynamic quality evaluation model for translation'. *The Journal of Specialised Translation*, 17. [Online] www.jostrans.org/issue17/art_obrien.pdf [accessed May 2014].

O'Hagan, Minako (2012). 'The impact of new technologies on translation studies. A technological turn?' In: Carmen Millán and Francésca Bartrina (eds), *The Routledge Handbook of Translation Studies*, pp. 503–18. London and New York: Routledge.

O'Hagan, Minako (2017). 'Crowdsourcing and the Facebook initiative'. In: D. Kenny (ed.), *Human Issues in Translation Technology*, pp. 25–44. London, UK: Routledge.

Olohan, Maeve (2004). *Introducing Corpora in Translation Studies.* London and New York: Routledge.

Olohan, Maeve and Elena Davitti (2017). 'Dynamics of trusting in translation project management: leaps of faith and balancing acts'. *Journal of Contemporary Ethnography*, 46(4): 391–416.

Papineni, Kishore, Salim Roukos, Todd Ward, and Wei-Jing Zhu (2001). *BLEU: A Method for Automatic Evaluation of Machine Translation*, IBM Research Report R C 22176 (W0109-022).

Pavel Terminology Tutorial, https://termcoord.eu/wp-content/uploads/2018/04/Pavel_ Silvia_and_Nolet_Diane_Handbook_of_Terminology-002.pdf [accessed 2019].

Project Management Institute (2004). *A Guide to the Project Management Body of Knowledge. (PMBOK® Guide).* 3rd ed. Newtown Square, PA: PMI Press.

Pym, Anthony (1993). *Principles for the Teaching of Translation*, pp. 100–16. Tarragona: Universitat Rovira i Virgili.

Pym, Anthony (2008). 'Professional corpora: teaching strategies for work with online documentation, translation memories and content management'. *Chinese Translator's Journal*, 29(2): 41–5.

Pym, Anthony (2010a). 'Text and risk in translation'. Intercultural Studies Group. Universitat Rovira i Virgili. www.researchgate.net/publication/283363313_Text_and_risk_in_translation [accessed 2019].

Pym, Anthony (2010b). 'The Translation Crowd'. *Tradumàtica* 8. www.fti.uab.cat/tradumatica/ revista/num8/sumari.htm# [accessed 2019].

Quah, Chiew K. (2006). *Translation and Technology.* New York: Palgrave Macmillan.

Risku, Hanna (2016). 'Situated learning in translation research training: academic research as a reflection of practice', *The Interpreter and Translator Trainer*, 10/1:12–28.

Robinson, Bryan J., Clara I. López Rodríguez, and María I. Tercedor Sánchez (2008). 'Neither born nor made, but socially-constructed: promoting interactive learning in an online environment'. *TTR: Traduction, Terminologie, Rédaction*, Vol. XXI (2): 95–129, Montreal.

Rohlfing, Katharina J., Matthias Rehm, and Karl Ulrich Goecke (2003). 'Situatedness: the interplay between context(s) and situation'. *Journal of Cognition and Culture*, 3(2), Leiden: Brill.

Samuelsson-Brown, Geoffrey (2010). *A Practical Guide for Translators*. Bristol, Buffalo, Toronto: Multilingual Matters.

Sánchez-Gijón, Pilar, Olga Torres-Hostench, Bartolomé Mesa-Lao (eds) (2013) *Conducting Research in Translation Technologies*. Oxford: Peter Lang.

Shuttleworth, Mark (2015). 'Translation management systems'. In: Chan Sin-Wai (ed.), *The Routledge Encyclopedia of Translation Technology*, pp. 687–91. London and New York: Routledge.

Shuttleworth, Mark (2017). 'Cutting teeth on translation technology: how students at University College London are being trained to become tomorrow's translators'. *Tradução em Revista*, 22: 18–38. 10.17771/PUCRio.TradRev.30595

Suojanen, Tytti, Kaisa Koskinen, and Tiina Tuominen (2015), *User-Centered Translation. Translation Practices Explained*. London and New York: Routledge.

TAUS Predictions Webinar, 21 January 2010. www.taus.net/events/user-calls/taus-predicts.

TAUS (2019). *DQF BI Bulletin – Q1*.

Toury, Gideon (1995). *Descriptive Translation Studies and Beyond*. 1st revised edition. Amsterdam and Philadelphia: John Benjamins.

Wagner, Emma, Svend Bech, and Jesús M. Martínez (2014). *Translating for the European Union Institutions*. London and New York: Routledge.

Wang, Vincent X. and Lily Lim (2017). 'How do translators use web resources?' In: Dorothy Kenny (ed.), *Human Issue in Translation Technology*, pp. 63–77. London and New York: Routledge.

Warburton, Kara (2015). 'Terminology management'. In: Chan Sin-Wai (ed.), *The Routledge Encyclopedia of Translation Technology*, pp. 644–61. London and New York: Routledge.

Wilks, Yorick (2008). *Machine Translation. Its Scope and Limits.* New York: Springer.

Wong, Cecilia Shuk Man (2015.) 'Machine translation in the Chinese University of Hong Kong'. In: Chan Sin-Wai (ed.), *The Routledge Encyclopedia of Translation Technology*, pp 237–51. London and New York: Routledge.

Zanettin, Federico (2015)'. Concordancing'. In: Chan Sin-Wai (ed.), *The Routledge Encyclopedia of Translation Technology*, pp. 437–49. London and New York: Routledge.

Zetzsche, Jost (2003–2017). *A Translator's Tool Box for the 21st Century. A Computer Primer for Translators*. Winchester Bay: International Writer's Group.

Zetzsche, Jost (2019). 'The 297th Tool Box Journal'. *The International Writers' Group*.

Zetzsche, Jost (2019). 'The 298th Tool Box Journal'. *The International Writers' Group*.

INDEX

Note: Entries given in **bold** refer to tables; entries in *italics* refer to figures.

acceptability 53, 96
accounting 2, 13, 136, 152
accuracy 53–5, **64–5**, 82, 84, 99, **104**
adequacy 53, 108
administration 2, 109, 136; public 71–2
administrative function 144
administrative skill 1
administrative tool 142; *see also* portal
AEM (automatic evaluation metrics) *see* metrics
AI (artificial intelligence) 52, 58, 86; strong and weak 135
algorithm 53
alignment 38–41, 81; automated 39
alphabetic language 12; *see also* non-whitespace language
API (application programming interface) 12, 56–8, 63, 80; connector 133–4, 143
authoring *see* copyright
automated speech recognition (ASR) 134–5
autosuggest 27, 38 *see also* predictive writing

benchmark 64, 96, 101: human translation 64, 93, 96; standard 96
Berthaud, S. 119
bilingual CAT tool format 28
bilingual file 2, 6, 100
bilingual format *see* format
bilingual glossary *see* glossary

bilingual reference 38, 100–1
bilingual revision *see* revision
BLEU (bilingual evaluation understudy) 60, 63, 65, 67, 96
BootCaT tool 83
bootstrapped corpora 82
Bowker, L. 96, 98–9
browser 2, 9; browser-based 144
business model *see* model

CAT tool 15–21, 24–30, 34–8, 51–9, 85–8; manufacturer 37, 41–2, 133; *see also* TEnT
cause-driven crowdsourcing 141
check *see* QA; revision
cloud-based tool 119; CAT tool 3, 13; *see also* SaaS (software as a service)
CMS (content management system) 143–4; *see also* TMS (translation management system)
code 7, 10, 11; of ethics 121; key 56; shortcut 69; source 98; writing 47; *see also* regex; tag
cognitive ergonomics 14, 21
cognitive friction 21
collaboration 3, 5, 13, 16, 79, 114
compatibility 2–3; 13–14; 39; *see* hardware and software
completeness 77, 99
concordance: CAT 30–1, 83–5; external 85; parallel 85; web 85; *see also* consistency

160 Index

confidential disclosure agreement *see* digital ethics/non-disclosure agreement
connector *see* API
consistency 26–7, 30–3, **64**, 71, 77
consumer-oriented crowdsourcing 142
content management system *see* CMS
context *see* match
conversion tool 2, 139; *see also* pdf
copyright 114, 116–23; authoring 122, 138, 143; digital material 98, 113, 122, 130; intellectual property 113–14, 117, 122–3; ownership 113–14, 116, 120; *see also* digital ethics
corpora: bilingual 39; digital 79; multilingual data 80–1
corpus 39, 60, 73, 79, 81–3; British National Corpus 85
corpus-based machine translation 53
criteria: assessment **104**; evaluation 62, 93–4, **104**; search 83; testing 64
Cronin, M. 141, 146
crowdsourced material 142
crowdsourcing 141–2; *see also* platform
customisation 99
customised TM 27, 37–8, 41, 50, 72, 137

data: centre 122; protection 119–20; sharing 119–21; *see also* metadata
database: external 25–7, 38, 86; internal 26, 69; *see also* file
deep learning 52, 54; *see also* machine translation
desktop-based CAT tool 136, 144
dialog box 10–11, 14, *29*, 30–3
dictionary 71, 78–82, 85; digital 79–102; sample-based 79; *see also* glossary
digital ethics 113; non-disclosure agreement (NDA) 115–16; *see also* copyright
digital material *see* copyright
digital platform 137–9; *see also* platform
directory *see* folder
Doherty, S. 64
domain 38, 58; knowledge 18; specific 37, 53, 63; suffix 78–9
DQF (data quality framework) *see* metrics
drop-down menu 10
Dunne, K.J. and E.S. Dunne 19

EAGLES 4, 59–60
edit distance 38, **55–6**, 64
editor: term extraction 73–4, 85, 88; *see also* translation/grid
efficiency 5, 55–6

Ehrenberger-Dow, M. and G. Massey 21
error: management 63, 65; repair 52; spotting 13; warning 42, 95, 100
error typology 64–5, 96, 105–6
extensible markup language (XML) *see* format; tag

Facebook 141
false positives, 27, 45, 48, 73, 86
file: clean 2; dirty 2; *see also* format; TBX; TMX; XLIFF
filter 3, 45–6; 95, 134 *see also* regex
fluency 53, **104**, 107–8, 135
folder: directory 2, 8; parent 7, *8*; see *also* subfolder
Forcada, M.L. 56, 63
format 41–6: bilingual 5; docx. 2–13; editable 2, 14, 30, 44; HTML 42; MS Excel 41; rtf 80, 100; source 30; target 47; *see also* interchangeable format; tag
formatting *see* tag
freelancer 20; freelance translator 94, 103, 132, 138; *see also* human resources
freeware 56
fuzzy *see* match
fuzzy match threshold 26

GALA (globalization and localization association) 12
glossary: bilingual 73; online 71
Google 12, 52, 63, 81, 83; Analytics 147; Cloud Translation 121; Translate 120
Gouadec, D. 96, 103, 122
Guerberof, A. 105–6

hardware and software 3, 123–5; *see also* in/compatibility
human resources 2, 18–20, 138; in-house translator 18, 103; project manager 16–20, 122, 144; *see also* freelancer; reviser; terminologist
human translation 55, 62, 64, 78, 96

image file 3, 40–1, 44; *see also* hardware and software; incompatability
incompatibility 124, 126
indemnity insurance 94, 115
in-house translator *see* human resources
input: consistency 57; data 65, MT 57–8
translator 57; user 12; *see also* output
interchangeable format 13, 40, 88, 124; *see also* XLIFF; TBX; TMX
interface 30, 41, 58, 138
internationalisation (i18n) 98

invoice 113, 134, 142, 144
ISO (International Organisation for Standardisation) 60, 77, 92–4, 101–4, 120

Jiménez-Crespo, M.A. 97–8, 111, 141
joined and split segments 27, 29, 39, 42

Kenny, D. 1
knowledge platform 141
KWIC (Key Word in Context) 81, 85

l10n (localisation) *98*
language: code 7; direction 27, 34; pair 11, 18, 44, 60, 63, 138; quality assurance 92; tag 7
language service provider 18, 80, 102
Levenshtein distance 108
leverage 5, 37, 54, 56
lexicographer 79, 82
licence 114; software 13, 134, 136–7, 144
linear 77–8, 100; *see also* nonlinear
linguist: contracted 34, 103; contractee 120–3, 127, 132, 136, 138; *see also* freelancer; freelance translator; reviser; subcontracted 121
LISA (Localization Industry Standard Association): model **64**
localisation 95, 97–9, 140–6
lookup 12, 26–7, 87, 134–5
LSP *see* Language Service Provider

machine translation: adaptive 54–60; integrated 12, 21, 26, 48, 51; neural 52–3, 60, 96, 107, 122; *see also* deep learning
management: business 2, 145; content 144; file 6, 24, 144; quality 60, 65, 98; risk 113–4, 122, 124, 128
mantra 14–5, 147, 149, 151
marketplace *see* platform
match: accuracy 55; context 26, 34, 87; fuzzy 26, 34, 37, 52–8, 86; perfect 26–8, 33, 37, 54; reversed 27; statistics 13; *see also* no match
metadata 33, 36–7, 53–5, 73–4, 120, 147; *see also* data
metrics 46, 52, 62–5, 96, 98; automatic evaluation (AEM) 63; data quality framework (DQF) 64–5; multidimensional quality (MQM) 64–5
Microsoft (MS) Office 2–3, 13, 24; MS Windows 1–3; operating system 3
model: business 137, 139; encoder 53 *see also* BLEU; LISA; metrics; TAUS
monolingual *see* revision

morphological change 69, 75, 84, 86
Mossop, B. 99, 105
MQF (Multidimensional Quality Framework) *see* TAUS
MS Word: competence 1; shortcut code *see* code; status bar 10; toolbar 10–11
Müller-Spitzer C. and A. Koplenig 79
Munday, J. 94

natural language processing 52
NDA *see* non-disclosure agreement
neural machine translation (NMT) *see* machine translation
no match 26–7, 30, 34, **36**, 105–6
non-disclosure agreement (NDA) *see* digital ethics
nonlinear 97, 142 *see also* syntagmatic
non-translatable 40, 92
non-whitespace language 28; *see also* alphabetic language
Nunes Vieira L. 106, 108
Nunes Vieira L. and E. Alonso 151

O'Brien, S. 96, 106
offline editor 137
O'Hagan, M. 142
Olohan, M. 85
on-demand software *see* SaaS
open-source software 3, 56
optimisation *see* search engine optimisation
output quality 65
outsource 15, 143
outsourced material 141; *see also* crowdsourcing
ownership *see* digital ethics

package 39–40; project 136; return 39, 136
paid crowdsourcing platform 141
paradigmatic 77, 107
parallel corpora *see* corpora
parent folder 7–8; *see also* subfolder
pattern matching *see* regex
pdf 40, **43–4**; *see also* format
platform 116, 125; marketplace 139, 142; translation 58, 138, 140, 143, 145; translator 4, 138; *see also* crowdsourcing; digital knowledge base; localisation; portal
PO *see* purchase order
portal 127, 134, 137, 142–4; *see also* platform
post edit machine translation (PEMT) 21, 61–2, 107–9, 141
post-editing (PE) 37, 54–5, 62, 102–3, 106

162 Index

post-editor 52, 92, 107–9
precision 7, 30, 64; *see also* recall
predictive feature 41, 53; typing 13; writing 38
pre-translate 27–8, 94, 140
preview 12, 29
process: conversion 3, 125; file 13, 42; revision 99; segmentation 28, 42; translation 13–17, 71–3, 92–4, 136–7, 144
professional organisation 4, 95, 116, 121
project management 17–19, 124–5; team 13, 19–21; translation 15, 125–6; *see also* project manager
project manager 13, 16–20, 33, 115, 122
propagate 27, 33, 58
pseudo-translation 42–4
purchase order (PO) 17, 34, 113, 144
push and pull approach 87, 140
Pym, A. 29–30, 78, 103, 122, 142

QA *see* quality
quality: assessment 65, 92–6; assurance (QA) 46, **64**, 77, 85–6, 92–5; check 20, 60, 92; control (QC) 74, 88, 93, 98, 104; estimation 55, 62–3; specification 93; TQA (translation quality assurance) 63, 92, 96

ranking: algorithm 146; order 4
recall 37, 45, 64, 69, 84; *see also* precision
reference: file 38–41, 85, 105, 122, 126; material 70–2, 80, 83, 85, 137; translation 55–6, 64, 96, 99; *see also* alignment
regex 44, 46–7, 95; pattern matching 46; *see also* filter
repetition 5, 34, **36**, 95
repetitive strain injury 11
review: bilingual *9*, 29–30; monolingual 52, 104; preview 12, 29; tab 11, 31; translation 17, 34, 53, 64, 102, 107; *see also* revision
reviser *17–18*, 94, 104–5, 112, 136
revision: bilingual 100–1; CAT tool 99–102, 105, 107, 136; model 95; monolingual 29; self- 17–18, 94, 100, 105; third-party 5, 17, 94, 101–2, 104, 150
ribbon 10–11, 44–5; CAT tool 11, 30–1, 34, *45*, 69; MS Word 10, *45*
risk: breakdown structure 124–5; factors 124–5, 127; management 114, 124, 127; response 124, *127*

SaaS (software as a service) 136, 143–4
sampling 79

score: edit distance **55**; error 52, 59, 63, 95, 102; MT 59, 63–4; underscore 7, 95
search: local 134; phrase-based 95, 146; tool 12
search engine 56, 62, 69, 84; optimisation 143, 146–7; MT 56; specialised 77
security: breach 121; breach of confidentiality 21, 113–15, 121–2; digital 115–18
seed 146; list 147–8
segment: source 4, 12, 26; split 27, 29; target 12, 26, 29, 80; subsegment 4; *see also* join; split
segmentation 28, 42, 84, 135; rule 28–9, 34, 46–7; *see also* subsegmentation
server 13–14, 42, 125, 132–3, 136–7, 144
sight translation 135; *see also* text to speech
smartphone 14, 38, 134, 143
software *see* hardware
source: file 6, 18, 98, 125–6; language 28–9, 32, 55, 104; text 42, 57, 73, 99, 115–16
speech recognition *see* automated speech recognition
speech technology *see* automated speech recognition
speech to text 134–5; *see also* automated speech recognition; text to speech
spellcheck 12–13, 41, 93, 99, 134
split *see* joined and split segments
standalone 2–3, 13–14, 52, 87–8
standard *see* ISO; quality standardisation
statistical machine translation 53, 121 *see also* neural machine translation
statistics 13, 34–6, 53
status bar *see* MS Word
storage system 6, 25
string 27–30, 37–8, 53, 55, 84, 98–99
subfolder 7–9
subsegment: matching 8, 36–7, 70; *see also* segment
subsegmentation 38, 90
syllabic language 12; *see also* alphabetic language
syntagmatic 77–8, 107; *see* also nonlinear

tablet 14, 119, 135, 143
tag; language 7, *see also* code; formatting 14, 41–2, 99
target: file 9, 39, 44, 95, 100; language (TL) 32, 42, 55, 60, 96, 147; text (TT) 34, 42, 53, 61, 96, 99–100

Index **163**

TAUS (Translation Automation User Society) 4, 37, 55–8, **65**, 81–2, 96; *see also* DQF (Data Quality Framework)

taxonomy 65

TBX (TermBase eXchange) 42, 79, 114, 124, 136, 139; *see also* interchangeable format; terminology database

teamwork 19–20

TEnT (translation environment tool) 1–2, 132; ASR *see also see* automated speech recognition; CAT tool; concordance; conversion tool; dictionary; translation management system

term: complex 73; definition **74**, 77; extract 73; extraction 13, 72–3, 88; lookup icon 87; pair 27, 37, 73–4, 84, 86, 88; search 13, 78; simple 73

TermBase eXchange (TBX) *see* TBX

terminologist 112

terminology database (Tmdb) 77–80, 83–8, 133–7

terms of business 119, 121, 130

terms and conditions 113–17, 121; translation services **117**

text genre 56

text to speech 134, *136*

threshold 54–5; match 26; *see also* fuzzy

TM *see* translation memory

TM editor 27, 45

TMS *see* translation management system

TMX (translation memory eXchange) 38, 41, 42, 58, 114; *see also* file; interchangeable format

transcreation 147

transfer 42, 116, 119–20; file 116, 119–25; of ownership 149; rights 148; rule 46

Translation Automation User Society *see* TAUS

translation editor/grid 36, 39, 41, 74, 99, 133

Translation Environment Tool *see* TEnT

translation grid *see* translation editor

Translation Management System (TMS) 56–7, 68, 136, 143; *see also* content management system (CMS)

translation memory (TM) database 3, 12, 25; edit distance 38; edit time 74; editor 27, 45; interchangeable 25–6, 38, 58; repair 45

translation project *see* project

Translation Results window 26–7, 38, 40, 69–70, 74, 84

translation unit (TU) 3, 12, 25–6, 39

Translators without Borders 138

TU *see* translation unit

usability 96

vendor 18, 21, 132, 139

vocabulary 71, 83; see *also* glossary

volunteer translation *see* crowdsourcing

web: corpora 82; localisation 97–9, 139–40; search 77–8; web browser *see* browser; web/cloud-based tool 21, 116, 119, 132–3, 137, 149

web content management system *see* content management system

weighting 55, 64

whitespace languages *see* alphabetic language

word count 2, 17, 33–4, 41; costing 26, 34; fees 34, 109, 123; pricing 15, 19, 21, 34, 139, 151; rates 14, 21, 26, 34

workflow 15–16, 140, 142–4; chart *16*–7; LSP *18*, 125, 136–7; translation 130, 132–3; translator 17, 58, 88

World Wide Web (WWW) 42, 78, 85, 146

XLIFF 2–3, 6, 13, 42, 93, 137; *see* also file

XML 3, 13, 80; see *also* formatting

Zanettin, F. 84

Zetzsche, J. 37, 53, 73, 81, 86, 88, 107

ZIP archive 39

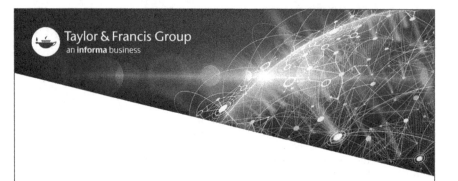

Taylor & Francis eBooks

www.taylorfrancis.com

A single destination for eBooks from Taylor & Francis with increased functionality and an improved user experience to meet the needs of our customers.

90,000+ eBooks of award-winning academic content in Humanities, Social Science, Science, Technology, Engineering, and Medical written by a global network of editors and authors.

TAYLOR & FRANCIS EBOOKS OFFERS:

A streamlined experience for our library customers

A single point of discovery for all of our eBook content

Improved search and discovery of content at both book and chapter level

REQUEST A FREE TRIAL
support@taylorfrancis.com